Single Women in Popular Culture

Also by Anthea Taylor

MEDIATING AUSTRALIAN FEMINISM: REREADING THE *FIRST STONE* MEDIA EVENT

Single Women in Popular Culture

The Limits of Postfeminism

Anthea Taylor

First published 2012 by
PALGRAVE MACMILLAN

Palgrave Macmillan in the UK is an imprint of Macmillan Publishers Limited, registered in England, company number 785998, of Houndmills, Basingstoke, Hampshire RG21 6XS.

Palgrave Macmillan in the US is a division of St Martin's Press LLC, 175 Fifth Avenue, New York, NY 10010.

Palgrave Macmillan is the global academic imprint of the above companies and has companies and representatives throughout the world.

Palgrave® and Macmillan® are registered trademarks in the United States, the United Kingdom, Europe and other countries.

ISBN 978–0–230–27382–5

This book is printed on paper suitable for recycling and made from fully managed and sustained forest sources. Logging, pulping and manufacturing processes are expected to conform to the environmental regulations of the country of origin.

A catalogue record for this book is available from the British Library.

A catalog record for this book is available from the Library of Congress.

10 9 8 7 6 5 4 3 2 1
21 20 19 18 17 16 15 14 13 12

Transferred to Digital Printing in 2012

For my parents, Rose and Maurice Taylor

Contents

Acknowledgements

The research undertaken for this project was made possible by both a University of Queensland Postdoctoral Fellowship and a University of Queensland Early Career Researcher Award. I thank the University of Queensland, and especially the Centre for Critical and Cultural Studies, for this investment in my work and for providing such a supportive research environment.

At Palgrave Macmillan, I wish to acknowledge Christabel Scaife (former Commissioning Editor) for championing the project in its initial stages, Felicity Plester for seeing it through to production, and Catherine Mitchell for her support and professionalism throughout the process.

A shorter version of Chapter 6 appears in *Feminist Review* (Issue 99, October 2011). I thank Palgrave Macmillan for their permission to use this material.

The cover image from *Bridget Jones's Diary* (2001) is courtesy of Photofest.

My friends and colleagues in the Centre for Critical and Cultural Studies (CCCS) at the University of Queensland deserve a special mention, especially Graeme Turner. In addition to his generous mentorship throughout my fellowship, I thank him particularly for his advice and encouragement in the final months of writing and for his insightful commentary on chapter drafts and the draft manuscript in its entirety.

I wish to express my gratitude to a number of people who provided feedback on specific chapter drafts: Melissa Bellanta, Marina Bollinger, Anita Harris, Camille Nurka, and Zala Volcic. I'd also like to acknowledge Fergus Grealy for his assistance in compiling the reference list. Diane Negra too deserves recognition for her thoughtful engagement with, and valuable feedback on, the draft manuscript.

Thanks to my family and friends for their support, especially my brother Owen, my sister-in-law Kirsty, and my delightful nieces, Isabella and Olivia, and Sarah Casey for her friendship, enthusiasm for this project, and humour.

Finally, this book is dedicated to my parents, Rose and Maurice Taylor, for all their love, support, and encouragement.

Introduction

Since the mid-1990s, the heterosexual single woman has been hyper-visible in Western popular culture. As the first generation since feminism's second wave moved into their 20s and 30s, a purportedly new subjectivity for women appeared to be gaining cultural currency in Western media culture. Indicative of this trend, *Sex and the City* seemed to celebrate the single woman of a certain demographic (white, financially secure, and heterosexual). She also appeared in popular fiction and film in the form of the loveable, scatty Bridget Jones and other similar 'chick lit' heroines. More recently, newspaper articles coining new labels for the single woman have been appearing with increasing regularity. Single women have variously been cast as 'freemales', 'TWITS' (teenage women in their 30s), and let's not forget that offensive age-specific appellation for mid-life women who date younger men: 'cougar'. As a consequence of the intense public focus upon her, the 'Single Woman' has even been pronounced a 'cultural obsession' (Dux & Simic, 2008, p. 77). Rather optimistically, I would argue, some critics have celebrated this as evidence of a 'new cultural affirmation' of being single (Macvarish, 2006), designating the current epoch '"the singles' century"' (Budgeon, 2008, p. 301). Indeed, the transnational proliferation of the 'SYF' (Single Young Female), an economically self-sufficient subject with extensive consumer clout, is said have heralded a 'New Girl Order' (Hymowitz, 2007). In this book, acknowledging the competing, contradictory discourses around women's singleness in popular culture, I interrogate such academic and popular claims about this supposed new cultural acceptance and celebration of singleness for women, attending to both texts that continue to position women's singleness as an aberration and others that attempt its refiguration.

1

Perhaps unsurprisingly, the single woman is a figure around whom broader cultural fears about feminism and about women's power and independence have always coalesced, as vitriolic attacks on nineteenth century spinsters attest. Even though the number of single women globally is said to be on the increase, it appears that the spectre of the spinster looms large in the popular imaginary (witness recent media coverage of Susan Boyle, the 'accidental' celebrity of *Britain's Got Talent*), even in narratives where she has apparently been refigured to accommodate the socio-political changes engendered by feminism (such as chick lit). As Virginia Nicholson points out, while single women may no longer be thought of as socially 'surplus' and there are reportedly more single person households and women are marrying less and at an older age in the West, contemporary media culture features more narratives of fear about 'lonely hearts and solitary singles than ever before' (2007, pp. xi–xii). Moreover, while the category 'single' encompasses those never married, widows, and divorcees (as well as those legally considered single though in a couple), the most visible and indeed the most anxiety-provoking single women in the Western mediasphere are still those who are not (or have not been) married. By and large, being single, although acceptable within certain temporal limits (mostly while women are yet capable of reproduction – more on the persistent trope of the biological clock later), appears to remain a socially interstitial subjectivity for women. It yet seems un-representable that a woman would actively choose for any length of time to remain partnerless or, rather, manless, for the single woman who preoccupies the cultural imaginary is invariably heterosexual. Concurrently, the single woman investing in becoming otherwise (also the most visible) is encouraged, and often congratulated, in her efforts to remedy her singleness and ensure the hegemony of hetero-patriarchy.

Historically, mainstream media culture has had an ambivalent relationship with the figure of the single woman, and the current context is no exception. The gesture of both 'capitalizing on and containing' the single woman has a long lineage and can at least be seen to date back to shifting representations of the 'single girl' in 1960s popular culture (Lehman, 2007, p. 28). In this sense, that single women are contested figures in the Western cultural imagination is nothing new. What is different about her current renderings is their emergence from a purportedly postfeminist representational environment, one that relies upon inherently contradictory discourses and assumptions about women – and single women especially. Postfeminism, rather than a simple backlash, signals how feminism is being reworked and renegotiated in media culture, often in politically troublesome ways. As Diane Negra notes, postfeminist media culture 'promulgates matrimonial panic', directing an increasingly 'diagnostic gaze towards single women' (2009, pp. 85, 61). Here, I am preoccupied with how such a gaze functions in a regulatory way that provides insight into the symbiotic relationship between postfeminist and neoliberal rhetorics. Building upon recent criticism on feminism, postfeminism, and neoliberalism in popular culture, I suggest that the single woman – in being both permissible (within specific limits) and repudiated – experiences the same discursive fate as feminism itself in contemporary media culture (see Gill, 2007, 2008, 2009; McRobbie, 2009; Negra, 2009). In particular, I consider how the reclamation of heterosexual romance that is central to the operations of postfeminism significantly delimits the kinds of narratives circulating about single women and the kinds of feminine subjectivities that are seen as inhabitable.[1]

Being partnered remains crucial to women's ability to become viable (and visible) subjects, and therefore viable citizens, in a way that it is not for men; the close textual analysis performed here explores this in depth. *Single Women in Popular Culture* is a cross-media study, consisting of detailed analyses of chick lit and the reverberations of the genre's most known heroine, Bridget Jones, reality television, self-help literature aimed specifically at single women, and blogs by single women, as well as attending (though in less detail) to journalism, popular non-fiction, film, and other television genres. Textual analysis of these various forms enables the identification of synergies, divergences, and inconsistencies across the cultural field to enable a broader mapping of how this figure comes to mean. That is, each of these modes of cultural production is approached in terms of their contribution to a broader, and ideologically fraught, cultural conversation over women's singleness. The texts upon which I focus have been produced predominantly in the United States, United Kingdom and, to a lesser extent, Australia. While recognizing that the 'cross-cultural traffic', especially between the US and the UK, suggests a high degree of 'discursive harmony' between these contexts (Tasker & Negra, 2007 pp. 13–4), I will also be attentive to cultural specificity and how this may work to delimit the readily available stories around women's singleness.

What I am calling the discursive shift from 'spinster to Singleton' is often used as evidence of a widespread cultural legitimation of single women. Focusing primarily on texts produced over the past two decades, here I examine not only the figure of the 'Singleton' but other forms of singleness visible in popular narratives to ascertain whether a broader cultural shift has in fact taken place or whether this figure continues to be one of discursive unease, seen as threatening to the dominant social order. Media provides the means through which women come to make sense of their singleness. Therefore, *Single Women in Popular Culture* asks what these texts make available for modern single women as well as where their assumptions are being contested. Rather than only looking at single women as objects represented by others, this book also attends to how women themselves are reworking and contesting limited representations of singleness through sites such as blogs and self-help style books that seek to revalue singleness as an identity and as a way of life. All the single woman narratives analyzed here are informed by (some kind of) feminism, enabling representations of this figure to be used as a way to track changes in the increasingly complicated relationship between feminism and media culture, especially in terms of postfeminism. Reading the single woman diagnostically, to help illuminate broader ideological tendencies and tensions around women and feminism, I use her to argue that feminist media and cultural studies must continue to cast a sceptical gaze over modern media culture while also acknowledging its imaginative possibilities.

In Chapter 1, 'Theorizing Women's Singleness: Postfeminism, Neoliberalism, and the Politics of Popular Culture', I situate this work in relation to relevant critical debates around media culture, postfeminism, and neoliberalism. In Chapter 2, 'From the Second-wave to Postfeminism: Single Women in the Mediasphere', I offer an overview of how single women have been discursively constituted in various sites of media culture over the past fifty years or so. Looking at journalism, popular non-fiction, film, and television, this chapter works to problematize the critical narrative that is gaining ascendancy about the newfound cultural acceptance and embrace of single women by underscoring the ambivalence that yet envelops this figure.

In Chapter 3, 'Spinsters and Singletons: *Bridget Jones's Diary* and its Cultural Reverberations', I analyze the figure of the 'Singleton' in what is routinely seen as the chick lit genre's foundational text, *Bridget Jones's Diary* (1996), as potentially – through its attempt to politicize and refigure singleness – representing a shift away from these dominant ways of representing single women. Despite its attempt to refigure singleness, however, the 'spinster' continues to represent the abject Other against which the Singleton is defined (as well as representing that which she most fears) but not without contradiction and indeed resistance on the part of Fielding's narrator. Moving beyond Fielding's novels, I also demonstrate what happens to the text's attempt to refigure singleness when

Bridget Jones steps off the page and begins her semiotic and political career in public discourse; that is, how she comes to inform constructions of women's singleness, as she indeed continues to do.

Chapter 4, 'Desperate and Dateless: Making Over the Single Woman', focuses on televisual single women in an ever expanding genre: reality television. This chapter engages with how the single woman is invariably seen to be on a desperate quest towards coupledom, including on *The Bachelor* and *Tough Love* in the US, and *The Farmer Wants a Wife* in Australia. It is in these narratives that the single woman-as-lack becomes most evident and men become figured as 'prizes' for which women must quite literally compete. In particular, conceptualizing so-called relationship reality series as a form of 'makeover' and 'life intervention' television, this chapter reveals how the behaviour of single women in these texts is monitored, regulated, and punished.

Chapter 5, 'Self-help and the Single Girl: From Salvation to Validation', addresses self-help manuals directed towards single women produced in the past few decades. Given that the purpose of self-help writing is seen to be the provision of tools through which the self can be 'corrected', how do these books approach the single woman as a 'problem' to be solved? Such manuals mobilize certain assumptions about both the single self and the other she is thought to crave that further demonstrate how postfeminist and neoliberal rhetorics intersect and bolster each other. This chapter demonstrates that such texts operate along a broad spectrum, from those that position singleness as an inherently undesirable lifestyle and identity that can (and must) be eradicated with the discursive assistance of these 'experts', through to those that position singleness for women as a viable and desirable choice.

In Chapter 6, 'Blogging Solo: Women Refiguring Singleness', I turn to the 'blogosphere' as an oppositional field where the meanings around singledom are contested, negotiated and rewritten. Drawing upon a number of blogs written by and for single women, and while cautious not to fall into the trap of 'digital optimism', I explore how self-generated content can provide the opportunity for discursive constructions of singleness that run counter to the narratives critiqued in earlier chapters. Within these blogs, writers aim to refigure women's singleness as well as providing resources, support, and a textual community where others can intervene in and contribute to the revaluation of single women. Moreover, it shows how these blogs, by acting to disrupt dominant media narratives around the woman without a man, can themselves work as instances of popular feminism and disrupt the hegemony of postfeminist logics.

1
Theorizing Women's Singleness: Postfeminism, Neoliberalism, and the Politics of Popular Culture

Single Women in Popular Culture presumes that popular media forms help provide the narratives through which we come to constitute ourselves/ are constituted as subjects. In the case of single women, such texts work to profoundly mediate women's understanding of being single (as they do other modalities of difference). When invoked in the public sphere, the idea of singleness appears with startling regularity as a problem to be rectified, despite concurrent depictions of (certain forms of) singleness as a permissible type of prolonged adolescence. In terms of how women's singleness is discursively constituted there is, therefore, a tension. At times the single woman appears to be celebrated – within specific temporal limits and for particular commercial purposes – and at others she continues to be pathologized, seen as a lamentable product of the pervasive feminist rhetoric that encouraged women to pursue independence and autonomy at the cost of a husband and, perhaps more importantly, a nuclear family.[1] Arguably there is nothing new about the single woman being a problematic figure in mainstream media culture and in Western discourse more broadly; currently, however, she is made-to-mean in a number of competing ways that speak to broader changes in how women (and indeed feminism) are being figured in so-called post-feminist media culture.[2] How do such intensely contradictory discourses operate alongside each other in various sites of popular culture? What is sayable about women's singleness, and by whom? What kinds of single women – in terms of age, race, sexuality, and class – are granted visibility? What ideological purposes do these representations serve? And how – and where – are they being contested?

This book presumes that the single woman, including the 'Singleton' of so-called 'chick culture', is a useful figure through which to critically engage with and rethink the relationship between Western feminism and modern media culture. In her shifting (or perhaps intractable) representations, this fraught relationship becomes magnified. The assumption is commonly made that, in what is purported to be the discursive shift from 'spinster to Singleton', the single woman has been irrevocably refigured. That is, she is now culturally celebrated where once she was denigrated. *Single Women in Popular Culture* disrupts this teleological narrative, which has been gaining currency in both popular and academic contexts, by demonstrating how the single woman remains a figure of discursive unease (or dis-ease) but in new and complicated ways that both incorporate and trouble feminism. In terms of women in media culture, the figure of the single woman is an interesting phenomenon in and of itself, but here I am also interested in how she can be used to cast light on the operations and logics of postfeminism. Moreover, I read the figure of the single woman *diagnostically*. As Douglas Kellner makes explicit in *Media Culture* (1995), diagnostic critique 'uses media culture to diagnose social trends and tendencies, reading through the texts to the fantasies, fears, hopes and desires that they articulate. A diagnostic critique also analyzes how media culture provides the resources for producing identities' (pp. 5–6). However, such critique also enables us to see how 'the ideological projects of media often fail' (Kellner, 1995, p. 5), something I show through, in particular, highlighting the narratives of women's singleness that run counter to those that dominate mainstream media culture.

Rather than using critical frames such as stereotyping or stigma (as many scholars of singleness have done), which both presume distorted representation and therefore an unmediated 'real' existing outside of how it is put into discourse, I foreground how such representations work to bring into being certain forms of creditable, or indeed discreditable, identities for single women (Reynolds, 2008). In this way, 'explicitly and implicitly, women are instructed by their environment (from the school room to women's magazines) in how to "become" a woman – a task that is never completed and is subject to constant revision' (Radner, 2010, p. 6). To build on this point, we are also 'instructed' in how to 'become' and indeed 'unbecome' single women, including through the types of popular cultural texts I engage with here. As a form of feminist cultural studies, this book presumes that how women are discursively constituted in the mainstream cultural field *matters*. But this need not imply some simplistic model focused on how 'positive' or 'negative' representations impact upon single women.[3] The limitations of such an approach have been well canvassed by media and cultural critics, not least because of the attendant assumptions about media effects on passive audiences and the (impossible) mimetic accuracy of representation. Instead, media is best conceptualized as one in a number of 'technologies of gender, accommodating, modifying, reconstructing and producing disciplinary and contradictory outlooks of sexual difference' (Van Zoonen, 1994, p. 41).

The type of feminist cultural criticism proffered here, then, is indebted to poststructuralist work on subjectivity, discourse, and representation. Accordingly, I suggest that singleness as a gendered form of difference is produced and negotiated in and through these mainstream cultural products. As a means of 'disciplining' women, in the Foucauldian sense, the intertextual network consisting of contradictory discourses around the single woman needs to be interrogated as a mechanism of power. Certain ways of being woman are legitimized in mainstream media culture through the exclusion and pathologization of others. Most obviously, it is heterosexual women who are the most visible in these popular narratives of singleness. While some of popular culture's 'Singletons' have short-lived affairs with women (such as Samantha Jones and her brief relationship with Maria in *Sex and the City*), heterosexual single subjects are those with which popular culture appears most preoccupied. It is not surprising that these postfeminist texts foreground such sexually normative women given that – as I demonstrate throughout – a core part of postfeminism is the re-embrace, naturalization, and indeed celebration of heterosexual romance (Gill, 2007; McRobbie, 2009). In light of the kinds of single women that are most visible in the popular imaginary, therefore, the focus here is necessarily on how postfeminist heterosexuality is enacted within and through such texts.

Although the fields of critical psychology and sociology have over the past few years produced a number of studies based on interviews with single women, focusing on the discursive resources they use to make sense of their singleness (Lewis & Moon, 1997; Reynolds & Wetherell, 2003; Sandfield & Percy, 2003; Simpson, 2006; Macvarish, 2006, 2008; Reynolds, Wetherell & Taylor, 2007; Budgeon, 2008; Reynolds, 2008), feminist media and cultural studies has not yet given this figure due critical attention – either through textual analysis or ethnographic research. That said, some feminist critics have briefly addressed the single woman as indicative of changes in how women more generally are represented in media culture. That is, she is a key figure in critical narratives that have located a seismic shift in the relationship between feminism and popular culture. For example, in *Redesigning Women: Television After the Network Era* (2006), Amanda Lotz uses the figure of Ally McBeal – whose broader cultural reverberations were evident when she appeared on the cover of US's *Time* magazine as an exemplar of the then burgeoning feminist 'third-wave' (along with the *Sex and The City* characters) – to posit this shift in media culture's attitude not only to single women but to feminism itself. Feminism, it is implied, has made these women possible, indeed representable. Likewise, in some instances of critical commentary on Bridget Jones (as Chapter 3 examines in depth), she is seen to embody the contradictions of being a feminine subject in late modernity in a way that suggests a fundamentally altered representational landscape (Genz, 2009, 2010). However, as Rosalind Gill argues (2007, p. 148) and as studies like Lotz's serve to illustrate, analyses of postfeminist media culture have tended to concentrate on just a few key texts (such as *Ally McBeal*, *Sex and the City*, and *Desperate Housewives*). While I too engage with some of these programmes when considering the broader intertextual environment in which the figure of the single woman comes to mean (Chapter 2), like Gill I am interested in turning to examples of cultural production that have received comparatively little (or no) attention from feminist scholars concerned with the figure of the single woman, including single women's self-help literature and blogs. Postfeminism is 'a comprehensive discursive system', thereby requiring analysis across diverse textual sites (Negra, 2009, p. 9). In attending to this wide range of texts, *Single Women in Popular Culture* offers a comprehensive, nuanced analysis of the broader cultural conversation in which the figure of the single woman is enmeshed.

Methodologically, my own analysis here is based on close readings of a number of popular cultural texts, with an emphasis on discursive formations and thus questions of power. While it is not necessary to restage debates over the claims that can be made via textual analysis as a methodology, it is worth making a few observations in this regard. Though of course women readers negotiate with these representations, creatively interacting and responding to the texts they choose to consume, textual analysis permits the identification of commonalities across the cultural field and enables the location of the single woman in a wider intertextual network. Without painting a homogenous picture here, there are undoubtedly some recurrent tropes, themes, and narrative patterns that have emerged in the broader, ongoing cultural conversation about what it means for (certain kinds of) contemporary women to be single that I have tracked, across various sites, in Western media culture. Even the most resistant of readers would find it difficult to refute the proposition that specific ways of thinking, speaking, and knowing singleness are foregrounded over others within postfeminist media culture, and that this process works to ensure that certain forms of feminine subjectivity are culturally legitimized over others – a process that itself has material effects. Such texts, of course, and the cultural work they do, can always be subject to contestation. My approach to media culture here is neither celebratory nor condemnatory but instead focuses on how these textual sites can at once be politically troublesome from a feminist perspective while potentially providing the tools to reimagine and refigure women's singleness.

In this regard, in the final two chapters I consider how single women writing self-help manuals or writing their lives via the blog form draw attention to the limitations of how women are coded in other sites of media culture. Such forms operate as vibrant pockets of discursive resistance in an otherwise fairly limited cultural conversation about singleness. Moreover, in the case of the blogs I examine, they problematize limited ways of figuring singleness and, implicitly, postfeminism. In this way, they show how the provision of alternatives to dominant ways of figuring singleness also requires the provision of alternatives to postfeminist rhetorics. That said, and as I explore in that chapter (as well as Chapter 5), the cultural impact of such texts is arguably not commensurate with more heavily promoted, and more widely consumed, texts that contribute to the broader meaning-making network around women's singleness. Nonetheless, such forms are politically and symbolically important in how they work to revalue singleness, as I will show.

As my analysis illustrates, rarely is a single woman in popular culture shown to be entirely reconciled to her singleness, itself one of the ways in which the threat she poses is managed. In terms of its popular renderings, women's singleness can be seen as a form of 'abject femininity' (Negra, 2009), an idea further explored here. Moreover, only single women who are clearly invested in the process to be otherwise – those on the 'quest to become unsingle' (DePaulo, 2006, p. 72) – as well as those that can be seen to be embody a normative femininity, are the most visible, and positioned as acceptable, within the texts of postfeminist media culture. Though there may be multiple forms of single femininities within women's lived realities, they are delimited and hierarchized in the textual sites to which I attend. In situating single women in a wider representational context, Diane Negra argues 'the vituperative and condemnatory discourses that often circulate in regard to single women' (2009, p. 61) are further evidence of an 'increased misogynist turn' in contemporary popular culture (2004, p. 4). This emphasis on the need for a feminist critical practice that facilitates a deconstruction of the binaries that continue to structure how women are publicly made to mean is certainly prescient. As Negra puts it, feminists need 'to hone critical modes of interrogating and interrupting the false dichotomies of idealized familial plenitude and vilified abject singlehood that currently prevail in U.S. [and other forms of Western] popular culture' (2009, p. 61). Following Negra's exhortation, *Single Women in Popular Culture* seeks to perform this kind of deconstructive, yet politically engaged, feminist critical practice and indeed argues that contemporary media culture, because of its increasingly complicated and ambivalent relation to feminism, actually necessitates such an approach.

The 'postfeminization' of media culture

Although popular feminism was for many years 'dismissed in favour of an authentic feminism which is "elsewhere"' (Brunsdon, 1997, p. 101), it is now axiomatic that mainstream media culture functions as one of the key public sites in the constitution of feminism. As numerous critics have shown over the past five years or so in particular (when theoretical debates about the status and politics of that shifting signifier, postfeminism, became most pronounced), contests over the meanings of feminism, and indeed between feminists, are now predominantly staged within the mediasphere. Media appropriations of feminism have been complex and diverse. The political consequences of such distillation continue to preoccupy feminist critics, who fear in particular the watering down of complex ideas and ideological critique, culminating in the emptying out of feminism's oppositional potential. But, as Rita Felski reminds us, feminism is an 'impure, porous public discourse' (2000, p. 201) and the idea that it exists (or indeed that it has ever existed) in a pure, non-commercial space beyond its 'media mediations' is simply unsustainable (Murray, 2004; see also Taylor, 2008).

Cultural conversations – and, most importantly, contestations – around gender and women's subjectivity occur every day within a media field that is now irrevocably inflected by feminism. To signal the way it is now 'simply part of the cultural landscape', Susan J. Douglas has coined the phrase 'embedded feminism' (2010, p. 9). The presence of feminism in mainstream media culture is often seen to be most obvious in the so-called 'new femininities' (Taylor, 2003; Gill & Herdieckerdorf, 2006), or what have even been called 'postfemininities' (Genz, 2009), believed to have proliferated therein over the past decade or so. In this way, as a number of critics concerned with how feminism has been taken up in popular culture have suggested, it is not only in overt engagements with the signifier 'feminism' that contests over its meanings are taking place. Indeed, it is predominantly in these popular cultural spaces where feminism (even if not explicitly named as such), and struggles over its meanings and thus its possible futures, are most visible.

Despite these popular engagements with feminism, to be partnered is yet seen as a universal feminine desire that cuts across class and race lines, therefore narratives about remedying singleness relentlessly populate movie and television screens, books, and popular music at an increasingly accelerated pace. Inter alia, the figure of the single woman provides a way into – and indeed a more nuanced way of approaching – debates about women, subjectivity, feminism, and modern media culture; especially around its 'postfeminization'. Indeed, 'any significant engagement with the popular cultural landscape of the last 15 years requires wrestling with the concept of postfeminism' (Negra, 2009, pp. 1–2). In and through these representations of the single woman, I argue, some very complicated arguments about women, feminism, and especially postfeminism are being staged.

Here I ask: what might this figure and her pronounced presence on the mediascape of the late twentieth–early twenty-first centuries tell us about the intersections of feminism and media culture? How have these dominant cultural logics of postfeminism affected how single women are now discursively constituted in popular culture? How is the threat posed by single women both represented and regulated? Where are the points where such regulation is unsuccessful or disrupted, especially by single women themselves? The often contradictory ways in which she is given to mean underscores the necessity for feminist cultural critics to be attentive to the politics of representation in a way that has been precluded by more optimistic readings regarding feminism's distillation in the mediasphere. Similarly, the increased presence of single women in various popular media forms is not in itself cause for celebration. Although (some) single women are hyper-visible in the public sphere, the politics of this (in)visibility – something to which I attend throughout – must always be taken into account. In focusing on the political specificities and ramifications of this over-determined relationship, I am not presuming, as Sarah Projansky so aptly puts it, that '"my feminism is right and popular culture's feminism is wrong" but rather that "my feminist analysis offers a particular critical perspective on the strengths and weaknesses of popular feminism"' (2001, p. 14). In line with this approach, some other feminist cultural critics have argued that postfeminism (in tandem with neoliberalism) has worked in particularly reactionary ways around the figure of the single woman and I draw upon and extend that work throughout. For example, Negra conjectures that 'postfeminism might be seen as particularly punishing in its relation to single women, having raised their cultural profile though without any corresponding enlargement of their status/options' (2009, p. 10; see also Leonard, 2009). The promotion of matrimonial and maternal subjectivities in postfeminist media culture, as Negra makes clear (2009, p. 5), relies upon the denigration and abjection of women's singleness.

Given, then, the ways that it works to delimit the forms of singleness that are visible in contemporary popular culture, it is worth noting that 'postfeminism' is a highly contested signifier, whose meanings (like any other) alter according to the discursive context in which it is deployed. The term can be found to possess currency in both popular and academic discourse, and in these sites it signifies in different ways.[4] In my analysis I am indebted to Angela McRobbie's recent work in *The Aftermath of Feminism* (2009). McRobbie has theorized postfeminism via the notion of 'double entanglement' (following Judith Butler), a term she uses to signal how feminism is simultaneously taken account of *and* repudiated in the modern public sphere: 'Post-feminism positively draws on and invokes feminism as that which can be taken into account, to suggest that equality is achieved, in order to install a whole repertoire of new meanings which emphasize that it is no longer needed, it is a spent force' (2009, p. 12; see also Tasker & Negra, 2007).

In this way, postfeminism cannot just be dismissed, as some critics have done, as a 'false feminism' (Kim, 2001); its relationship to feminism is much more complicated than such an assertion permits (though its politics are indeed dubious). The dual process of both adapting and disavowing feminism theorized by McRobbie is especially apt to the position of the single woman in the dominant cultural imaginary: 'What makes contemporary media culture distinctively postfeminist, rather than prefeminist or antifeminist, is precisely this entanglement of feminist and antifeminist ideas' (Gill, 2007, p. 161). Here I explore how this 'suturing' of feminism and antifeminism – upon which Gill, following McRobbie, remarks – plays out in specific and complicated ways around the figure of the single woman. Like feminism itself, and through a series of complex representational manoeuvres, I argue that the contemporary single woman is allowed, endorsed, even celebrated; yet simultaneously disavowed as that which must be pitied, scorned, and emptied of her oppositional potential. That is, the contradictions and tensions that I am mapping around the figure of the single woman are indicative of the contradictions and tensions that are constitutive of postfeminism *itself*.[5] Moreover, as I will show, though postfeminist discourse represents one of the key ways in/through which feminism has been reworked and comes to circulate in today's media culture, postfeminism is also subject to contestation therein. That is, the 'tenets of mainstream postfeminism' can be 'unsettled' from within (Negra, 2004). Via such 'unsettling', other forms and ways of figuring feminism can be seen to be in operation and used as the means through which different stories of women's singleness are able to be articulated.

Although not explicitly used in relation to the single woman, feminist critics have invoked terms such as 'retrosexism' (Whelehan, 2000) and 'enlightened sexism' (Douglas, 2010) to mark the pernicious ways in which this taking account of feminism has, in many instances, permitted some deeply reactionary narratives about women to (re)surface in ways that can seem difficult to attack – given their claims to exist in a period of comparative gender equality and ostensibly profound feminist achievement. This too is the case with the single woman who is often seen as at once a professional triumph and a personal failure: 'As the professionally successful but often interpersonally challenged women of postfeminist culture confirm, the aspiration of being fabulous, strong, and professionally independent is counterposed with the desire to secure a heterosexual partnership, and often their successful coexistence is deemed both unlikely and unrealistic' (Leonard, 2009, p. 11). According to such narratives, which arguably work to manage the threat posed by the woman without a man, public/professional competency equals private/personal incompetency. This idea – that women's success in the public sphere has come at the price of the private – resurfaces throughout the texts of postfeminist media culture. Women's singleness, in such accounts, comes to be figured as a failure of feminism (an explicitly levelled charge considered further in the next chapter). Moreover, as Sheryl Vint argues, in 'making the right man the solution to the dilemmas of gender discrimination' popular texts position feminism as having been mistaken or exaggerated 'because love is real, natural, and unchanging, preventing us from ever imagining a world in which most men treated women badly' (2007, p. 163).

The difficulty of negotiating these tensions between fairly traditional forms of femininity and a rhetoric of agency inspired by feminism is commonly seen as a quintessentially postfeminist dilemma, exemplified by the so-called 'postfeminist singleton' (Genz, 2009; 2010). However, I would argue that the presumed universality of this feminine desire to be coupled puts under strain the celebratory argument that the 'postfeminist singleton occupies a multivalent and paradoxical space between dualities' (Genz, 2010, p. 115). In contrast, here I argue the single woman is an important figure through which to consider not only how 'subjects are governed, disciplined or regulated in ever more intimate ways' but how ideas of 'choice, agency and autonomy' can be seen to have 'become central to that regulatory project' (Gill, 2008, p. 443). Given this, representations of the single woman help illuminate how postfeminist and neoliberal logics are, in many respects, mutually reinforcing.

Postfeminism and/as neoliberalism

Postfeminism relies upon, indeed helps to construct, a particular version of the single feminine self. Here I will show that what Rosalind Gill identifies as the 'makeover paradigm' integral to postfeminism (2007, p. 156) applies in very specific, and often reactionary, ways to single women. As Gill remarks of this paradigm, 'This requires people (predominantly women) to believe, first, that they or their life is lacking or flawed in some way; second, that it is amenable to reinvention or transformation by following the advice of relationship, design or lifestyle experts and practising appropriately modified consumption habits' (2007, p. 156). As I suggest throughout, a key way in which to discredit singleness is to insist that the single woman be made over into something else; or at least be seen to be in the process of transformation. She cannot be allowed to stay the way she is – consistent with this logic, and as I have noted, the most visible single woman in postfeminist media culture is she who proves her profound wish to be otherwise; this is the very condition of her possibility. The single woman quite literally lacks an-other, something which in the rhetoric of neoliberalism she can easily rectify through various forms of self-labour. Postfeminism, as Gill argues, resonates powerfully with neoliberalism: 'the autonomous, calculating, self-regulating subject of neoliberalism bears a strong resemblance to the active, free-choosing, self-inventing subject of postfeminism' (2007, p. 164). Postfeminism, then, is in effect neoliberalism gendered feminine and articulated to feminist-inspired discourses of autonomy, freedom, and choice for women. Indeed, some critics even use the term 'neoliberal postfeminism' (Vavrus, 2007) to signal their ideological symbiosis.

   In addition to Gill's work on the intersection of postfeminism and neoliberalism, my use of the term 'neoliberal' is indebted to the work of political philosophers such as Wendy Brown. Economically, neoliberalism refers to limited State intervention and the privileging of the market; its emphasis on the privatization of state assets and services has morphed into a broader rhetoric around how citizens should behave. Neoliberalism, in terms of cultural politics especially, signals the extension of this economic rationality into realms not directly related to the State but which nonetheless perform the work of governance in a way that benefits it (Brown, 2003). As Wendy Brown argues, 'neo-liberalism normatively constructs and interpellates individuals as entrepreneurial actors in every sphere of life. It figures individuals as rational, calculating creatures whose moral autonomy is measured by their capacity for "self-care"'. According to Brown, therefore, neoliberalism 'carries responsibility for the self to new heights' (2003, p. 3).

Despite the extreme focus on self that marks neoliberalism, the centrality of the (male) other – particularly in texts bearing what Gill calls a 'postfeminist sensibility' – remains paramount, and indeed neoliberal rhetorics extend into the realm of interpersonal, and especially romantic, relationships. This contradiction is at the heart of postfeminist neoliberal rhetoric, where the idea of women's choice – 'just pleasing themselves and following their autonomously generated desire' (Gill, 2007, p. 154) – is used to justify women's investment in, for instance, traditional romance scripts. Women are no longer indoctrinated into believing a man will make them happy, they now (apparently) actively *choose* to believe he will, and this is seen as cause for a postfeminist celebration. In contradistinction, Gill sees this as a 'messy suturing of traditional and neoliberal discourses': 'In this modernized, neoliberal version of femininity, it is absolutely imperative that one's sexual and dating practices be presented as freely chosen (however traditional, old-fashioned or inegalitarian they may be – involving strict adherence to rules, rationing oneself and not displaying any needs)' (2007, p. 154). So what might popular culture's intensive efforts to ensure women are partnered, imploring them to do the work to sustain and bring about such partnerships, tell us about neoliberalism (and indeed postfeminism) and its role in sanctioning certain modes of being and relating?

As I will make clear, the single woman is implored to discipline herself in particular ways to transcend or makeover this inherently undesirable identity. However, sometimes she is shown to need assistance in this process and therefore what Bourdieu calls 'cultural intermediaries' are called upon to help make her over, especially in the realm of reality television (see McRobbie, 2009). Developing this point, in Chapter 4 I argue that dating reality television operates essentially as a form of 'makeover' television, not simply through its pronounced attempt to make women unsingle, but in how it monitors and seeks (to varying degrees) to regulate single women's behaviour. In Chapter 5, I return to these questions and consider how the single woman is exhorted to change in the context of a broader self-improvement culture (Rose, 1996, 1999). More broadly, drawing upon Foucauldian informed ideas about technologies of the self and governance, here I am concerned with the role media culture plays in attempting to regulate the single subject who is gendered feminine – a regulation that is inextricably linked to the postfeminist valorization of romance and heterosexual coupledom.

Postfeminist discourse retreats from the politicization of intimate relationships that characterized second-wave feminism and 'romanticis[es] heterosexual romance' (Hammers, 2005, p. 169; Dow, 1996). In particular, I am concerned with how this overt embrace of heterosexuality, via fairly unreconstructed romance narratives, became a marker of postfeminism (and came to be seen as *the* central desire, and personalized dilemma, of young modern women) and the impact that this has had on the kinds of discourses circulating about the single woman over the past few decades. The idea of 'having it all', routinely described as the dilemma with which all postfeminist media texts engage, has particular implications for how single women are constructed. Of course, 'having it all' is a highly gendered discourse (not to mention its assumptions about race and class), as the negotiations it invokes are seen to be solely the province of women; that women having both public and private identities is still seen to be problematic (in a way that it never was for men) points to the very necessity of feminism as a political project not to its success. The trope of 'having it all', signalling career *and* men and the family their attainment signifies, equates with 'having' more than just oneself – it means, most emphatically, *not* being single. The question, too, invoked by this so-called postfeminist dilemma – 'Why should women have to give up (hetero)sexuality in order to have a professional career?' (Projansky, 2001, p. 80) – implies that not having a man is a sacrifice as opposed to a potentially desirable option. The single woman who does not object to or fear her own singleness, therefore, embodies a glitch in this postfeminist representational economy, and there are a number of ways in which she is symbolically dealt with; as I seek to demonstrate here throughout.

In terms of shifting representations of single women (as well as feminism itself), sexuality is integral: 'The major representational change mediated by popular culture in regard to femininity is an open acknowledgement of female sexuality and the right to sexual pleasure' (Smyczynska, 2007, p. 130). Perhaps unsurprisingly, it is through renderings of the single woman that such a shift is most visibly enacted; it is her sexuality and its public display with which many popular narratives are preoccupied. Accordingly, the figure of the single woman in contemporary media culture cannot be extricated from what has been called the 'striptease culture' (McNair, 2002) of the early twenty-first century. As Attwood argues of the characters from *Sex and the City*, 'this particular figure has become very prominent in popular culture as a "chic" signification of post-feminist, postmodern bourgeois sexual identity, and of the pornographication which Brian McNair documents' (2006, p. 86). Indeed, the single woman who is ostensibly 'celebrated' in popular culture is a particular type of sexualized subject and evidences what Attwood calls a 'new form of sexual address to women' (2005). That women can, and do, practice their sexuality not only outside long term monogamous relationships, but entirely by themselves – though mediated by various products (lingerie, sex toys, porn) – is presumed and reinforced within contemporary media culture, including through advertising and television programmes such as *Sex and the City* (Attwood, 2005, 2006). The contemporary single woman, as all the texts I examine here illustrate, is by no means presumed asexual. On the contrary, as characters like *Sex and the City*'s Samantha Jones exemplify, she is often hypersexual – performing a type of excessive (hetero)sexuality, indeed a 'man-like' pursuit of sexual pleasure (her constant refrain within the series is of wanting to have sex like a man or without emotional investment). What Sarah Projansky (2001, p. 79) has called 'prosex postfeminism' positions 'sexual interaction with men as a core desire for women' and mobilizes negative assumptions about feminism's critique of heterosexuality: '[T]hese representations assume the centrality of heterosexuality in women's lives in opposition to what postfeminist discourses portray as antisex feminism' (2001, p. 83). Desiring a man, and acting upon this desire, is then seen as a postfeminist act. This question of how women's sexuality is performed, and indeed regulated, in the texts of mainstream media culture, and how this can be seen as a marker of postfeminism, will be considered here at various points.

If we accept the argument that there has been a discursive shift in terms of these public figurations of the single woman, something I question throughout this book, it must follow that the way heterosexual relationships and marriage in particular are rendered meaningful and valuable must also have experienced a shift or in some way responded to this. But have the dominant mythologies around 'the One' or soul mates been likewise refigured? No study of how single women are figured in popular culture can ignore this question, for it is through and against such narratives that the single woman comes to be seen as problematic. That is, these representations and the conflicting discourses in which the single woman is enmeshed are key to the maintenance and mythologization of heterosexuality – the single woman is the Other against whom 'normal' (i.e. coupled) women are discursively constituted and brought into being as particular gendered and sexed subjects. Postfeminism, it seems, is by no means post-compulsory heterosexuality; indeed, the two discourses seem, in popular culture, to be entirely consistent and mutually reinforcing. That is, postfeminism (further) normalizes and universalizes heterosexual coupledom. In the next section, I interrogate the continued hegemony of compulsory heterosexuality and how it helps to ensure that certain, deeply ideologically loaded, stories of women's singleness continue to proliferate, despite claims about its widespread cultural acceptance.

Romance, marriage, and compulsory heterosexuality

In her polemic, *Against Love*, Laura Kipnis argues:

> Has any despot's rule ever so successfully infiltrated every crevice of a population's being, into its movements and gestures, penetrated its very soul? In fact it creates the modern notion of a soul – one which experiences itself as empty without love. Saying 'no' to love isn't just heresy, it's tragedy: for our sort the failure to achieve what is most essentially human. And not just tragic, but abnormal.
>
> (2003, p. 22)

In many respects, the study of how single women are constructed is necessarily also a study of how these ideologies around romantic love operate in our media saturated environment. In this way, this book also underscores how deeply heterosexuality is naturalized and how heteronormativity operates in new and sophisticated ways within contemporary media culture. Acting as a critique of the 'heterosexual imaginary' and the ideological labour that both perpetuates it and renders it invisible, this book can be situated within the field of what Chrys Ingraham has identified as 'critical heterosexual studies' (1999) as well as the burgeoning field of 'singles' studies'.

Since Adrienne Rich's infamous essay on 'compulsory heterosexuality' (1980), feminists have attempted to lay bare the cultural and symbolic work that undergirds the institution of heterosexuality. Accordingly, it is axiomatic within feminist studies that 'heterosexuality is a site for the social construction of gender, and that heterosexual sex is a primary instrument through which we are constructed *as women* and *as men*' (Kitzinger & Wilkinson 1994, p. 76, original emphasis). Moreover, being in a romantic (heterosexual) relationship has historically been conceptualized as the key marker of mental health and maturity in modern Western societies (Storr, 1988; Geller, 2001). Choosing a life of solitude remains an 'oddity' (Brown, 2006, p. 202), especially for women whose identities are commonly seen, in psychoanalytic terms, to be intersubjective (Benjamin, 1990). It is still perceived to be one of – if not the – central choices that *all* citizens will make, and indeed that *makes* all citizens.

The relentless privileging of this form of relationship serves to undermine other forms of affect and non-familial bonds, revealing the continued valorization of heterosexual coupledom as the only legitimate form of cathexis.[6] For Negra, this is part of a postfeminist representational economy wherein femininity is codified and essentialized, with women believed to be 'bound together by a common set of innate desires, fears, and concerns' (2009, p. 12). These desires, as she extrapolates, are those relating to heterosexual partnerships and mothering, areas which come to be seen as the only avenues for 'legitimate' affective investment for women (Negra, 2009, p. 9). Postfeminism's embrace and unremitting promotion of heterosexuality forecloses the possibility of the feminine subject negotiating a new relationship with the self, retreating instead to a world that continues to privilege – or at least valorize the relationship with – the (male) other. The single woman, therefore, is written out (or worse) of the dominant narratives of this signifying economy.

The enduring power of the 'heterosexual imaginary', and its naturalization, necessarily has a significant impact on how single women are figured in Western media culture. As Chrys Ingraham argues, appropriating Althusser's work on the Lacanian imaginary in relation to his study of ideology, the operation of the 'heterosexual imaginary' is concealed, thereby leaving institutionalized heterosexuality unexamined. By refusing to subject it to critique in our day-to-day existences:

> [W]e don't explore how it is learned, what keeps it in place, and the interests it serves in the ways it's currently practiced. Through the use of the heterosexual imaginary, we uphold the institution of heterosexuality as timeless, devoid of any historical variation, as 'just the way it is' while creating social practices that reinforce the illusion that as long as this 'is the way it is' all will be alright in the world. Romancing – creating an illusory – heterosexuality is central to the heterosexual imaginary.
>
> (1999, p. 16)

Given then that heteronormativity is central to the maintenance of this imaginary, it (via the State) also requires that subjects situate themselves in relation to the married/single binary, such as on census forms, even when they would rather refuse to do so (Ingraham, 1999, p. 17). This assumption about the universality of a desire for heteronormative coupledom helps to ensure that the woman-without-a-man (and especially without a marriage certificate) is largely perceived as lack.[7]

Despite some commentary on the shifting cultural significance of marriage and its patent impermanence in the twentieth and twenty-first century (with the divorce rate in the West widely acknowledged to be one in two), the cultural currency of institutionalized heterosexuality, through marriage, remains firmly in place. It continues to function as an institution whose borders are jealously guarded (witness the virulent opposition to same-sex marriages) Indeed, it has been argued that it is due to the declining significance of marriage and heightening divorce rates, not to mention the reduced economic imperative for women to marry, that efforts to maintain it as a site of privilege and value in terms of social status have become more pronounced (Koropeckyj-Cox, 2005, p. 96). Although singleness is largely figured as a transitory state, statistics reveal that it is increasingly marriage which is the transitional period with, for example, the majority of Americans now spending a greater proportion of their lives single than married (DePaulo, 2006). Nonetheless, as Geller (2001, p. 104) argues, becoming engaged, and ultimately married, is still largely viewed as a form of redemption for single women, a type of 'social victory', despite narratives of progress around the purported acceptance of women's singleness. For Geller, 'the notion of matrimony as destiny for women is as deeply entrenched in our own culture as it has been in any past era' (2001, p. 382). The rhetoric of coupledom is also used by and about gay and lesbian couples (Budgeon, 2006), who in seeking the privileges afforded by the institution of marriage serve to buttress its ideological power and, concomitantly, heterosexuality itself (Ingraham, 1999, p. 166). As all these critics suggest, the idea of a singular relationship, a marital one especially, to meet all of a person's 'affective and physical needs' continues to be vigorously promoted (Ingraham, 1999, p. 162).

As texts constructing the single woman as a problem to be solved (most obviously through marriage) indicate, postfeminist popular culture has clearly taken 'a hypermatrimonial turn' (Negra, 2009, p. 81). So while single women have perhaps never been so visible in popular culture, this also applies to her married counterparts: wives. The single woman is, as Anne Kingston has called her to signal how she represents the Other of married women, an 'unwife' (2004). Further evidence of this intense preoccupation with wives can be found in the proliferation of, and audience investment in, contemporary television programmes about wives, including in the field of reality shows: *The Real Housewives of New York* (as well as other areas in the States such as Atlanta and Orange County), *Mob Wives*, and *Army Wives*. Further, the intense media frenzy in the lead up to the Royal Wedding of Prince William and Kate Middleton has also witnessed the preoccupation with weddings and the enduring affective investment in the aspirational Cinderella narrative which suggests much about class as well as gender. The excessive media attention to this wedding could be seen as one of the most intense instances in recent history of what has aptly been called 'matrimania' (DePaulo, 2006).

Being a straight single woman, particularly for a prolonged period, is often seen as a failure to perform heterosexuality adequately or appropriately, especially in terms of the defiance of its key institution: marriage. Single women, and specifically those who self-consciously choose it, represent embodied resistances to the regulation of intimate relationships and thereby act as threats to be managed. In accordance with what Geller (2001) has called the 'matrimonial fetish,' there is a tendency to disallow the agency of singles, a gesture which serves to undermine transgressive potentialities of singleness: 'most unmarried persons are viewed as victims who have defaulted to singlehood, rather than as powerful agents who have established and maintained personal relationships that fulfil their own preferences and desires' (Byrne & Carr, 2005, p. 89). As I will show, the refusal to concede such agency continues to position singleness as an illegitimate way of being in the world for women. It is also an important way of further normalizing heterosexuality and coupledom.

In terms of the cultural work being done to ensure its hegemony, including through the circulation of ideologies of romantic love, patriarchal capitalism is said to be 'in a continual state of crisis management' (Ingraham, 1999, p. 21). That is, the symbolic labour being undertaken to shore up this situation is immense. In this vein, Angela McRobbie has shown how the symbolics of heterosexual desire have had to be reworked to account for modern socio-political changes in women's status in the West. That is, changes to (some) women's lived realities, particularly in terms of economic independence, have meant that popular culture has become a central site in ensuring the continued desirability of heterosexual desire. As McRobbie says, 'confronted with the prospect of women becoming less dependent on men as a result of participation in work and with the possible destabilization of gender hierarchy which might ensue, it becomes all the more important for the Symbolic to re-secure the terms of heterosexual desire' (2009, p. 62). And it is this frame that helps ensure, and indeed *requires*, that the single woman remains a figure of profound difference, invoked as that which women fear either remaining or becoming. In fact, remedying singleness is big business, with the United States Bureau of Statistics recently noting that the number of 'dating service establishments', including Internet-based services, was 904 in 2009, an industry that employs 4,300 people and generates $489 million in revenue (US Census Bureau News, 19 July, 2010). The expansion of this industry, centred on rectifying singleness, speaks to both the commercial and ideological interests being served by the promotion of this 'marital economy' (Geller, 2001). The explosion of such businesses, with their promise of assisting putatively forlorn singles, itself can be seen as an instance of what Bella DePaulo calls 'singlism'.

'Singlism', 'matrimania', and feminism

There is no doubt that much feminist attention, especially in the field of history and literary studies (work I further consider here in Chapter 3), has been directed towards the spinster as an important political fig-ure working to disrupt the circumscribed femininities available in the nineteenth century. However, over the past few decades the work of asserting singleness as a viable way of being for women has not been as pronounced. Though more recent writers like Elaine Trimberger (2005) and Bella DePaulo (2006) have addressed women's singleness, as have the bloggers I spotlight here in Chapter 6, 'feminist writers have not generally challenged the stigma attached to single women' (Rosa, 1994, p. 115). In fact, Rachel Moran (2004) has comprehensively demonstrated how second-wave feminism effectively 'forgot' the single woman. As she argues, the liberal feminist agenda, as the most dominant form to have found voice in the Western public sphere, was focused instead on transforming heterosexual partnerships into equitable relationships. The consequences of this are substantial; Moran suggests that feminism has 'failed to deliver a satisfying conception of life outside of marriage, even as women increasingly find themselves in this situation' (2004, p. 278). So although feminism, including from within the academy, has worked to address how various modalities of difference work to consti-tute women's subjectivity, singleness – as a very real form of difference that impacts upon women both symbolically and materially – has only comparatively recently been viewed as a form of difference worthy of critical or indeed political attention.

In her groundbreaking work in this field, American psychologist and public commentator on singleness, Bella DePaulo, coined the term 'singlism' (2006) to denote various forms of discrimination, both direct and indirect, material and symbolic, against those without partners. As well as drawing attention to limited media constructions of singleness, she outlines how privileges for the coupled are entrenched at a governmental level through specific policies and legislative measures. In particular, DePaulo emphasizes the need for a shift in the cultural imaginary to enable singleness to be valued as more than simply a transitional state, an idea which underpins this study. Appropriating Betty Friedan's (1963) rhetoric, DePaulo argues that singlism 'is the twenty-first century problem that has no name' (2006, p. 2). Likewise, as mentioned, she uses 'matrimania' to signal Western culture's hyper-investment in marriage and wedding culture: 'The narrative structured by singlism and fuelled by matrimania is the only story that has been told of our lives' (DePaulo 2006, p. 235).[8] Although DePaulo does not recognize the potential of counter-narratives to disrupt these limited stories (something to which I turn in the final two chapters especially), their cultural pervasiveness is unquestionable. Indeed, those failing to live according to this dominant narrative continue to be judged, often harshly, for their non-compliance.

Of the enduring affective power of this heterosexual imaginary, particularly for women, Lauren Berlant observes: 'People who are unhinged or unhitched, who live outside the normative loops of property and reproduction, are frequently seen both as symptoms of personal failure and threats to the general happiness, which seems to require, among other things, the positioning of any person's core life story in a plot of love's unfolding, especially if that person is a woman' (2008, p. 172). Indeed, as she intimates, to be 'unhitched' is largely equated with being 'unhinged'. This plot of which Berlant speaks continues to dominate in mainstream media culture as the romance genre, and its audience base, further expands. In addition, the social value of the ritual of the wedding ceremony appears undiminished. In fact, weddings, 'massively promoted by consumer culture', are said to be experiencing a 'new popularity' (McRobbie, 2009, p. 21). To suggest its market success even in times of financial crisis, the wedding industry – or what Ingraham in *White Weddings* dubs the 'wedding industrial complex' – has been referred to as 'recession proof' by Wall Street analysts (1999, p. 26). As her study underscores, it is a multi-billion dollar, global business and thus the promotion of such institutionalized heterosexuality has commercial as well as ideological causes and effects. Moreover, it is also implicated in the rhetoric of happiness.

As Sarah Ahmed's recent work on happiness and its politics illuminates, happiness itself is yet seen to be as contingent upon romantic partnership and marriage especially. The 'promissory logic of happiness', she observes, is evident around the 'idealisation of marriage' (2007, p. 12). The single woman, conversely, especially in popular narratives like *Ally McBeal*, is a figure of profound unhappiness and its central character Ally is throughout seen to mobilize such 'promissory logic'. If only she were not lonely – that is, if she were partnered – her happiness would be guaranteed (or so she presumes). Singleness is therefore routinely excluded from narratives of how happiness can be attained (though some writers examined here in Chapter 5 contest this). Indeed, in the reality television series *Tough Love*, the aberrance of the single woman is represented as having produced profoundly unhappy subjects who must be made over into partnered ones as the only way to transcend this dismal state. How single women are publicly figured thereby works to aid in the continued circulation of such assumptions about marriage as integral to the modern individual's – and especially a woman's – happiness, including apparently for some feminists.

In 'Marriage Envy' (2006), Suzanne Leonard outlines how some so-called 'third-wave' feminist writers have failed to engage at any length with the prospect of women living a life without a long-term partner. Conversely, they appear to have been at pains to recuperate marriage as a legitimate feminist choice: 'Thus, it is fair to say that a newly pro-marriage culture has emerged, one that curiously cuts across sexual, gender, racial, class, and political lines, even as debates rage across the country about who should be able to enter into this highly coveted relation' (Leonard, 2006, p. 44). As Leonard explains, third-wave women writing on marriage, such as Patricia Payette in the collection *Jane Sexes It Up* (2002) and others writing in *Young Wives' Tales* (2001), seek to justify their own implication in it rather than to challenge it as an institution of privilege and exclusion.

Although there are indeed many discursive and ideological differences between them, the intersections of postfeminism and third-wave feminism become visible on this issue.[9] As Astrid Henry (2004a) emphasizes, an embrace of women's sexual agency and the pleasures of heterosex in particular represents one of the key ways that third-wave writers seek to differentiate themselves from what they – in the dominant rhetoric of generationalism – figure as the Mother feminism (i.e. the second-wave). This third-wave reclamation of heterosexual romance has then been positioned as a reclamation of feminism itself (Van Slooten, 2006), opening it up to those women who refused to identify with feminism because it was seen to be anti-men and, more importantly, anti-romance. In this regard, Van Slooten celebrates texts like *Ally McBeal* and *Bridget Jones's Diary*, which she hopes will ultimately enable women to 'find a place where romance and feminism will be happily married' (2006, p. 52). While recognizing of course that many heterosexual feminists may invest in and enjoy such 'romance', its wholesale celebration risks not just excluding women who do not identify as heterosexual but also women for whom such a 'marriage' remains undesirable, critically and/or personally. As I illustrate throughout, this reclamation of heterosexuality and romance works in significant ways to delimit the kinds of subjectivities that are made visible and possible for single women.

This focus, then, on recuperating marriage common to both (some) third-wave writing and postfeminism has led to a silence about the politics of women's singleness and a failure to grasp the need to position it as a viable way of being in the world. 'Feminism, it seems', as McRobbie observes, 'robbed women of their most treasured pleasures, i.e. romance, gossip and obsessive concerns about how to catch a husband' (2009, p. 21), and now, given this allegedly postfeminist context, these can all be reclaimed: 'Feminism was anti-marriage and now this can be shown to be a great mistake' (McRobbie, 2009, p. 20).[10] In this frame, searching for – and sustaining – a successful romantic partnership with a man (through marriage especially) becomes the ultimate act of postfeminist agency (as well as a repudiation of second-wave feminism). Feminism is therefore seen to be responsible for giving 'women the desires that have made them unhappy' (Ahmed, 2010, p. 53). To follow this logic, it is postfeminism that allows women to (re)engage with what makes them most happy (i.e. men). Postfeminism becomes therefore a reaction against what Ahmed has called 'the feminist killjoy' (2010).[11] Furthermore, although the rhetoric of choice is central to postfeminism (and indeed, as I argued earlier, neoliberalism), the 'choice' to remain single is rarely foregrounded as a viable one in the way the 'choice' to be partnered seems to be. (Of course, I recognize when invoking the idea of choice around women's singleness that this is itself a 'choice' not available to all women either within or outside of Western cultures. That is, some women continue to have no choice but to choose heteronormative coupledom and the symbolic and material privileges it affords.)

The ways in which postfeminism invokes the idea of choice has been explored by Elspeth Probyn. In the postfeminist discourse of 'choiceoisie', choices for women, such as career or family, are seen as individual ones, abstracted – as she notes – from the conditions of choosing (1997, p. 131); that is, the political and cultural contexts that make some choices possible and indeed seem more viable than others are obscured from view (see also Dow, 1996). For those investing in institutionalized heterosexuality (such as through marriage) the ostensibly pro-feminist rhetoric of choice is deployed as a way of 'obviating feminist critique by underscoring the agency' of the women making such choices (Vavrus, 2007, p. 52). Indeed, the constitution of oneself as a desirable (and desiring) heterosexual subject – performing a certain type of femininity and 'choosing to attract the male gaze' – is also seen to be integral to postfeminism (Dubrofksy, 2005, p. 131; Projansky, 2001; Gill, 2007). Feminism is believed to have done its work such that the kinds of tech-nologies of gender that feminists formerly scrutinized no longer need to be critiqued and can instead be reclaimed and celebrated; this frame, of course, has specific ramifications for how women's singleness is figured in the texts of postfeminist media culture. If a core part of a postfemi-nist or indeed 'postfeminine' subjectivity (Genz, 2009) for women is an embrace of men (and their gaze), where does this leave the single woman for whom finding a man is not a central priority? Bridget Jones in particular, for McRobbie, is seen to exemplify this tendency to rel-egate feminism to the past in order to (re)embrace traditional feminine desires and subjectivities (2009, p. 20). In my chapter on Bridget Jones, I explore this issue in more depth.

'Globalization of Singlehood'

For some critics, the apparent rise in the numbers of singles is an inter-national trend, prompting claims about the 'globalization of single-hood' (Kaufmann, 2008). In this vein, 'successful singles narratives' are said to proliferate in public discourse, resulting in proclamations about 'the international symbolic presence of new archetypes of singleness' (Macvarish, 2008, p. 10). However, the heterogeneity presumed by such arguments is simply not borne out by the media texts scrutinized here; prolonged singleness for women is rarely constituted as a viable ontol-ogy in these popular narratives. Although it might be expected that such demographic shifts would lead to singleness being reconceptual-ized in popular consciousness 'in a positive – or at least neutral – way' (Gill & Herdieckerdorf, 2006, p. 496), the cultural vocabulary being used to make sense of these socio-political changes remains limited and inherently contradictory. As I demonstrate throughout this book, the assumption that this is a lamentable state – even when women explicitly articulate a preference for life without a partner (co-habiting or otherwise) – remains firmly in place. Moreover, as Tanya Koropeckyj-Cox argues, it seems remarkable that while the numbers of singles are increasing, and forms of discrimination on the basis of 'race, ethnicity, disability, and sexual orientation are less tolerated', stereotypes and prejudices against single people continue to be widespread (2005, p. 91; DePaulo, 2006).

To mark the apparent social shift and ostensible valorization of single-ness, it remains common for publications, both critical and popular, to use the term 'new single woman' (Whitehead, 2003; Trimberger, 2005; Lotz, 2006). But how does this deployment of the 'new' function, what ideological purpose does it serve? In *Feminism and the Materialist Politics of Discourse*, Rosemary Hennessy (1993) has spoken of how the moniker 'new woman' has at various times operated as a way of updating the patriarchal imaginary without substantially disrupting its symbolic anchors. This is likewise the case, I would argue, with the 'new single woman', who – consistent with the broader cultural logics of postfemi-nism – appears to have been refigured but whose threat to dominant hetero-patriarchal ways of both being and signifying is diffused by a series of representational manoeuvres which position her at best with ambivalence, at worst with derision and contempt. Of postfeminism and especially its reclamation of romance, Sue Thornham notes 'if pop-ular media have become the arena in which competing narratives jostle for legitimacy, it is important to remember that the public narratives which result are always themselves contested spaces, in which claims to newness must always be evaluated in the light of far older (meta-) narratives which may lie just below the surface' (2007, p. 81). Not only are these claims of 'newness' overblown, they can function to mask an underlying investment in fairly traditional gender narratives.

The suggestion that women now benefit from a 'new cultural affirma-tion of single living' (Macvarish, 2006) often emerges from the assump-tion that interpersonal relationships have been transformed through 'reflexive modernity' and individualization. Such a climate has purport-edly led to the destabilization of both traditional kinship models and heterosexual partnerships. Relationships based on romantic love are believed to have been decentred, making way for new, diffuse forms of intimacy (Macvarish, 2008). If such relationships are no longer norma-tive, then the possibilities for singleness to be seen as a prolonged stage along the life course, as opposed to simply a transitory state, become clear. In this vein, in *The Transformation of Intimacy* (1992), Anthony Giddens argues that 'confluent love' represents a democratization of intimacy, where couples are in partnerships only to the extent that they are seen to be mutually beneficial (see also Bauman, 2003). For women, 'plastic sexuality' (Giddens, 1992), the expression of sexuality detached from reproduction, is believed to lead to new relationship permutations, although feminists have questioned how this ostensible 'sexual democracy' actually plays out at the material level in ways that benefit women (Hazleden, 2004). Moreover, rather than addressing 'post-traditional intimacies' (Budgeon, 2006), there remains a critical tendency to focus on the heterosexual couple (usually those with children), 'thus rendering invisible the range of intimacies falling outside this form but which nonetheless are being practised in everyday life' (Budgeon, 2008, p. 302).

When women's singleness is considered within sociological literature, as Roona Simpson points out, it is routinely seen as problematic, including in Ulrich Beck and Elizabeth Beck-Gernsheim's *The Normal Chaos of Love* (1995) and Giddens' *Transformation*. These key sociological texts on the changing nature of personal relationships as a result of reflexive modernization 'both implicitly assume sexually based coupledom as the foundation for intimate relationships; consequently, the experiences of those outwith couple relationships are relatively disregarded' (Simpson, 2006, p. 1). As Simpson notes (2006, p. 1), the perceived 'problem' of single women is evident in this comment from Beck and Beck-Gresham: 'there is another problem emerging, affecting those women who pursue an independent career but must in many cases pay a high price, the loneliness of the professionally successful woman' (1995, p. 63). *Single Women in Popular Culture* positions itself against some of these previous critical accounts that, despite these claims about the deprioritization of coupledom and intimacy transformed, reinscribe the sense of women's singleness as an aberrant and inherently undesirable way of being.

Although I am primarily concerned with how the apparent increase in women's singleness is given meaning, rather than locating the cause of such an increase, shifts in how singleness is both understood and lived are commonly said to be tied to changes in modern adulthood more broadly. For Heath and Clever, broader transformations such as women's increased employment and the concomitant changes to the organization of their private lives; a new 'post adolescent' phase on the life course; and new models for conducting interpersonal relationships are all significant factors related to singleness becoming viable as an extended period for more people (2003, p. 35). For some, these shifts commenced with Generation X (Watters, 2003). Generation X is often referred to, following Douglas Coupland (1991), as the 'slacker generation' and, for many commentators, this generation appear too 'slack' to get married. Over the 1990s and 2000s in Australia, where I work, local versions of programmes centred on such slackers and single 'urban families' like *Friends* included *The Secret Life of Us* (or the UK's *This Life*) and *Last Man Standing* (itself especially interesting for its treatment of the single man). Others have held feminism responsible for creating a generation of professionally successful, yet apparently miserable because uncoupled, women. In *Unhooked Generation: The Truth About Why We're Still Single* (2006), Jillian Straus focuses on Generation X, lamenting that the numbers of single women in their 30s is one of the 'inadvertent effects of feminism', and this kind of accusation has become relatively commonplace in the media's accounts of women who have been too choosy or too focused on their career to find a partner – something I explore further in Chapter 2. There are also the periodic moral panics around single women, manifest especially around the notion of a 'man drought' (Salt, 2008), and this is intensified when the subject of women's childlessness is raised.[12]

Defining singleness

As a number of critics have argued (Byrne & Carr, 2005; DePaulo & Morris, 2006), single women cannot and should not be viewed as a monolithic group (though there is little diversity in their representation in popular culture). The meanings of women's singleness have of course shifted and been reworked over time, in line with (and in some cases constitutive of) broader socio-political changes in women's status. As with other aspects of subjectivity, there is 'no enduring, essential and fixed nature to singleness' (Reynolds, 2008, p. 151). Moreover, singleness is a relational category; that is, 'the meanings of singleness are in dialogue with the meanings of marriage, with each category shifting in relation to the other in response to wider societal change' (Holden, 2007, p. 6). The category of 'single' itself is not homogenous and women's positioning in relation to it shifts along the life course: divorced, widowed, in a relationship but not married, etc. Furthermore, other aspects of the single woman's identity may be more important in terms of being positioned subordinately. That is, other modalities of difference overlap with women's singleness and it therefore cannot be considered an isolated aspect of subjectivity. And indeed, the claiming of an identity as a single woman signifies in different ways according to how it intersects with these other forms of difference. Moreover, adopting the position of single woman as an identity – a political gesture performed by many of the bloggers considered in my final chapter – can work to reinscribe the limited and limiting binary of married/single.[13] There are, as has been widely argued of identity more generally, considerable limitations in trying to fix singleness as an identity; it is neither a desirable nor entirely possible gesture. In terms of who I invoke when discussing singleness, like DePaulo (2006), I refer to those who are not in a committed romantic partnership. Furthermore, as DePaulo emphasizes, it is also important to be aware that 'there is a hierarchy of single people, and older singles who have never "achieved" marriage are at the very bottom. They are the most infantile singles of them all' (2006, p. 113). As I discuss further in the next chapter, this idea that a woman without a man exists in a state of arrested development is common; the selfish single is dubbed insufficiently mature to value the many sacrifices made by wives and, most importantly, mothers.

Although women's singleness is heterogenous, the women upon which my analysis focuses are predominantly in their 20s and 30s (though some older and younger women feature intermittently), heterosexual, not married or in committed partnerships, and without children; these are the most visible, as well as some of the most problematic, single women in the popular imaginary. Popular culture's portrayals of divorced or widowed women have their own specific limitations (think Courtney Cox's deeply problematic portrayal of the 'cougar' in the sitcom, *Cougartown*), but having at least once 'defeated' their singleness (and more often than not fulfilled their procreative function) they are imbued with a form of cultural capital that eludes the single woman.[14] Therefore, while 'single again' women face unique disadvantages and have been conceptualized in public discourse as 'failures' (Sandfield, 2006), my focus in this book is largely on never married women who (choose to) live without a long-term partner; they are the ones rendered especially problematic in the hegemonic narratives on which this book focuses.

Moreover, mirroring the elisions of much of mainstream media culture, 'given that the central figure of postfeminist discourses is a white, heterosexual, middle-class woman' (Projansky, 2001, p. 12), the whiteness and class privilege of these highly visible single women cannot be ignored and I will attend to this in individual chapters. Within the postfeminist discursive frame, '"woman" is meant to stand for all women but does through the lens of whiteness' (Projansky, 2001, p. 74). In this way, these figurations of single women largely reinscribe the process of 'whitewash' in which media culture has long been shown to be implicated (Gabriel, 1998). As previously emphasized, because they are the most visible, my analysis centres on heterosexual single women. Single lesbian women within popular culture are rarely foregrounded, except perhaps in programmes such as *The L Word* but even this series – consistent with other forms of postfeminist media culture – is thoroughly driven by characters' quests to become unsingle and, in the case of Bette Porter and Tina Kennard especially, the pursuit of a nuclear family unit. Further, the lesbian woman who is un-partnered is arguably seen as less threatening to the dominant hetero-patriachal order as she is not seen to be actively performing her supposedly 'deviant' sexuality via a romantic relationship.

One final note on the parameters of this study; it is in some respects impossible to critically examine the single woman without also, even briefly, mentioning the single man. Negra has argued that the single man in contemporary popular culture is now being rendered problematic in a way similar to his feminine counterpart:

> Postfeminist representational culture is preoccupied with distinctions of age and generation and it is adept at searching out and 'rehabilitating' those who don't fit its heteronormative, consumerist, domestic script. While in this respect its most frequent target has been the single woman, recent popular culture reflects an increasing interest in the single man. In a (perverse) spirit of gender egalitarianism, deficient/dysfunctional single femininity is now increasingly matched by deficient/dysfunctional single masculinity in a number of high-profile films and television series.
>
> (2006)

Such popular representations of this 'dysfunctional masculinity' are certainly worthy of further interrogation. However, as Jill Reynolds argues of her own choice to focus exclusively on women's relation to certain discursive constructions, singleness is a 'gendered category that works differently for men and for women' (2008, p. 22). Moreover, it remains the case that single women – especially those choosing not to have children – have been historically seen as a threat to the hetero-patriarchal social order in ways that men have not.[15] Attending to the 'discursive climate for single women', Reynolds emphasizes, is a legitimate project in and of itself and this book, therefore, is most concerned with how single women continue to be figures of profound cultural anxiety, while also drawing attention to how they are intervening to challenge limited representations. By way of background to those that follow, in the next chapter I provide an overview of how single women have been publicly represented since the 1960s.

2
From the Second-wave to Postfeminism: Single Women in the Mediasphere

Introduction

In this chapter, as a way of contextualizing the more detailed textual analysis in those that follow, I provide an illustrative snapshot of how single women have been figured in the Western public imaginary since the early 1960s. Though by no means an exhaustive account, I attend to key texts, including newspaper articles, books, films, and television, with the most significant cultural reverberations from over the past 50 years.[1] As Betsy Israel remarks in *Bachelor Girl: The Secret History of Single Women in the Twentieth Century* (2002): 'More so than any other living arrangement, the single life is deeply influenced – *haunted* may be a better word – by cultural imagery. And the single woman herself has had a starring role in the mass imagination for many years' (2, original emphasis). It is the various ways in which this 'starring role' has been played, especially over the past two decades, that concerns me throughout this chapter and indeed this book. Commencing my analysis with the present, and engaging especially with journalistic constructions of women's singleness from Australia, the United Kingdom and the United States, I work backwards to consider some of the most prominent single women in Western popular culture's history. I do this as a way to disrupt the common teleological narratives of progress that often mark critical discussions of how single women, and women more broadly, are represented in media culture. Often embodying precisely the types of feminine subjectivity for which feminism fought (independent, financially autonomous, ambitious, sexually fulfilled), the figure of the single woman, as I have suggested, is a key nodal point in the increasingly complex interactions between feminism and popular culture.

33

In this chapter, unlike some other critics, I argue that it is difficult to map a linear narrative onto the figure of the single woman that takes us from limited representations to something more progressive (or indeed vice versa). Although there have undoubtedly been changes, it is not possible to read them according to any simple model of evolution.[2] The proposition that there has been a significant discursive shift from 'spinster to Singleton' in terms of how the single woman is publicly made-to-mean, and that she is now comparatively celebrated, is unsustainable if we take an historical overview of how and where she has appeared over the past five decades, as well as spotlighting the politics of these representations. Instead, such an overview indicates that there is a persistent ambivalence around this figure which reveals not just cultural anxieties about the woman without a man but about feminism itself.

As many feminist scholars have shown, the form of feminism to have found voice, and indeed to have been incorporated into, mainstream media culture is the liberal variety that focuses on women's integration into the masculine public sphere and their access to previously masculine forms of privilege. Accordingly, it is through the figure of the 'White, straight, single, professional women working in a supposed man's world' (Dow, 2002, p. 260) that feminism most obviously manifests in various forms of popular cultural production. The single urban career woman has also borne the brunt of attacks against the feminism she has come to stand for and which has been charged with causing upheavals in modern sociality, intimate relationships, and an apparent decentring of gendered subjectivity. However, while Bonnie Dow has suggested that feminist identity comes to be publicly represented through this figure, when it comes to the texts with which I am most concerned, it is *post*-feminist identity that is most clearly articulated in and through single women in media culture. That is not to say that an engagement with feminism is not staged through these single characters; on the contrary, it is a particular approach to feminism that marks them out from their literary, televisual, and cinematic predecessors.

These narratives around single women, and their prominence from the mid-1990s onwards, can be seen as part of what McRobbie (following Foucault) identified as a 'discursive explosion' around femininity which was preoccupied with its 'ambiguous relationship to feminism' (1994, p. 158). That such a 'discursive explosion' can be seen to have been largely channelled through the figure of the single woman, as I argue here, is perhaps not surprising, as feminist gains facilitated more diverse subjectivities for women and saw what have been dubbed 'new femininities'[3] being staged, and in some cases valorized, in the mediasphere. The texts in which single women now so prominently feature – those which have 'taken feminism into account and implicitly or explicitly ask the question "what now?"– are "vital to the construction of a new gender regime"' (McRobbie, 2009, p. 21). Accordingly, how these single women negotiate feminism and the kinds of gendered subjectivities that are possible in the late twentieth and early twenty-first centuries is played out in complicated ways in various sites of contemporary popular culture.

Celebrating singleness? Single women in the noughties

There is little doubt that since the 1990s (if not earlier) the single woman has occupied a prominent, if ambivalent, position on the Western media landscape. In particular, as previously remarked, the millennium is said to have ushered in a 'new cultural affirmation of single living' (Macvarish, 2006), manifested within the texts of popular culture especially. Tracking this apparent shift, sociologist Jean-Claude Kaufmann argues: 'Something really did happen at the turn of the millennium. The atmosphere suddenly changed. Bestsellers like *Bridget Jones*, and cult series such as *Friends* and *Ally McBeal*, were unashamed celebrations of the single life' (2008, p. 115; see also Clements, 1998). Similarly, in popular discourse, the single woman was said to have 'come into her own' (Edwards, *Time*, 28 August, 2000). This celebratory rhetoric aside, the single woman (or a certain version thereof) was certainly made more visible in the noughties; she was on our television screens, in our movie theatres, and in the pages of popular fiction. Indeed, so hypervisible was this purportedly 'new single woman' that she was even addressed – indeed quite literally hailed – in a song by American pop songstress Beyonce, who implored 'all the single ladies' to 'put [their] hands up'. However, 'All the Single Ladies' (2008) functioned as more of a cautionary tale to commitment-phobic boyfriends who had missed the proverbial boat by failing to seal the deal with a marriage proposal. The song warns men that they are easily replaceable should they not fulfil this universal feminine desire. The song's refrain – 'if you liked it then you should have put a ring on it' – with its subject seeking to make her erstwhile paramour jealous by seductively dancing with another man, is hardly an anthem for the oft elided pleasures of singledom. Infact, in its emphasis on the engagement ring, it serves rather to valorize and glorify marriage as the teleological destination of a committed heterosexual relationship – at least as far as women are concerned.

In addition to popular music and their fictional incarnations in chick lit novels, film and television, in the 2000s single women also started to become a more urgent topic of public discussion in overtly factual media forms, with their newsworthiness seeming assured. Indeed, fictionalized Singletons became the catalyst for broader news engagement with the increasing numbers of actual single women in the West.[4] Given how news discourse works to construct reality (as opposed to simply reflecting it), the import of these pieces, and the rhetorical strategies they mobilize, should not be underestimated. Such stories form a key part of the intertextual network around women's singleness which this study tracks. Though the boundaries between the two have been thoroughly destabilized, it is worth noting that stories on women's singleness continually appear not just in so-called tabloid newspapers but in broadsheets as well. Throughout the 1990s and over the last decade, several journalistic pieces that sought to come to terms with women's singleness, often invoking the rhetoric of a 'man drought' while yet attempting to celebrate single living and the redundancy of romantic partnerships, appeared in newspapers in Australia, the UK, and the US. One of the most noteworthy of these was published in the US' *Time* magazine in August 2000. Its cover story was entitled 'Who needs a husband?', complete with a photograph of the emblematic singletons: the four glamorous stars of *Sex and the City*. This was not the first time that *Time* magazine had used a popular cultural text as a point of entry into broader socio-political ruminations. In 1998, it had caused a stir when another well-known single character from the small screen, Calista Flockhart (as Ally McBeal), appeared on its cover with American feminist luminaries Susan B. Anthony, Betty Friedan and Gloria Steinem, posing the equally provocative question: 'Is feminism dead?' (29 June, 1998). In the accompanying article, 'Feminism: It's All About Me!' (Bellafante, 1998), the fictionalized figures of Bridget Jones and Ally McBeal were invoked to answer this question in the affirmative; such representations of pathetic, desperate single women were seen as proof of feminism's metaphorical burial; but more on Ally, Bridget and the alleged death of feminism later.

Not only are these covers, and the articles they preview, suggestive of the broader cultural reverberations of these postfeminist heroines, they also reveal the way that debates around feminism, women and representation are now routinely staged in the mainstream media. The 2000 article boldly, and somewhat hyperbolically, proclaims 'single women, once treated as virtual outcasts, have moved to the centre of our social and cultural life', with its author citing not only Bridget Jones and the women from *Sex and the City* as evidence of this 'major societal shift' but also the female leads from television dramas like *Judging Amy* and

Providence (Edwards, 2000). Offering statistics on the increasing numbers of single women, the article identifies single women as a 'blockbuster consumer group' with much 'clout' and declares the symbolic death of the spinster. However, quoting Sarah Jessica Parker, the article also reveals its ambivalence about the phenomenon it claims to be cataloguing: 'Parker regales single friends with tales of how boring married life is and how much luckier they are to have freedom and fun. Does she really believe it? "Well, no", she admits. "It's just a fun thing to say to make single people feel better"' (Edwards, 2000). The condescension here is palpable and positions the happily – perhaps smugly, as Bridget Jones would say – married Parker in opposition to her *Sex and the City* character (who will be considered later in this chapter).[5]

The 1996 publication of *Bridget Jones's Diary*, and the release of its film adaptation in 2001, precipitated debates around women and singleness in newspapers and magazines that continue to this day. Photographic stills from the film commonly accompany newspaper articles about single women, using Renee Zellweger's Bridget as a visual shorthand for a series of assumptions and discourses around single women. It is also worth noting that the perpetual use of the iconic Bridget in these articles, part of what has been dubbed 'the Bridget Jones effect' (Whelehan, 2000, p. 141), functions to reinscribe the normative whiteness that predominates when women's singleness is visible in the mediasphere. Despite being a fictional figure, the affable yet neurotic Bridget is routinely invoked as evidence of broader, global social shifts, as is *Sex and the City*'s Carrie Bradshaw. One news report, citing a survey revealing that Australian unmarried women outnumber their married counterparts for the first time since World War 1, discursively links these infamous 'Singletons' as evidence of this social trend: 'The Mosaic 2008 analysis reveals 51.4 per cent of women are opting for the singles lifestyle in a new phenomenon billed as "Bridget Jones meets Sex and the City"' (12 March, 2008, 'SPUDS, Single Women Taking Over Australia', news.com.au).

Referring in its title to 'The Bridget Jones Economy', an article in *The Economist* also uses Fielding's heroine to identify global demographic shifts and to discuss their economic implications[6]:

Bridget may be a caricature, but only just. Her creator, Helen Fielding, has drawn someone much more human and recognisable than the elegant and wealthy young New York singles in the TV shows 'Friends' and 'Sex and the City'. Yet all three portray people who dominate and shape the rich world's city life, not just in

New York and London, but increasingly in Tokyo, Stockholm, Paris and Santiago: well-educated, single professionals in their 20s and 30s ... Bridget and her friends have begun to show up in the census figures.

(22 December, 2001, *The Economist*, p. 68)

While another commentator, again making assumptions about the transnationality of this phenomenon, deploys Carrie in much the same fashion in an article entitled 'The New Girl Order':

Yes: Carrie Bradshaw is alive and well and living in Warsaw. Well, not just Warsaw. Conceived and raised in the United States, Carrie may still see New York as a spiritual home. But today you can find her in cities across Europe, Asia, and North America. Seek out some trendy shoe stores in Shanghai, Berlin, Singapore, Seoul, and Dublin, and you'll see crowds of single young female (SYFs) in their twenties and thirties, who spend hours working their abs and their careers, sipping cocktails, dancing at clubs, and (yawn) talking about relationships. Sex and the City has gone global; the SYF world is now flat.

(Hymowitz, 2007, p. 1)

And despite these problematic assumptions about mimetic accuracy (not to mention cultural imperialism), these articles are telling in regard to the broader cultural reverberations of not just Fielding's Bridget but other single figures from popular narratives. What they reveal is how these characters are being used as an interpretive framework through which putatively global socio-cultural shifts can be publicly read. As Joke Hermes argues, 'Here we have a new type of heroine that attracts audiences and sparks debate, not just amongst those who consider themselves feminists, but also outside these hallowed halls' (2006, p. 80). While the originality of these figures is contestable, Hermes' point regarding the way they have come to occupy a space, and precipitate dialogue around gendered subjectivity, outside the academy is prescient. In Chapter 3, I return to these concerns as I address the various cultural uses to which Bridget, as the exemplary 'Singleton', has been put.

Some predict that these demographic shifts have irrevocably altered the socio-political landscape and have ushered in new forms of stigma-free subjectivities for millennial single men and women. For example, in November 2000, *Life* magazine, of Britain's *Observer* newspaper, featured

'The Singles Issue', where it pronounced the 2000s the 'Singles Century' (5 November):

> In this week's magazine, we celebrate the single life. For the first time, being single is a proactive lifestyle choice, like the car you drive, the food you eat, or the books you read. People are no longer willing to settle for settling down. The single stigma has faded away (the more there are, the less likely they are to be pitied). Friends are the new family ... There's been a significant shift in attitude, a feeling that singletons may be alone, but they certainly aren't lonely. Again and again, the people in this issue use the word 'freedom' to describe their lives. They've got the financial control, the network of friends, and the confidence to be independent.

Mobilizing the discourse of the 'urban tribe' (Watters, 2003), as well as singleness as a choice for those with certain class privileges, the article argues that there has been a significant cultural shift in regards to attitudes towards singles. In these accounts, singles are 'the standard-bearers of a joyous and inventive freedom' (Kaufmann, 2008, p. xiii). Rarely do such articles exhibit an awareness of the various forms of discrimination, symbolic and/or material, encountered by single women; though this work of politicizing women's singleness does occur in other representational spaces, like the blogosphere (as my final chapter demonstrates). This disavowal of the stigma attached to singleness is common, as is this emphasis on single women as a key market segment. An article in *Businessweek* similarly pronounces:

> Yes, it's the age of the single woman, with broad implications for both the culture and the economy. They certainly don't see themselves as spinsters, old maids, or crazy Miss Havishams – the negative stereotypes of yesteryear. Unmarried women are buying houses, driving sport utility vehicles, bearing or adopting children, and rising to positions of influence.
>
> (Arnst, 1998)

Co-existing with this more overtly celebratory rhetoric within the journalistic field, it is also routine to position women's singleness as part of a prolonged adolescence.

Demographers regularly coin terms to encompass this apparently 'new' form of single woman, and, indicative of the newsworthiness of such a subject, journalists over the past decade or so have been devoting entire articles to, and helping bring into circulation, such ideologically loaded terms. Underpinning many of these signifiers is the assumption that heterosexual single women are invalid citizens, not having reached 'proper' adulthood, and the thirty-something woman without children especially is seen to exist in a selfish state of arrested development. Recent Australian media attention to an alleged social phenomenon dubbed 'TWITs' – teenage women in their thirties – is indicative of how this trope of the single woman-as-adolescent operates: 'TWITs are putting serious relationships and parenthood on hold, instead choosing to continue partying and enjoying the freedoms they discovered in their teens' (Hale, *Herald Sun*, 2 August, 2009). However, the 'TWIT' is not the only moniker being used to connote the single woman's perceived selfishness and self-absorption. Engaging in a meta-commentary on these media-generated appellations, a similar article appeared in the Australian broadsheet, the *Sydney Morning Herald* (Brett, 7 April, 2008).

Focusing on Hollywood, the article's portrayal of variously described singles also appears indebted to the heroines that pepper the mediascape of the twenty-first century: 'nowadays there's a whole new set of positive buzzwords that are putting solo-femme status on the hot Hollywood map. Quirkyalones, un-marrieds and proud singletons are making a sassy comeback with cocktails in their hands and expensive stilettos on their feet.' The relation of such figures to conspicuous consumption is clear through the invocation of 'expensive stilettos' which have come, especially in light of Carrie Bradshaw's fetishistic attachment to her Manolo Blahniks, to metonymically signal the single woman's purportedly high income, (implicitly selfish) ability to spend money on luxury consumer goods, and failure to act in the financially responsible manner of her married counterpart. This equation of singleness with selfishness, narcissism, hedonism, and immaturity – as is common (DePaulo, 2006) – recurs throughout these journalistic constructions of modern single women. (Along these lines, in the 1990s a Japanese sociologist coined an offensive term for singles still living with their parents that was rapidly taken up by journalists and applied especially to single career women: 'parasite single'.[7])

Like these Australian examples, both *The Observer* (Davies, 2008) and the *Daily Mail*[8] in the UK appeared preoccupied with a new form of social subjectivity for women in 2008: the 'freemale'. A *Daily Mail* article entitled 'Rise of the freemale: The women who'd rather be single than share their time and money' (Rees & Ballinger, 2 June, 2008) sees this phenomenon exemplified by celebrities such as Kylie Minogue and Cameron Diaz.[9] It commences: 'The number of single women has hit an all-time high, a study has shown – and most of them aren't looking for love. They apparently choose to be alone, and rejoice in a life where they can spend time and money as they wish. This new breed of singleton has been dubbed a "freemale", because she chooses her freedom over a family' (Rees & Ballinger, 2 June, 2008). The use of the phrase 'they apparently choose to be alone' once again evidences the inability to recognize women's agency when it comes to being without a man, and the suggestion that they do not 'share their time and money' implies the selfishness with which single women are routinely charged. A follow up article a few days later – once again accompanied by a photograph of Bridget, with the caption: 'Sad Singleton: Bridget Jones (Renee Zellweger) bemoans her solitary status' – is even more critical of this male-free subjectivity, with the unambiguous title: 'Forget this tosh about "freemales" – single women who say they are happy are lying' (Spurr, 2008). Relating the story of a conversation at a party with a 'perfectly made-up thirty-something woman', the journalist reveals her own inability to accept the woman's description of herself as 'happily single'. Instead, she confides to her readers:

> Who did she think she was kidding? In fact, do you believe any single woman over 30 is being honest when she claims to be happy that way? I don't. What's really going on behind that confident demeanour and fulfilled exterior is crushing loneliness and desperation ... They know it, and I know it, but they're too embarrassed to admit it: that's why they end up as single, lying females trying to protect some semblance of their dignity.
>
> (Spurr, 2008)

The incredulity of this journalist, and indeed her sheer contempt for single women's self-narratives, reveals a deeper cultural anxiety regarding a woman's inability to exist without a man that persists despite celebratory claims to the contrary.

Optimistic proclamations about the public refiguration of singleness are also evident in some academic work in this area. For example, Jan Macvarish (2008, p. 8) argues that 'the portrayal of the dilemma of contemporary singleness has shifted in the past six years from anxiety about how romance might come about for thirty-something singles to reconciliation to indefinite or permanent singleness as an affirmed lifestyle choice'. Such assertions, I would suggest, are not readily substantiated when one takes a close look at the meanings and anxieties publicly circulating, across a variety of media platforms, around women's singleness especially. Moreover, as I have previously observed, singleness is only allowable within certain temporal, not to mention class and racial, limits. Other single women continue to be publicly abjected, coded as dysfunctional spinsters; a prime piece of evidence to counter the more celebratory accounts of how single women are constituted in contemporary media culture, and indeed in society more generally, is the case of *Britain's Got Talent's* 'accidental celebrity', Susan Boyle.

Throughout 2009, international reportage about Boyle saw the deployment of a series of problematic, yet familiar (or, I would say, recalcitrant), tropes and caricatures about single women; the following article title is exemplary in this regard: 'Singing Scottish spinster becomes a global sensation' (*Sydney Morning Herald*, 17 April, 2009). As Negra points out, Boyle's presence in the mediasphere was potentially subversive, rendering visible women who 'live off the postfeminist grid', but ultimately these possibilities were shut down: 'The spectacle of an unprettified midlife woman claiming public visibility briefly opened the door to a different kind of understanding of the single woman but then firmly closed it again' (2010, p. 61). Almost without exception, much was made of the fact that she had never been kissed and lived alone yet with the spinster's perennial best friend, a cat. But Boyle's positioning in the media has not been without its critics. As Joan Smith (2009) argues in *The Guardian*, rather than being dubbed a spinster, with all its derogatory connotations, 'Boyle could have been described in a less pejorative way as a single woman who'd spent much of her life looking after her sick mother – like a lot of other women in Britain, in other words – but it is her difference that has been played up during the weeks of intense media coverage.' Smith continues, likening media treatment of Boyle, especially the presumed disjuncture between a beautiful singing voice and an 'unseemly' exterior, to a 'freakshow'.[10] The ways in which Boyle was constructed and received functioned not only to 'shore up conceptions of acceptable/"unacceptable" norms of femininity' (Holmes, 2010, p. 76) but to reinforce distinctions between 'acceptable' and 'unacceptable' forms of singleness for women. Attractive, glamorous, consuming subjects clearly on the hunt for men, like those from *Sex and the City*, appear permissible whereas those like Boyle are not. While it is often assumed that the term 'spinster' has fallen out of common parlance, even a cursory glance at news coverage of Boyle suggests that it maintains its currency. Such examples further suggest, as Germaine Greer in her characteristically polemical style remarks, that 'though the free expression of contempt for "old maids" is now anathema, fundamental contempt for the unattached female is still in place' (1999, p. 246).

That singleness is a newsworthy, and lamentable, attribute when it comes to prominent women in the public sphere is also well exemplified by a recent Australian example. In January 2011 the first woman (and at only 38), the Australian Labor Party's Lara Giddings, was appointed Premier of the Australian state of Tasmania. The day after she was sworn in, one of the country's broadsheets, *The Australian*, proffered an article that focused on how her successful career in politics had prohibited her search for a man. The journalist suggests that one of the 'sacrifices' she had made to reach this pinnacle of political life includes 'failing, so far, to find a life partner' (Denholm, 25 January, 2011). Indicative of the notion of singleness as a personal deficit, the fault of career-driven women, the article nevertheless codes Giddings as recuperable by adding the phrase 'so far'; that is, as the article's title tells us, 'Leftist Lara Giddings Still Looking For Mr Right'. Similarly, much press coverage of Australia's first woman Prime Minister, Julia Gillard, has focused on the fact that she is not married and especially that she has no children (though, unlike Giddings, she does have a long term partner).[11]

When single women function in/as news, it is invariably framed in a narrative that either works to infantilize them (even if simultaneously couched in celebratory rhetoric) or to mourn their manlessness, but more importantly, the childlessness that this state implies. One of the biggest threats posed by the single woman is that she may remain childless or, to use the term used by advocates in this area, 'childfree'. Or, perhaps, worse – that she will take advantage of reproductive technologies and become a mother while yet single. In Australia in the mid-2000s, journalist Virginia Hausseger (2005) explicitly blamed feminism for her own so-called 'social infertility', asserting that feminism effectively downplayed the 'biological clock' in such a way that women refused to concede its validity and consequently found themselves childless. Similarly, Danielle Crittenden's *What Our Mothers Didn't Tell Us: Why Happiness Eludes the Modern Woman* (2000), produced in the US, foretells the dangers of prolonged singleness for women. In these narratives, the single woman becomes a social problem primarily because her 'manlessness' hinders the fulfilment of her 'natural' feminine role. Women's desire for an autonomous identity, and especially for a career, is seen to have had dire personal consequences – especially in terms of reproduction.[12]

Crittenden, along these lines, warns the single woman 'there is a price to be paid for postponing commitment' (2000, p. 62) – that men will be in short supply and her fertility will be on the decline: 'Alas, it is usually precisely at this moment – when a single woman looks up from her work and realizes she's ready to take on family life – that men make themselves most absent. This is when the cruelty of singleness really sets in.' That is, when she discovers that, in terms of their temporal flexibility vis-à-vis procreation, 'Men will outlast her' (67) and, having spent so many years on her own, immersed in work, such a woman will 'end up inadvertently extending the introverted existence of a teenager deep into middle age' (69) – it seems she risks becoming a 'TWIT'. As this rhetoric illustrates, all women are believed to conceptualize their singleness as lamentable because all women are believed to innately desire children, thus illustrating the undiminished currency of biologically essentialist discourses in the public sphere. Moreover, the trope of 'having it all', and indeed its impossibility, is routinely invoked as a way of establishing the limitations of feminism. Rather than attributing the 'failure' to negotiate the difficulties of full participation in both the public and private spheres to institutional factors, the political is reconstituted as personal and trajectories such as 'retreatism' and 'opting out' are foregrounded as viable solutions for women with children (see Probyn, 1993; Vavrus, 2007; Negra, 2009).

In addition to the self-help manuals considered here in Chapter 5, a number of popular books have taken the single woman as a problem to be analyzed (and then rectified), including Barbara Dafoe Whitehead's *Why There are No Good Men Left: The Romantic Plight of the New Single Woman* (2003) and, more recently, Lori Gottlieb's *Marry Him: The Case for Settling for Mr Good Enough* (2010). The fact that many women in the West are successful and highly educated (of course these are the most privileged) is now seen as responsible for their regrettable singleness; high achievers have high expectations – unrealistic ones apparently. In *Why There are No Good Men Left* (2003), Whitehead argues that the emphasis on achievement for girls in their school years in particular is responsible for the deferral of love; women succeed at school, in the tertiary system, and then build a career where once they focused on finding husbands (p. 61). For Whitehead, the success of cultural products like *Sex and the City* and *Bridget Jones's Diary* can be attributed to a 'pervasive anxiety on the part of unmarried women'. Through such an assertion, she fails to acknowledge the role of these texts themselves in fostering such anxiety. While she applauds the achievements of young women, facilitated by what she calls the 'girl project', readers can also detect more than a hint of nostalgia for a period in which doubts, insecurities, and the inability to find a mate did not plague women. These women are highly successful, she emphasizes, but they are patently miserable – because single. Although she does not position her account against feminism, there is undoubtedly an implied critique that its ostensible success in producing these ambitious, intelligent young women has an underside the social consequences of which – an apparent 'crisis in dating and mating' (2003, p. 1) – are only beginning to become clear.

In these popular accounts, being single is seen as a tension between 'tradition' and 'nature' and feminism; for example, recent debates about women's inherent 'pickiness' when it comes to choosing a mate and the idea that they should 'settle' have seen the playing out of this tension in public discourse, especially in relation to Lori Gottlieb's *Marry Him: The Case for Settling for Mr Good Enough* (2010). The rhetoric of 'settling' presumes that being single is so utterly undesirable that any man will do. So personally fearful is Gottlieb of a life of perpetual singleness that she published this manifesto for 'settling' to deter other single women from making the mistakes she made with men and which led to her having a child on her own. The book had its genesis as an article for the *Atlantic Monthly* (March, 2008) that effectively sought to shift the blame for women's widespread singleness to women themselves. Coming particularly under fire were what she deemed to be women's unrealistic expectations, which feminism had fostered. In 'Marry Him!' she conjectures: 'ask any soul-baring 40-year-old single heterosexual woman what she longs for most in life, and she probably won't tell you it's a better career or a smaller waistline or a bigger apartment. Most likely, she'll say that what she really wants is a husband (and, by extension, a child)'. For Gottlieb, 'every woman I know – no matter how successful and ambitious, how financially and emotionally secure – feels panic, occasionally coupled with desperation, if she hits 30 and finds herself unmarried.'. Gottlieb simply does not allow that this maxim does not apply for all women; to those who disagree with her about this gnawing worry, she scoffs, 'either you're in denial or you're lying' (March, 2008). There is simply no representational scope, in her narrative, for women to remain contentedly single. As I have suggested, though the rhetoric of 'choice' is central to postfeminism, it is rarely operationalized around women's singleness.

Commentators such as Crittenden, Whitehead, and Gottlieb are deeply invested in the idea that all single women's lives are miserable, with otherwise successful, professional women tortured by regrets regarding their romantic attachments (or rather lack thereof). This trope of 'settling' ties into the 'time panic', especially around marriage and motherhood, through which modern women's lives are most commonly read (Negra,

2009). In this way, 'female adulthood is defined as a state of chronic temporal crisis' (Tasker & Negra, 2007, p. 10). This emphasis on time anxiety has been seen as distinctly postfeminist, directed most pointedly towards single women: 'In postfeminist culture the single woman stands as the most conspicuously time-beset example of contemporary femininity, her singlehood encoded as a particularly temporal failure and a drifting off course from the normative stages of the female lifecycle' (Negra, 2009, p. 61). In order to 'beat the clock' and be compliant with these hegemonic life stories, therefore, both in terms of finding a partner and having a baby, women's expectations must be lowered considerably.

As these works of popular non-fiction suggest, the ways in which single women are publicly figured reveals persistent anxieties about feminism and women's power. Women now have power, but are supposedly miserable. Feminism is charged with taking these women high up the corporate ladder, but leaving them husbandless; making them high achievers educationally, but leaving them childless. (The class biases of such assumptions, too, are obvious.) Gottlieb perceives feminism to be at the heart of this apparent 'crisis' that has created, as Whitehead similarly argues, a generation of discontented women; one of her chapter titles is unambiguous in this regard: 'How feminism fucked up my love life'. Therefore, for these conservative commentators at least, the inability to accept that women can be satisfied without a masculine other derives from and indeed perpetuates – at least in part – popular narratives not only about the immense success of feminism, in liberal terms, but also about the very misguided-ness of feminism as a political project. Success in the public sphere, the implication is, comes at the price of happiness in the private. As Monica Dux and Zora Simic argue in *The Great Feminist Denial*, the 'Single Woman's story' is often positioned as a 'contemporary morality tale ... in which feminism is usually portrayed as the principal villain' (2008, p. 77). As one journalist asserts, again using Bridget Jones to exemplify the supposed meaningless, hedonistic single lifestyle, 'my childless contemporaries and I are the fallout generation from the sexual revolution, the real-life Bridget Jones' who spend their evenings getting drunk instead of reading bedtime stories' (Mulvey, 2006). Here, 'reading bed stories' is seen as legitimate behaviour, against the vacuous socializing of drunken singles. Such feminist-blaming popular narratives, which reinscribe the pathologization of singleness, form part of the intertextual web in which the single woman comes to signify.

As these examples suggest, while the majority of mainstream newspaper articles on the 'problem' of women's singleness focus on white women, Felicia D. Henderson has shown how 'countless newspaper articles ... have bemoaned the "plight" of single, black women' (2009, p. 375). These articles, she implies, construct a racially specific man drought and black single women are doubly Othered: 'According to these reports, the situation is dire for the single black woman hoping to be married: She is too accomplished and black men are too few' (Henderson, 2009, p. 375). For example, as Henderson notes, in 'Singled Out: In Seeking A Mate, Men and Women Find Delicate Balance' (8 October, 2006), which appeared in the *Washington Post*, Krissah Williams argues that the fact that 'half a million more black women than men are college graduates' results in a 'widening interracial battleground over class and gender'. So, here, again, the single woman is cast as a victim of her own (not to mention feminism's) success.

These attitudes have their own histories, of course, and for the remainder of this chapter I sketch out how the single woman has been discursively constituted in mainstream media culture since the early 1960s, as part of the process of tracking how feminism has been taken up, negotiated and rewritten therein. The most obvious place to start, in this regard, is Helen Gurley Brown's *Sex and the Single Girl* (1962), the prototypical feminist self-help book that is often credited with instigating this alleged seismic shift in cultural attitudes towards single women.

Sexing the single girl: Helen Gurley Brown and 1960s prototypical popular feminism

Prior to the period of intense activism around women's rights that became known as the second-wave of feminism in the late 1960s–early 1970s, the question of women's liberation was, albeit perhaps more obliquely than in the radical feminist tracts that came to characterize the movement, receiving public attention. Popularly, the single woman, in particular, was believed to require advice on how to live a more ful-filled, and in many ways empowered, life. She apparently faced unique dilemmas, both personal and professional, that necessitated friendly yet authoritative intervention. The so-called 'single girl', as a subject position not without its limitations, was therefore called into being in the early 1960s within the pages of Helen Gurley Brown's prototypical popular feminist book, *Sex and the Single Girl*. As I (2008), and many oth-ers have previously argued, popular non-fictional texts have been key in constituting feminism's public identity and also for helping to contest certain ways of circumscribing femininity, and in this regard Brown's book is no exception. When published in America in July 1962, *Sex and The Single Girl* went straight to the best-seller list and remained there for almost seven months (Douglas, 1994, p. 68). Helping to raise the book's public profile even further, its film adaptation, starring Natalie Wood as the single sex expert 'Dr Brown' and Tony Curtis as the cad she reluctantly falls for, appeared in 1964.[13]

Brown's work is not without its limitations, including its so-called 'girling' of the single woman. The use of the appellation 'girl' in the book's title signals the infantilization of the single woman that, in many respects, is visible to this day. However, her deployment of the term 'girl' can be seen as a strategic gesture to render the subject (and the subject matter) of her book less threatening. As Hilary Radner argues, 'Her girlishness also responds to and contains the anxieties that a woman no longer under the yoke of patriarchy (if still subject to the whims of capital) might evoke' (1999, p. 10). That notwithstanding, the agency of Brown's single girl cannot be denied nor can her extensive plans for how this agency could be best exercised in a patriarchal economy she acknowledges values women in certain ways over others. Though she has commonly been written out of feminist histories of the women's movement, and indeed out of the feminist canon, over recent years some scholars have sought to recuperate the protean feminist discourse of the woman who was to become *Cosmopolitan's* editor.[14]

Her two popular feminist books, *Sex and the Single Girl* (1962) and *Sex and the Office* (1964), are remarkable for their views on women's sexual agency and desire. With Brown's popular (feminist) texts in the early 1960s, the single woman morphed from dowdy, asexual spinster to a pleasure-seeking, unabashedly sexual subject and the politics accordingly shifted: 'Less sexually bold than might be imagined, the book was more significant, at a time when any unmarried woman over 25 already felt herself stigmatised "the spinster", for its celebration of being single' (Winship, 1987, p. 106). There was nothing undesirable about the single girl in Brown's account. But while, as some critics have recently emphasized (Genz, 2009; Scanlon, 2009), Brown's assertions about women's sexual agency are laudable, the end game was yet to find and secure a mate; the single girl of her popular texts would conceivably, at some point, 'settle down'. In this regard, a contemporary review of her book in *The Nation* quipped that a more apt title would be: *Sex and the Single Minded Girl* (Lehman, 2007, p. 33). The idea of making a political choice, or even a choice at all, out of living a single life as nineteenth century feminist self-professed 'spinsters' had done, then, had been lost.

The single girl, for Brown, might choose to enjoy this transitory state but she would never choose to indefinitely embrace this liminality.

'The single woman', Brown argues,

> far from being a creature to be pitied and patronized, is emerging as the newest glamour girl of our times. She is engaging because she lives by her wits. She supports herself. She has had to sharpen her personality and mental resources to a glitter in order to survive in a competitive world and the sharpening looks good. Economically she is a dream. She is not a parasite, a dependent, a scrounger, a sponger or a bum. She is a giver, not a taker, a winner and not a loser.
>
> (2003, pp. 5–6)

Her narrative centres on singleness as a new feminine mode of being in an urban context, and precedes the 'new single girl at large in the city' narrative (Crozier, 2008, pp. 58–9) typified by programmes like *The Mary Tyler Moore Show* and, of course, latterly *Sex and the City*.[15] The act of situating women in the city, imbuing their presence therein with a kind of taken-for-grantedness, working to naturalize the feminine body in that space, is in itself an important symbolic move in the early '60s (and indeed later). The single girl's literal relocation from the domestic to the traditional masculine public sphere becomes in Brown's rendering not only possible but utterly desirable. Her advice to the increasingly visible single woman is pragmatic and practical – she provides a set of tools, with an insider's canniness, for negotiating a socio-political context that allows, indeed relies upon, the single woman's labour while expecting her to adhere to a fairly traditional feminine script in all other regards. She does not seek to suture these contradictions but accepts them as part of the lived reality of the modern single woman. And although Brown views women's singleness as a transitional state, this is certainly not all it is – it is a period in which her public and private identities can be developed relatively unfettered by a man. That is not to say that Brown fails to recognize how patriarchy works to delimit women's lives and subjectivities but rather to underscore the centrality of women's agency in Brown's account. For Brown, the single girl's identity predominantly comes from her positioning in the workplace not (like previous generations of women) the home (Radner, 1999, p. 12). 'A job', she tells readers, 'gives a single woman something to *be*' (Brown, 2003, p. 89, original emphasis). Further highlighting the way work functions to provide an autonomous identity, and setting the single girl in opposition to the wife (whose lot she concedes is easier than that of the single girl who has to forge her own identity), she adds: 'A single woman is known for what she does rather than whom she belongs to' (Brown, 2003, p. 89).

Sex and the Single Girl is undoubtedly a form of self-help book, an instruction manual that covers everything from recipes for the single girl's dinner parties, make up tips, where to meet men, financial advice, through to how to 'manage' an affair with a married man. As she argues, though more than worthy of the effort, the task of enjoying single life can be arduous and the self is indeed a project upon which much labour must be expended: 'there is a catch to achieving single bliss. You have to work like a son of a bitch' (Brown, 2003, p. 8). (This emphasis on various forms of self-labour continues in self-help literature for the single woman to this day, as Chapter 5 here illustrates.) Brown's often witty, and indeed risqué for the time of its production, narrative voice confides in her readers, using personal experience as an authorizing discourse. She speaks from the other side: she was the single girl of/to whom she speaks but, with a sigh of relief, married in her late 30s. Her observations and instructions are bolstered by her tales of her own successful enactment of these life-altering strategies; she can be trusted because she has *lived* it. Basing her advice on personal experience, Brown, as Scanlon argues, both fits neatly into the category of expert and exceeds it: 'In *Sex and the Single Girl* readers encountered, as she put it, an older confidante who celebrated rather than attempted to contain female sexuality' (2009, p. 9). As Scanlon further notes, the book's publisher, Bernard Geis, suggested 'that many readers wrote letters claiming that Brown served them even better than did psychiatrists, offering them pride in their single status and the means of talking back to those who wanted to marry them off' (2009, p. 10). Therefore, her book resonated with single women readers, who appreciated Brown's legitimation of their 'Single Girl' identities.

In and through Brown's book women's singleness became both visible and viable in the public imaginary; in this regard, its feminist credentials seem impeccable. That said, her emphasis on sexuality as a significant form of capital for the single woman renders the book's relationship to feminism a little more ambiguous. Further, paradoxically, Brown's book is at once an unashamed celebration of the single girl's life and an advice manual on both dating and comportment. In particular, much of the book is devoted to embodiment as Brown advocates the single girl's mastery of the 'technology of sexiness' (Radner, 1999, pp. 15–16).

Through this assumption of a performative femininity, as opposed to any innate or natural one, Brown's work was indeed innovative. Moreover, it appeared around the time the contraceptive pill was becoming more widely available and the so-called 'sexual revolution'[16] was burgeoning, with women's sexuality becoming detached from reproduction and recognized as not confined to the marital boudoir: 'Theoretically, a "nice" single girl has no sex life. What nonsense! She has a better sex life than most of her married friends. She need never be bored with one man per lifetime. Her choice of partners is endless and they seek *her*' (Brown, 2003, p. 7, original emphasis). Sex for women, like a living space solely their own (Brown, 2003, p. 119), within *Sex and the Single Girl* is seen as one of life's essentials and she even provides a chapter devoted to schooling readers in 'How to be Sexy' (Chapter 4). Brown, through both her non-fiction and in editing *Cosmopolitan*, is now seen to have influenced public conceptualizations of women, sexuality, and even feminism in important ways.[17] However, in the 1970s, it was television and popular fiction rather than second-wave feminist polemics that seemed to take up her discursive construction of the 'Single Girl' and reaffirm the possibilities of the identity she had envisioned.

Television is now no stranger to the single career woman in the city, but the way she has been dealt with, not surprisingly, shifted over time (Dow 1996; Dubrofsky, 2002, p. 267). *The Mary Tyler Moore Show* began in 1970 on America's CBS and is said to have offered 'television's first single woman truly attempting to "make it on her own"' (Scanlon, 2009, pp. 132–3). As Dow argues, Mary is the character against which subsequent televisual independent working women have been judged; her 'shadow' said to 'hang over them' (1996, p. 25). Much feminist criticism has been produced in relation to *Mary Tyler Moore*; in terms of the positioning of the single woman within popular culture, her presence on the televisual landscape is significant. The programme's theme song makes explicit its focus on an independent woman negotiating modern life: 'You're going to make it on your own.' The prevalence of such single working women figures in popular culture at this time is said to have been a response to the demands of feminist organizations, such as Friedan's National Organisation of Women (NOW), which placed '"improving images of women in media"' high on its agenda in the late 1960s as well as to advertisers' desire to capitalize on this new market of autonomous women (Lehman, 2007, p. 12). In this way, Mary Tyler Moore was evidence of how liberal feminism was being incorporated into the mainstream media in the 1970s (Dow, 1996, p. 50; Genz, 2009).

In addition to characters like Mary, other prominent independent women in the 1970s could be found in the pages of popular second-wave feminist novels such as Erica Jong's *Fear of Flying* (1973); although most well-known for its articulation of the idea of the 'zipless fuck' (exemplified by a public sexual encounter with a stranger), the novel also explicitly addresses the politics of women's singleness, foregrounding its outsider status. Narrator Isadora Wing, though married for parts of the novel, self-reflexively interrogates the institutional privilege of marriage and notes: 'It is heresy to embrace any way of life except as half of a couple. Solitude is un-American ... a woman is always presumed to be alone as the result of abandonment, not choice. And she is treated that way: as a pariah. There is simply no dignified way for a woman to live alone' (in Whelehan, 2002, p. 28). These ideas are echoed in 1990s literary texts, especially chick lit novels like *Bridget Jones's Diary*, of which 1970s popular feminist fiction is said to be a precursor (Whelehan, 2005). However, in the decade prior to this genre's emergence – the 1980s – single women's sexuality and increased presence in the public sphere evoked fear and anxiety, especially in film.

Backlash; cinematic single women as 'toxic feminists'

In *Backlash: The Undeclared War Against Women* (1991), Susan Faludi famously argued that alongside proclamations of women's equality and success in the public sphere in the 1980s ran counter-narratives foregrounding their misery:

> This bulletin of despair is everywhere – at the newsagent's, on the TV set, at the cinema, in advertisements and doctors' offices and academic journals. Professional women are suffering 'burn-out' and succumbing to an 'infertility epidemic'. Single women are grieving from a 'man shortage'. *The New York Times* reports: childless women are 'depressed' and 'confused' and their ranks are swelling.
>
> (1991, pp. 1–2)

Part of the backlash meticulously and polemically catalogued by Faludi included popular narratives around the alleged 'rising mental distress of single women', claims which she notes were never substantiated by epidemiological studies (1991, p. 55). In spite of some of the conceptual limitations of Faludi's thesis[18], she deftly illustrates how single women in the 1980s especially were quite literally pathologized (seen to be suffering from various forms of mental illness) across media, from the more overtly 'factual' genres like news and magazine articles to Hollywood blockbusters. Although actual studies of single women's lives and their expectations begged to differ, 'conventional press wisdom held that single women of the 1980s were desperate for marriage – a desperation that mounted with every passing unwed year' (Faludi, 1991, p. 33). She recounts the infamous *Newsweek* story that a woman over 40 was more likely to be murdered by a terrorist than to find a husband, which itself helped to discursively constitute the man drought around which there came to be such intense moral panic in 1980s media, particularly in the United States.[19]

For Faludi, such mainstream narratives were part of an all pervasive 'backlash' against second-wave feminist gains. In her analysis, nowhere was this backlash more evident than around the single woman, especially those without children. Women's success in the public sphere was juxtaposed with their patent failure in the private; that feminism was responsible, and had to be held to account, for this misery was taken as a given. This narrative continues to gather traction, particularly in recent books about women's declining fertility and childlessness which mobilize the 'barren womb' style discourses so thoroughly unpacked a few decades ago by Faludi (Hewlett, 2002; Cannold, 2005; Hausseger, 2005). It was not simply that women were single which acted as the source of angst but that they were single *and* successful in the traditionally masculine world of employment. Hollywood film from this era is particularly instructive in this regard, so for the remainder of this section I briefly interrogate the kinds of feminine singlehood that circulated in some of the most prominent of these texts.[20]

In popular film of the 1980s and early 1990s, the single woman (and especially the single childless woman) became a figure of abject horror, harbouring barely sublimated rage, murderous urges and profound jealousy towards those living the patriarchal nuclear familial dream. Hollywood films such as *Basic Instinct* (1992), with a highly eroticized, ice-pick wielding Sharon Sharon or *Disclosure* (1994), featuring Demi Moore as sexual harasser, as well as *Fatal Attraction* (1987) all mobilize the trope of the castrating, often sexually voracious, woman in a position of power (Leonard, 2009, p. 81).[21] In particular, it is Alex Forrester, the seemingly deranged 36-year-old protagonist of *Fatal Attraction*, who most is commonly cited as evidence of the media backlash against feminism (Faludi, 1991; Walters, 1995). Indicative of its success, the film is said to have earned $100 million in its first four months at the box office (McRobbie, 2009, p. 37). *Fatal Attraction*, and its cultural reception, has received much analysis so I will only briefly attend to it here.

Fatal Attraction is, unsurprisingly, routinely seen as a cautionary tale against women's single subjectivity; not only is it unviable, it is punishable by death (and an especially gruesome and brutal one at that).[22] While the film is as much about a perceived precarious masculinity, for which feminism is implicitly responsible, as it is about the potentially destabilizing effects of women's sexual autonomy and singleness, for this study it is the figure of Alex that is of most interest. This is especially the case as she continues to function as the spectre of the transgressive single woman haunting the popular imaginary; warning women that she is who they could become and warning men that she is who they should steer clear of at all costs. As Angela McRobbie remarks, 'because Alex played by Glenn Close became a kind of evil, insane, hate figure (a contemporary witch) she also entered the popular imagination of younger women as someone they must avoid ever becoming in their pursuit of independence alongside love, sex, marriage and motherhood' (2009, p. 35). The cultural reverberations of this vengeful character continue, as her invocation in *Bridget Jones's Diary* suggests (see Chapter 3).[23] Moreover, the trope of the 'bunny boiler' (an act committed by its single protagonist) has entered popular lexicon, short-hand for an obsessive, intense single woman whose attention is essentially unwanted and, given the fate of the bunny, apparently psychotic. And, similarly, in the early 1990s another film overtly argued that there was nothing more terrifying than a *Single White Female* (dir. Schroeder, 1992). In this film, the trope of the mentally unstable single woman so well established in Lynne's text is entirely reinscribed. Like the 'bunny boiler', in popular discourse the identification of a woman as a 'single white female' invokes Hedy's (Jennifer Jason Leigh) 'unhealthy' emulation of Allie (Bridget Fonda) as well as the general threat posed by a woman fitting this moniker – a threat that, like in *Fatal Attraction*, must be violently eliminated.[24]

Alex Forrester (Glenn Close), seemingly competent, agentic career woman and Dan Gallagher (Michael Douglas), lawyer and family man, meet at a work function then begin a 48-hour affair while his wife is out of town with their daughter. After Dan ends their tryst, Alex refuses to accept that it is over and the remainder of the film tracks her unraveling: 'what begins as a tale of a man's violation of the trust of his loved ones turns into a misogynistic rant against the social posture and sexual autonomy of the independent woman' (Babener, 1992, p. 26). Alex comes to symbolize not just the single woman but the single *working* woman, that product of feminism that became the scapegoat during the Reagan era for a series of social ills, including the breaking down of

the nuclear family (Leonard, 2009, p. 69). While not explicitly identified as a feminist, Alex is undoubtedly seen to represent feminist values;
she is figured as 'the emasculating personification of toxic feminism'
(McNair, 2002, p. 152). She deploys throughout feminist-informed
discourses around egalitarian relationships and her very brazenness,
including in terms of sex, is implicitly attributed to feminism (Leonard,
2009). Moreover, *Fatal Attraction* can be seen to exemplify what Barry
Grant refers to as 'yuppie horror films', among which he also counts
Poison Ivy, Single White Female, and *Desperately Seeking Susan*. For Grant,
these films resemble horror films in how their evil protagonists function
as the repressed Other of 'the individual psyche of collective culture'
(1996, p. 8). In this way, Alex disrupts Dan's privileged 'yuppy' lifestyle,
functioning as an embodied threat to his privileged material existence.

Through their lack of a man, single women have often been associated both with lesbianism and feminism (which themselves have been
routinely conflated in the popular imaginary). However, in so-called
'backlash' films like *Fatal Attraction*, not only is the female protagonist
avowedly heterosexual, it is her insatiable sexual appetite that symbolizes her threat to the entire hetero-patriarchal social order and its central institution, marriage. Historically, the cultural anxieties around the
single woman are perhaps most evident in the film noir figure of the
femme fatale (Creed, 1993). While masculine fears of women's sexuality
have been described psychoanalytically as *vagina dentata*, the Freudian
idea exemplifying men's fear of castration, the voracious sexuality of
the woman operating outside the confines of a marital relationship,
of a woman who cannot be defined in relation to a masculine other,
is seen as especially potent.[25] Dan and Alex's love-making is frantic
and she is figured throughout as predatory and sexually insatiable. Her
suicide attempt after Dan announces he is leaving after two nights of
illicit sex positions her as mentally unstable, a threat not just to Dan
and his family but to herself. Her deficiency – that she has no man – is
seen as both cause and effect of her apparent mental instability. Though
initially coded as a successful, independent career woman, following
their affair's end, the film entirely strips Alex of an independent subjectivity and she exists only in relation to Dan (Joshel, 1992). Alex is
seen to be controlled by her emotions, which are deemed excessive and
which, despite her initial allure, ultimately render her repugnant to Dan
(Dubrofsky, 2009, p. 363).

The infamous line 'I'm 36 years old, it may be my last chance to
have a child', when Alex announces to Dan that she is carrying their
child and intends to keep it, locates the film firmly in relation to the

'man drought' and 'barren womb' discourses circulating at the time of its production and reception (Faludi, 1991). It is not just a sexually and economically independent woman the film renders fearful but one whose metaphorical biological clock is loudly ticking. Throughout, the film stages an opposition between the 'legitimate' subjectivity of Beth – stay at home mother and wife – and the 'illegitimate' subjectivity of Alex – the career woman embodying the ultimate lack. Indeed, the film's denouement features the physical playing out of the conflict that has underpinned the diegesis; this literal battle between Beth and Alex figures Dan as a highly coveted prize. As Dow argues in light of the fact that it is Beth and not Dan who finally eliminates the threat posed by the psychotic single woman, 'Dan doesn't get to be the hero because he is the *prize*' (2006, p. 126, original emphasis).

For Faludi, given the punishment meted out to Alex, the film's title is a misnomer: 'In the end, the attraction is fatal only for the single woman.' The film's conclusion emphasizes that 'the best single woman is a dead one' (1991, p. 152). *Fatal Attraction* is perhaps an extreme example of popular culture's acrimony towards single women, but its ongoing presence in the cultural imaginary suggests that the trope of the hysterical and delusional woman-without-a-man continues to register fears about women's singleness (and the feminism with which it is seen to be linked). For example, lest it appears such psychotic feminine figures are a thing of the past, it is worth noting that the sequel to *Single White Female* was not released until 2005 (dir. Samples) and made explicit the derangement of said single woman in its subtitle: *The Psycho*.

For some critics, though, the fictional single women of 'backlash cinema' like Alex – despite the way she is constituted as a dangerous predator – can be recuperated. Nina Auerbach, for example, argues that the figure of the 'old maid', whom she believes has been 'ferociously modernized' in *Fatal Attraction,* could function to 'revive our [feminists'] belief in the old maid's power' (1991, pp. xii–xiii). In this way, '*Fatal Attraction* and its ilk should remind even women who hate it that we *have* set ourselves outside conventional norms and that our most vibrant role is that of the outsider' (Auerbach, 1991, p. xiii, original emphasis). As I will suggest, however, the empowering liminality implied here by Auerbach has been excised from discursive constructions of the single woman in the late twentieth/early twenty-first centuries. The single woman is no longer an outsider figure, existing on the margins, but has conversely been thoroughly incorporated into the mainstream, and, as noted in Chapter 1, she is – like feminism itself – simultaneously permissible yet disavowed.

'Chick culture' and postfeminism in the 1990s

While in the 1980s the single woman was deemed such an intense threat to patriarchal order, and to the nuclear family itself, that she had to quite literally be eradicated, the growth of what has been called 'chick culture' in the 1990s witnessed a more ambivalent approach to her that is often seen to be a product of the broader mainstream adoption of feminist discursive frames. Around this time, a seemingly 'new' rendering of the single woman came to feature within the pages of the chick lit novel and its filmic manifestations. Chick lit, in terms of popular narratives centring on single women, was only one part of a broader intertextual network making seemingly autonomous, empowered women their focus. Ferris and Young argue that such texts are best seen as part of a broader cultural phenomenon dubbed 'chick culture' (2008, p. 1). For them, chick culture signals a 'new visibility of women in popular culture'; a 'deliberate address to female audiences; and is 'vitally linked to postfeminism' (2008, pp. 2–3). It encompasses chick lit; what they call 'chick TV programming' (in which they include shows like *Sex and the City*); chick flicks; music; magazines; and blogs (2008, p. 2). 'Chick culture' represents in many ways a feminized form of popular culture that responds to, and indeed helps make sense of, shifts in women's subjectivity engendered by feminism. Arguably, audience desire for recognition of shifts in their lived realities drove such changes, as did advertisers' targeting of independent single women as a distinctive consumer category with considerable spending power.

As a film genre, chick flicks represent – by and large – a form of romantic comedy. In the tradition of many a Meg Ryan movie (*When Harry Met Sally, Sleepless in Seattle, You've Got Mail*), it seems women within popular culture are still intensely preoccupied with finding, securing, and keeping a man, as more recent films like *He's Just Not That Into You* (based on the self-help book of the same name) evidence. In the 2009 adaptation (dir. Kwapis), a number of the film's female characters are obsessed with decoding signals from the opposite sex and to interpreting the vagaries of communication between men and women. In fact, the trope of the single woman miserable and unfulfilled without a man, and consumed with how to remedy this situation, recurs throughout Hollywood films from the 2000s. For example, in films like *The Wedding Date* (2005, dir. Kilner), where the heroine Kat (Deborah Messing) pronounces herself 'single and miserable' and accordingly hires a male escort to fend off queries about her singleness at a family wedding and in *27 Dresses* (2008, dir. Fletcher), where the 'always a bridesmaid never a bride' adage is mobilized to signify that the heroine, Jane Nichols (Katherine Heigl), has not quite reached the privileged status of 'bride' (a fact, of course, that she laments especially as her sister becomes engaged to her long-term crush).[26]

In terms of television, in the mid-late 1990s a series of narratives focusing upon the lives of professional single women in urban contexts proliferated (Negra, 2004). Women privileged by their class, race, education, and employment status filled mainstream media culture. The women from *Friends* and *Ally McBeal*, as well as their descendants, those from *Sex and the City*, are routinely seen to offer something original in terms of television's engagement with the figure of the single woman. Being single comes to be a 'consistent character attribute' in such series, although the degree to which singleness is incorporated into the actual narrative varies (Lotz, 2006, p. 92). Some of these mainstream stories featuring the Singleton, though seemingly recuperative, in effect continue to render the single woman troublesome – including *Ally McBeal*.

Ally McBeal: 'Bridget Jones with a law degree'[27]

Ally McBeal, created by David E. Kelly, ran for a total of five seasons (1997–2002, Fox) and revolved around the eponymous heroine's personal and professional lives, though the latter often simply stood as a backdrop to the incessant melodrama enacted in the former. A lawyer at fictional firm, Cage and Fish, Ally's fantasies about marriage and motherhood routinely play out through her auditory and visual hallucinations, a key way in which 'the mise-en-scene privileges Ally's inner world, experience and emotions' (Moseley & Read, 2002, p. 245). Ally is a self-professed neurotic, with much of the programme featuring her engagement with various therapists; her speech is often halting and tentative, and she is routinely seen to be childlike (in Season 5, for example, she rides a scooter to work). Like other single women in public discourse, she is regularly categorized (by other characters) as self-absorbed and selfish; something the programme itself facilitates by its singular focus on her inner life. Her mental stability, or lack thereof, is a recurring theme within the narrative; she ponders: 'How did I get to be such a mess? (1.4[28]). One of the other characters, firm partner John Cage, describes her as 'riddled with emotional deficits' (5.1), while her flatmate and district attorney, Renee, tells her 'emotionally, you're an idiot' (1.8). These deficiencies are seen as both cause and effect of her manlessness. Ally is not ambivalent about her singleness; she clearly deplores it (in the final season this sense of lack softens somewhat but only because she becomes a mother).

By representing the heroine's unconscious fears and desires, and by incorporating her voiceover narration, the programme urged viewers to identify with Ally (Douglas, 2010, pp. 109–11). The infamous dancing baby, a computer generated image, accompanied by the song 'Hooked on a Feeling', makes its first appearance mid-way through season one (1.11). Indeed, it is the baby's ubiquitous presence – a none too subtle reference to her ticking biological clock – in Ally's psyche that cause others to recommend she see a therapist (1.14), which she does until the end of the series, further reinscribing the sense of singleness as a pathology (the primary topic for discussion with these various therapists are her relationships, or lack thereof, with men). Technically, the series is innovative and experimental; ideologically, it is more conventional. However, even aesthetically, by midway through its second season, *Ally McBeal* was failing to deliver on the new directions promised by the first season, regressing to the 'unidimensional range of normality typical of earlier sitcoms' (Nochimson, 2000, p. 25).

The intertextual relation of Ally and Bridget Jones has been commonly invoked in feminist criticism and is a testament to the transnational cultural flow of these discourses around the figure of the single woman. Some critics, eliding their cultural specificity, see them both as indicative of a global contempt towards single women: 'The problem with Bridget and Ally is that they are presented as archetypes of single womanhood even though they are little more than composites of frivolous neuroses' (Bellafante, 1998).[29] For others, Ally McBeal is believed to dramatize (like Bridget) 'the problems, struggles, and contradictions facing contemporary young women' (Moseley & Read, 2002, p. 239). Professionally, there are clear differences between these two 'Singletons'. Ally's competency in the courtroom rarely comes into question; unlike Bridget, she is professionally adroit and frequently wins her cases. In the final season, the firm is even rebadged 'Cage, Fish and McBeal' as she is made partner. Moreover, the court cases in which the firm becomes involved often centre around issues relevant to feminism – especially sexual harassment, pornography, gay marriage, workplace discrimination based on appearance, censorship, prostitution, and sex discrimination (though the firm's approach to such issues is often unorthodox and not necessarily sympathetic to feminism).

In the diegetic world established by *Ally*, the public and the private blend throughout, with the firm's unisex toilet rather unsubtly signifying the destabilization of the professional/personal binary and gender boundaries in the workplace and around which the entire series revolves (Moseley & Read, 2002, p. 245). In staff meetings, the firm's lawyers – especially Ally – regularly discuss their romantic dilemmas, again implying this public/private permeability that structures the entire series. Finding herself working in a firm with her now married childhood sweetheart, Billy, Ally frequently laments that her life has not gone 'according to plan':

> I had a plan – my whole life, I had a plan. When I was 28, I was gonna be taking my little maternity leave, but I would still be on the partnership track. I would be at home, at night, cuddled up with my husband reading 'What to Expect When You're Nursing' and trying cases. Big home life, big professional life, and instead, I am going to bed with an inflatable doll, and I represent clients who suck toes. This was not the plan.
>
> (1.17)

In spite of all her achievements in the public sphere, without love, Ally's life is seen to be profoundly lacking and love's promise dominates her thoughts; for example, each night she sings 'Goodnight, my someone' to herself (Season 1).

The text often self-consciously draws attention to how Ally has been a figure of controversy, especially for feminists, as she herself acknowledges: 'I am a strong, working career girl who feels empty without a man, the National Organisation for Women, they have a contract out on my head' (1.5). *Ally McBeal*, and its eponymous heroine's positioning in relation to feminism, has been a heated topic of debate both publicly and within the academy (Moseley & Reed, 2002; Ouellette, 2002; Lotz, 2006; Van Slooten, 2006). The much cited *Time* magazine cover located her (by associating her with feminist luminaries like Gloria Steinem) firmly within debates about the future, or rather the death, of feminism that were being staged in the 1990s predominantly along generational lines. Indeed, once again self-reflexively invoking these feminist debates around the show's central character, in one episode Ally tells John Cage that she dreamt she featured in *Time* as the 'face of feminism' (2.12). Undue attention was given to the length of the protagonist's hemline and the purportedly anorexic body of the actor who played her (Calista Flockhart); whether she was an appropriate 'role model'; and if she was antifeminist.[30]

For L. S. Kim, implying that there is a 'real' or authentic feminism that is being distorted by its media representations, programmes focusing on 'the so-called working girl (or single girl in the city) seem to proffer a feminist tone or objective, but it ultimately seems to be a false feminism' (2001, p. 323). As a number of feminist critics have shown, feminism is now made-to-mean predominantly within the textual spaces of main-stream media culture, and given the common recognition that there is no one singular form of feminism, it is untenable to propose a feminism untainted by its interactions with media culture. Kim claims that such shows are both 'postfeminist/antifeminist' (2001, p. 322), and while sympathetic to her politically engaged reading, this simple conflation of postfeminist with antifeminist is a troublesome slippage. It is, however, commonly enacted in feminist criticism of single-woman-centred pro-grammes like *Ally McBeal*.[31] This identification fails to acknowledge how feminism is used and comes to inform millennial and post-millennial constructions of feminine subjectivity. Postfeminism is more com-plicated than its neat conflation with antifeminism allows, as I have argued in Chapter 1. It also presumes that feminism's greater diffusion in the mainstream necessarily has lamentable political consequences; and while this may, in some instances, be the case, the multiplicity of feminist appropriations necessitates a more nuanced critical approach. Accordingly, I am not concerned with dismissing programmes like *Ally McBeal* as antifeminist but I am interested in rendering visible their politics and how their incorporation of feminism produces a hybrid-ized form leading to potentially less than progressive representations of contemporary women and their singleness.

In terms of her singleness (and her perception of its inherent unde-sirability), Ally McBeal seemed to offer little that feminists could cel-ebrate.[32] Her anxiety and neuroses over that very singleness pre-empted the kinds of anxious subjectivity that would be played out over and over again in the 1990s and 2000s, most notably through Bridget and her chick lit cohort. As Susan J. Douglas remarks, 'Ally McBeal gave women a new postfeminist subjectivity to try on and inhabit, accomplished yet insecure, riddled with ambivalence and contradiction' (2010, p. 108). For many critics, it is popular culture's seeming embrace of single female characters attempting to negotiate these tensions – to 'have it all' – that renders them quintessentially postfeminist. They are seen to embody the difficulties of 'navigating between the achievements of feminism and the demands of femininity' (Douglas, 2010, p. 108). The paradox of this postfeminist identity is evidenced by the following quotation from Ally herself: 'I'm a lawyer, I'm independent, I've got the world at my fingertips and I am woman – and if he doesn't love me, I don't know what I'm going to do' (4.5). Viewing Ally as a postfeminist heroine, many feminist cultural critics position her as simply speaking to the single woman's efforts to combine the personal and the professional. As Genz argues, 'The postfeminist Singleton [among whom she counts

Ally] endeavours to find a subject position that permits her to hang on to the material and social gains fostered by the women's movement as well as indulge in her romantic longings' (2010, p. 138). This focus on the desire for a man to complement her comparatively more successful professional life means that there is no space within the diegesis for the legitimation of singleness.

For Ally (and indeed the other female members of the ensemble cast), despite her myriad accomplishments in the public sphere, 'being single was akin to a death sentence' (Douglas, 2010, p. 110). For example, in one episode, Ally applies for a court order to allow her former school teacher, now an ill elderly woman, to be induced into a coma. The reason: because in her dream life she is married with three children, while in reality she has no one (except a priest and Ally). Here, then, being in a coma – effectively dying – is figured as preferable to living as a single woman with no family (2.11). Episodes frequently end with Ally, a solitary figure walking down the street, accompanied only by a melancholy ballad to signal her isolation. So acute is Ally's sense of emptiness, at times she even sleeps with a male blow up doll dubbed 'David'. Making explicit this anxiety, she confesses in an interior mono-logue: 'Part of me has always thought life has no meaning until you get to share it with someone' (4.1). Defeating singleness is a serious project for Ally, for which she will go to extreme lengths, including ramming a 'cute' driver with her car in the hope of securing a date. As she tells the unsuspecting motorist, 'I'm almost thirty, I'm single. I don't meet many prospects and when I do I will damn well run them down' (3.12). And, although she remains single, Ally ultimately does not end up alone as she finds herself a mother.

In a neat, if thoroughly implausible, narrative twist in the final season (5.11), it is revealed a daughter has been conceived via a mistaken use of Ally's eggs which had been donated to a fertility clinic for research purposes many years prior. Her ten-year-old daughter, Maddie, arrives and Ally tells her that perhaps it isn't a man she has waiting for all these years but her; Ally's singleness is recuperable only via her adoption of a socially laudable subject position: Mother. Moreover, the series con-cludes on a note of maternal sacrifice and her singleness is eclipsed. In the series finale (5.21) Ally resigns so she can relocate to New York for the sake of her daughter (who is having difficulty adjusting to life in Boston). Her career, in the final instance, is uncertain as she tells fellow partner Richard: 'They have law firms in New York.' Given the final epi-sode, 'it seems that having a career, for Ally, was kind of a pit-stop on the way to motherhood' (Dubrofsky, 2002, p. 273). While she did not 'choose' to have a child, she did choose the child over her professional life. Through motherhood, it seems, Ally finds gendered fulfilment, suggesting the ways in which postfeminism often inscribes nostalgic gender scripts. Another popular television programme, released the year after Ally concluded, revolving around the lives of four single women, seems to offer more possibilities in terms of challenging the illegitimacy of women's singleness.

Sex and the City: Ambivalent singlehood

Although *Sex and the City* (1998–2004, HBO) has also attracted much critical attention, including an entire edited collection of essays, *Reading Sex and The City* (Akass & McCabe, 2004), it is impossible in a study of this nature not to engage with the cultural contribution it made to refiguring women's singleness.[33] *Sex and the City* explicitly bears its indebtedness to Gurley Brown's prototypical feminism in its title. Signalling *Sex and the City*'s intertextual relation to Brown's work, Kingston remarks: 'It was Helen Gurley Brown's *Sex and the Single Girl* updated and brought to cable' (2004, p. 219). It is undoubtedly the case that television programmes like *Sex and the City* were made possible by second-wave feminism; in terms of characterization, plot and dialogue, and the sheer types of feminine identities it foregrounds, the influence of feminism permeates the series. The four central characters are, if perhaps not self-identified as such, at the very least implicitly feminist and are a testament to the distillation of feminism into Western popular culture of which I have already spoken. Moving in and through urban space in each episode (as opposed to being confined to any particular site), these women are *flaneuses*, taking pleasure in their relatively unhindered mobility in the formerly masculine space of the city (Kim, 2001, pp. 329–30). Like others depicted in the mainstream media, they also appear to use their sporadic singleness as periods of self-development (Macvarish, 2008).

Rather over-statedly, however, *Sex and the City* has been said to give women 'permission to stay single in style' (Scanlon, 2009, p. 57). The question this begs, of course, is which women and for how long? Furthermore, in terms of the friendships at the narratives' centre, much has been made of the series' enactment of a kind of utopian postfeminist sisterhood. A new way of being (single) for women is believed to have been enacted and celebrated in and through the series; new forms of sociality and the privileging of non-familial bonds have seen it critically rendered 'queer' as well as suggesting that life without a man is indeed livable: 'What made *SATC* different was that it regularly suggested that this family of four could be enough to make up a life, a life still worth living without the husband and baby, a life led outside the historic feminine and feminist script' (Gerhard, 2005, p. 46). Such celebratory comments obscure the series' racial, sexual, and class politics, and how it constitutes certain types of feminine subjects 'legitimate' singles and thereby excludes others. They also fail to recognize that the model of sisterhood the show is believed to have ushered in to popular culture has not actually carried over into more recent texts. For example, this form of non-biological sisterhood has more recently been challenged through reality TV programmes like *Keeping Up with the Kardashians* and dramas such as *Brothers and Sisters* which continue to privilege familial bonds as the basis for supportive relationships between women. Similarly, the new Australian programme, *Offspring*, which borrows the diary-style voice-over confessional of the Bridget Jones' franchise and visualizes the heroine's fantasies in a way that is reminiscent of *Ally McBeal*, also privileges the biological family over the 'urban' one.

The show's glorification of conspicuous consumption can be seen to be consistent with the broader cultural logics of postfeminism; as Negra argues, 'luxury consumption' is celebrated within postfeminism, where capitalism becomes 'salvation', signaling 'unapologetic class stratification in America' (2009, pp. 118–19). This stratification is not only present in *Sex and the City* but is glamorized, especially through the series' emphasis on haute couture and, most blatantly, designer shoes. The four women's lifestyles require a high disposable income and in the instances when the apparently gauche subject of money is raised, there is always a friend standing by with a \$30,000 Tiffany engagement ring to pawn (4.16). In this way, and in line with postfeminism, the show positions the act of consumption as a key marker of the single woman's independence (Lehman, 2007, p. 232); according to this logic, these four women must be some of the most independent on television! As this series makes patently obvious, the single woman is seen as especially significant in marketing terms, and – in line with postfeminist and neoliberal rhetorics – the ability to enjoy single life is tied to consumption: 'The glorification of this single girl narrative is highlighted by her right to choose to consume items such as men, food, dialogue, and commodities, and the pleasure she receives from those acts of consumption' (Gennaro, 2007, p. 273). In this vein, the 'single girl narratives' that are most permissible – such as *Sex and the City* – are those which invoke a 'perpetual adolescence', itself based on and fostering of perpetual consumption (Gennaro, 2007, p. 273).

Despite its emphasis on a particular type of consuming feminine subject, the series does work to expose the fissures in the dominant ideologies around gender and heterosexuality; demystifying them to reveal the double standards and exclusionary social practices that privilege the coupled. In more celebratory instances of criticism, the series is said to make 'a persuasive case for the single life, but also for the need to expand notions of the family in ways that accommodate recent changes in women's lives' (Nelson, 2004, p. 85). For Nelson (2004, pp. 88–9), 'these women are not the pathetic, neurotic or psychotic portraits of single women past (and, too often, present)'. Indeed the show does regularly draw attention to the stigmatization of women's singlehood and, in particular, makes explicit the limitations of co-habitation and marriage on women's selfhood. But while these four women may be shown to enjoy their singleness, it is certainly not positioned as a state that they have actively chosen or wish to prolong.

In the series pilot, its heroine (though arguably there are four) describes herself to the unsubtly dubbed 'Mr Big' as a 'sexual anthropologist'. A number of critics have celebrated the series for offering 'a refreshing alternative to most mass-media depictions of female sexuality' (Henry, 2004b, p. 82). It is apparent that the focus on women's agency and sexual pleasure do broadly position it in a feminist discursive realm. Its non-judgemental approach to women's sexual desire rendered the series unique. Sex in a relationship, sex while single, sex with oneself, sex with a woman – all these possibilities are explored, to a greater or lesser degree, within this series. Not surprisingly, sexuality has been seen to be central in programmes focusing on single women because of 'their characters' liberation from the marriages that have limited the available stories about women' (Lotz, 2006, p. 87). Frank discussions about sex and the individual women's sexual practices feature in every episode over the show's iconic cocktail, the Cosmopolitan, or their weekly brunch. In this way, *SATC* can be classified a 'dialogical sitcom' wherein 'the dialogue is the action' (Gennaro, 2007, p. 252). These conversations between the four women, where nothing appears taboo, often operate as forms of consciousness-raising sessions, where sexual double-standards and heteronormative expectations are deconstructed by the four friends. As Jane Arthurs argues, 'The series publicly repudiates the shame of being single and sexually active in defiance of the bourgeois codes that used to be demanded of respectable women. It self reflexively interrogates media representations of the single woman although the emotional power of these residual stereotypes is acknowledged' (2003, p. 85). Moreover, each character represents a different side of singleness, permitting a wider exploration of women's experiences and identities.

The four faces of singleness

The four *SATC* protagonists each has a different, though sometimes over-lapping, way of performing and negotiating their singleness (including through its, even if temporary, elimination). Indeed, it could be argued that in proffering four different types of single women, the programme entails a little conceded diversity and heterogeneity in the popular representation of women's singleness. Samantha in particular is often lauded as providing a non-judgemental approach to women's sexuality, allowing her sexual expression to continue unfettered and without moralizing: 'Samantha represents the sexual revolution in its entirety' (Kim, 2001, p. 329).[34] While Charlotte is described as a 'cheerleader for love', repeatedly invoking the idea of 'the One', the most pronounced contestations of how single women are subordinately positioned come from Miranda. But she, often seen as the most overtly feminist character proffered by the series, is as preoccupied with becoming unsingle as the rest of the characters. That said, the series' explicit critique of this preoccupation is regularly articulated by her. Carrie, in many ways, represents an amalgam of her three faux sisters, and as the 'voice' of the programme she directs each episode, interpreting incidents in all their lives in her voiceover, as well as focalizing the action through the question she poses, ostensibly for her newspaper column, in each episode. Her guiding questions include: 'Is there a cold war between marrieds and singles?' (1.1); 'Are we simply romantically challenged or are we sluts?' (3.5); 'Can we have it all?' (3.10); 'To be in a couple, do you have to put your single self on the shelf?' (4.14); 'Are we the new bachelors?' (5.7); and 'When will waiting for the one be done?' (6.12). *Sex and the City* not only features single women characters, but stories that engage with the prosaic elements of being single (Lotz, 2006, p. 99). That is, it is not merely that single women are at the series' centre but single-ness itself is explicitly interrogated therein, and it is this distinguishing factor that marks it out from other programmes focusing on urban professional single women. Moreover, a feminist-informed vocabulary is evident throughout characters' dialogue and Carrie's voiceover.

The programme intervenes to disrupt limited depictions of women's singleness in two key ways. Firstly, it explicitly addresses how women's identities are shaped and delimited by certain societal expectations around femininity and heterosexuality, drawing attention to and often satirizing the way single women are marginalized and devalued.

Secondly, it challenges the centrality of the search for a male significant other (upon which the series itself relies for its narrative drive) by
foregrounding alternative bonds and relationships, especially between
the four women themselves, but also by having the characters' self-
reflexively address the ways in which they prioritize men at various
stages in their lives, at some cost to their independent identities. That
said, as has often been pointed out, at the series finale, each of the four
characters is partnered while the romance between Carrie and Mr Big
drives the entire series; even when not together, or when Big is physically not part of an episode, he remains an absent presence.

The series', or rather its heroines', preoccupation with romantic
attachments is regularly critiqued from within. For example, in 'Take Me
to The Ballgame' (2.1), Miranda articulates her frustration vis-à-vis the
centrality of men: 'Does it always have to be about them?' Meanwhile,
Carrie's ambivalence towards marriage in particular is witnessed in an
episode where this disdain comes to be quite literally written on her
body ('A Woman's Right to Shoes', 6.9); while trying on wedding dresses
with Miranda, she comes out in hives and, in extreme distress, struggles to be freed from the dress and all it symbolizes. This very visceral
reaction mirrors an earlier episode; in 'Just Say Yes' (4.12) Carrie vomits
when she finds an engagement ring in Aidan's bag. Indeed, throughout
the series, Carrie persistently expresses concerns about what a committed relationship would do to her identity as a single woman. In 'All
that Glitters' (4.14), she tries to find a way to negotiate the competing
demands of these subjectivities; as she puts it, she 'tries to find a way for
my single self and my couple self to co-exist'.

In her analysis of these issues, Negra argues that '*Sex and the City* origi-
nates with the recognition that single women retain if not quite on the
same terms, the status of "social problem" they have long held' (2004,
p. 1). The series frequently works to problematize this positioning of single woman as social ill, attempting to disrupt the way women's singleness
is put into discourse. As the women play a card game – 'Old Maid' –
Miranda remarks of the ideologically loaded discursive inconsistencies
between single men and women, 'Why do we get stuck with old maid
and spinster, and men get to be bachelors and playboys?' (5.3). In 'They
Shoot Single People, Don't They?' (2.4), Carrie is photographed for the
cover of *New York* magazine. The story, which has been pitched to her as
'Single and Fabulous' eventually appears as 'Single and Fabulous?' The
interrogative shifts the tenor of the article significantly and the episode
engages with how singles (and women in particular) are publicly figured. Much to her horror, the photograph used is of a hung-over, tired,

chain-smoking Carrie and the shift from exclamation mark to question mark forces her to interrogate her own attitude to singleness. Carrie concludes it is better to be alone than to simply be with a man for the sake of it, and the episode ends with her eating in a restaurant on her own, with – as Arthurs remarks – 'no book to read as armour' (2003, p. 85), thus challenging the idea that single women cannot enjoy a meal on their own without being deemed tragic, pathetic, or lonely.

In 'Four Women and A Funeral' (2.5), high achieving lawyer Miranda takes out a mortgage on her first apartment; the refrain throughout the episode is 'So, it's just you?' and she is forced to tick the 'single' box on the associated paperwork. This episode explicitly deals with various forms of symbolic and material discrimination against single women, critiqued particularly by DePaulo (2006). When Miranda inspects the apartment, an elderly neighbour tells her that the previous owner, 'a single woman, died in that apartment, wasn't found for a week and rumor has it, the cat ate half her face'. Invoking Bridget Jones' fear of being eaten by Alsatians, as well as the ubiquitous trope of the cat-loving spinster, this episode positions itself as part of a broader conversation around the fears of single women. After moving in to the apartment, Miranda nearly chokes on Chinese takeaway, inducing a panic attack, and she cries to Carrie over the phone: 'I'm going to die alone.' As Negra remarks of this episode, 'In actively confronting the mythologies that stigmatize the single female household and the ownership of property by single women and exposing their irrationality, this episode differs from mainstream chick flicks that tend to uphold such mythologies even while subjecting them to gentle comic treatment' (2004, p. 7).

Social rituals also commonly come under scrutiny, especially in relation to how single women are positioned as outsiders. For example, in one episode Samantha hosts a 'I don't have a baby shower' (1.10). Meanwhile, in 'A Woman's Right to Shoes' (6.9), Carrie tells Miranda: 'If you are single, after graduation there isn't a single occasion where people celebrate you.' In this episode, Carrie tallies up the amount she has spent on friends' engagements, weddings, bridal and baby showers and when her shoes are stolen from a married friend's apartment, she registers at Manolo Blahnik for a replacement pair. Furthermore, when Miranda's mother dies in 'My Motherboard, Myself' (4.8), she speculates about reactions to her singleness at the funeral: 'Ignore the coffin, there's a single 35-year-old woman walking behind it … that would be the real tragedy.' While Miranda, however, is not alone (her urban family accompany her to the funeral), once again the series draws attention to the way single women are read in specific social contexts (i.e. as deviant and worthy of pity).

In 'The Freak Show' (2.3) the programme inverts the idea of single women as freaks, as it tracks a series of horrendous dates endured by Carrie with decidedly freakish men. In this respect, it makes clear that while femininity, and women's professional subjectivities especially, may have been reconfigured in the wake of second-wave feminism, masculinity has failed to be likewise reordered (Whelehan, 2010, p. 160), and it is this disjuncture that provides the gendered conflict upon which the series pivots. 'The Agony and the Ex-Tacy' (4.1) is another episode that deals explicitly with how single women are perceived and highlights the strategies employed to combat negative reactions. Miranda's self-deprecating humour is shown as a means strategically used to 'avoid the pity party' and the 'don't worry, you'll find someone looks'. Ultimately though, Miranda finds that she is not the only woman reverting to such tactics to manage reactions to her non-normative status, as a married friend is shown to do the same in relation to invasive questions about her lack of children.

Continuing its efforts to explicitly make meaning of women's singleness, in 'Bay of Married Pigs' (1.3) the series explores how single women are perceived as threats, with married women fearing that they seek to pounce on their vulnerable husbands. The trope of war between single and married women is repeatedly deployed in Carrie's voiceover in this episode. Wives have been seen as the 'chief punishers of single women', forcing to them to conform and renounce their status as 'unwife' (DiCicco, 2010, p. 92), and this particular episode certainly positions wives in this manner. There are other moments in the series, however, that are more ambiguous in relation to women's prolonged singleness. In 'Splat' (6.18), the 40-year-old party girl plummets to her death, to which Carrie remarks: 'If you are single in New York after a certain age, there is nowhere to go but down.' Here the series acknowledges the maxim that it helps to perpetuate: that women's singleness has a shelf-life. This satirical depiction is nonetheless a cautionary tale, juxtaposed as it is with *Vogue* editor, Enid Mead's (not insignificantly played by *Murphy Brown*'s Candice Bergen) desperation to be partnered and heartfelt plea for Carrie to find her someone eligible in the same episode.[35]

While the television programme concluded in 2004, *Sex and the City*'s enduring market appeal is evidenced by the commercial success of the two films that tracked the four characters since the series' conclusion, though the representational politics of both worked to contradict the more progressive elements that were seen to mark the series.[36] The series' finale (Season 6) has each of the women paired off in committed relationships, offering a form of conventional narrative closure that the programme more broadly seemed to be working to resist. In this sense, although Carrie's concluding voiceover foregrounds the importance of the relationship 'you have with yourself' (6.20), 'the finale tells us that the real point of the show has been to place these sexually powerful, economically independent women in traditional heterosexual relationships' (Mabry, 2006, p. 204). Nonetheless, in a number of ways the series as a whole does attempt to shift the terms of debate around single women, to refigure singleness from what Jill Reynolds has called a 'discreditable identity' (2008, p. 5) to one that can, and indeed deserves, a form of cultural legitimation it has heretofore not been granted. As Negra observes, *Sex and the City*, while limited in terms of class privilege and affluence and how it celebrates a 'perpetual girlhood' for its characters, 'occupies vitally important space in a social and representational environment that regularly pronounces judgment over childless, unmarried and/or professional women' (2004).

For one writer, the series (along with *Ally McBeal*) offers a bleak overarching narrative about single women: '"The new single girl, tottering on her Manolo Blahniks from misadventure to misadventure, embodies in her very slender form the argument that not only is feminism over. It also failed: look how unhappy the 'liberated' woman is! Men don't want to marry her!"' (D'Erasmo in Shalit, 1999, p. 6). Without being celebratory, it is important not to simply presume that the feminist potential of any of these mainstream single-woman narratives is lost because of their protagonists' desire for relationships with men, tempting though this position is. Indeed, part of the appeal of popular texts like *Sex and the City* is that they posit, and relocate, women's sexuality from the realm of monogamous relationships and marriage especially to a more fluid space where myriad encounters are possible and socioeconomic factors do not lead women, and lock them, into emotionally unsatisfying relationships. Nonetheless, that romance and the search for coupledom features so prominently in all these popular single-women focused texts is telling. But that is not all that features, as *Sex and the City* illustrates.

Conclusion

As we shall see throughout *Single Women in Popular Culture*, and as this chapter has argued, the mass-mediated figure of the single woman offers a salutary reminder of the dangers (or at the very least the limitations) of attempting to impose any ideal of linear 'progress' in terms of the meanings circulating around her. As Deborah Siegel remarks, 'The story of this

Single Girl's alleged triumph – the story behind the headlines – is one far more complex and a great deal less sanguine than a cursory glance suggests' (2002, p. 3). This proposed representational trajectory – single women were once culturally denigrated but as mainstream cultural production took account of feminism and other shifts in social subjectivity they became celebrated figures of women's incontestable autonomy and independence – comes under strain the minute we spotlight the myriad contradictions and the ambivalence that continue to mark public renderings of this figure (Siegel, 2002). And, of course, while at times she is undoubtedly seen as problematic and is pathologized, the ways in which she comes to mean – and the impact of the broader postfeminist representational climate on that – requires a refined critical practice. Instead of leveling 'the same "old" feminist criticisms' (Whelehan, 2010, p. 160) at the texts of postfeminist media culture, as Whelehan reminds us we may be prone to do, the current representational climate necessitates a reflexive interrogation of the kinds of analytical tactics that may now be appropriate for feminists: 'Postfeminist culture does not allow us to make straightforward distinctions between progressive and regressive texts. Nevertheless, it urgently requires us to develop new reading strategies to counteract the popularized feminism, figurations of female agency, and canny neutralization of feminist critiques in its texts' (Tasker & Negra, 2007, p. 22). It is such reading strategies I seek to offer here. As my preoccupation throughout is to interrogate this ostensible shift from spinster to Singleton, and to unpack the kinds of representational politics it signals, the next chapter takes the character responsible for coining this term – Helen Fielding's Bridget Jones – as its focal point.

3
Spinsters and Singletons: *Bridget Jones's Diary* and its Cultural Reverberations

Introduction

Feminist commentators have emphasized the regularity with which figures like Bridget Jones (along with those from *Sex and the City* and *Ally McBeal*) feature in critical engagements with the single women of postfeminist media culture, noting in particular how this functions to elide other forms of difference and femininities (Gill, 2007). My own choice to focus predominantly on Bridget in this chapter, however, results from the way she continues to culturally reverberate, especially in contemporary press engagements with the 'problem' of the single woman. By looking not just at the original novels featuring Bridget but at the ways in which she came to subsequently circulate, taking on an independent symbolic life beyond the pages of Fielding's original texts, I am able to consider the cultural uses to which the text (or, more aptly, its heroine) has been put. As it is often seen as the genre's 'ur-text' (Ferris & Young, 2006, p. 4), this chapter initially contextualizes *Bridget Jones's Diary* within the chick lit genre, before offering a detailed engagement with Fielding's text (and, to a lesser extent, its sequel and film adaptations), and how its heroine has come to mediate public constructions of women's singleness from the mid-1990s to the present.

As the previous chapter intimated, Fielding's creation, Bridget Jones, is without doubt the most highly visible single woman of Western postfeminist media culture to date. While, as a number of feminist critics have shown, origin stories can be problematic due to their exclusions and assumptions about linearity, privileging one particular history over others, the continuing cultural reverberations of Fielding's iconic Bridget suggest that it is imperative that we return to the textual site seen as genealogically responsible for the emergence, and subsequent popular circulation, of a new term for single women in the 1990s: 'Singleton'. Moreover, given it is the Singleton that is often invoked as evidence of popular culture's supposed newfound embrace of the single woman – the rhetorical move that I have called 'from spinster to Singleton' – Bridget, in her various incarnations, represents a fitting place to start the detailed textual analysis that forms the basis of *Single Women in Popular Culture*.

Much condemnation of *Bridget Jones's Diary* has focused on what is seen to be her utter desperation to be unsingle, which has in many senses reinscribed the kinds of criticisms previously levelled at the romance genre as a feminized (and hence historically devalued) form of popular culture.[1] While the novel is of course a reconfigured romance narrative, the picture is more complicated than readings deploring outright Bridget's often obsessive search for a man allow. Within *Bridget Jones's Diary* romance is not in any simple way glorified over the uncoupled life; Fielding's narrative teases out the process through which coupledom is ultimately foregrounded as a viable way of overcoming singleness, but not without ambivalence. Although the novel in the final instance proffers the closure of a traditional romance narrative, Bridget herself articulates, and exists within the tensions created by, the competing discourses around women's singleness identifiable in other popular cultural sites. However, when the heroine escapes the text and comes to circulate in broader public discourse, such contradiction and ambivalence is rendered all but invisible. Before offering a close reading of *Bridget Jones's Diary*, and the consideration of Bridget as a public figure, the next section briefly reviews the single woman genre it is believed to have spawned: chick lit.

Postfeminist Romance? The constitutive elements of 'chick lit'

As an ever-expanding global publishing phenomenon and as a form clearly if ambivalently indebted to feminism, the so-called 'chick lit' novel is one of the key textual sites in which modern women's singledom is rendered meaningful. Indeed, chick lit has been explicitly positioned as a literary response to the increasing numbers of single women, attending to the struggle to make their singleness intelligible (McClanahan, 2003, p. 41). Chick lit, in terms of sales, has undoubtedly been one of the most significant generic developments in late twentieth century fiction (let alone women's writing in general). In their engagement with feminism, such narratives are preoccupied, not with feminist identity as such (itself a diverse and shifting subject position), but with giving meaning to the social, political, cultural, and juridical shifts which have repositioned and broadened the 'scripts of femininity' (Ussher, 1997) available to (some) Western women. Like other forms of cultural production, popular fiction – including chick lit – can work as an important site of ideological struggle, intervening in the complex process of 'renegotiating female subjectivity' (Cranny-Francis, 1990, p. 187). In this way, while heterosexual relationships are pivotal in these narratives, crucial also is the process of self-construction in which narrators engage (Umminger, 2006).

In *The Feminist Bestseller*, Imelda Whelehan argues that chick lit is a form of 'postfeminist narrative of heterosex and romance' for readers who believe themselves too 'savvy' for more traditional romance writing (2005, p. 186). These literary texts – being preoccupied with women's self-monitoring and surveillance of the body; naturalizing (some form of) feminism as 'commonsense'; focusing on individualized choice and empowerment; and by situating women as 'empowered sexual subjects' – clearly embody a 'postfeminist sensibility' (Gill & Herdieckerdorf, 2006, pp. 498–500). Moreover, as I have argued in Chapter 1, they (along with other texts like 'chick flicks') perform the cultural work of recuperating heterosexuality and romance, thereby necessitating that the single woman be seen as in need of transformation – a process tracked by chick lit novels. They are generally realist, with varying degrees of the comic, and adapt many of the conventions of the romance novel. First-person is the genre's most common mode of narration, a device through which heroines' innermost thoughts and insecurities around singleness can be textually foregrounded.

Narrators of these texts are invariably young heterosexual women, in their mid-late 20s/early 30s, single urban professionals, and more often than not their normative whiteness is presumed via its invisibility and the novel's lack of attention to any markers of racial difference.[2] Their implied reader is presumed to mirror their protagonists, if not in terms of class and racial privilege, then in terms of being an urban single who profoundly desires to be otherwise. The narrator and her network of woman friends are those who have most benefited from liberal feminist reformism, their occupation of the public sphere and participation in the circuits of capitalism is taken for granted. In terms of her sexuality, the chick lit narrator is without question heterosexual and, within the genre, although a gay man routinely features in her circle of friends, an exploration of non-normative sexualities is all but invisible (Benstock, 2006, p. 254). The heroine is often beset by anxieties over her weight,[3] but her greatest source of anxiety is her manlessness.

Protagonists and their cohort are seldom (if ever) low paid, unskilled workers, but commonly have a relatively high disposal income and therefore embody a high level of class privilege.[4] They are often conspicuous consumers and designer clothes are, if not purchased, highly coveted, thereby the emphasis on luxury consumption that Diane Negra (2009) argues is a constitutive element of postfeminism is certainly operative within the pages of chick lit.[5] While they consider their jobs important, this is 'largely because they supply the means for an urban lifestyle that is dedicated to consumption' (Philips, 2000, p. 239). In line with chick culture's heavy reliance on female friendship networks, these novels commonly celebrate women's intersubjectivity and privilege bonds of sisterhood over traditional familial ties. The chick lit narrator cannot do without her friends, and a self-help confessional culture forms the backdrop of many narrativized lunches/dinners/drinks over which she frequently laments the bastardry of the opposite sex. The sameness of these women friends is invariably juxtaposed with the difference of the object on whom their conversation is centred: their masculine (would be) partner. In the self-help era of 'men are from mars, women are from venus', the incommensurability of the sexes – as in earlier texts by women writers like Jane Austen – is underscored and put to great comic effect (Whelehan, 2002, p. 50).

Although the chick lit heroine's financial independence via her workforce participation is assumed, the realm of the professional seems more often than not to provide a background, or indeed acts as an encumbrance, to her central preoccupation: finding and securing a man. At the commencement of most chick lit novels, the narrator is without a love object (or is experiencing the demise of a relationship) – a condition she frequently laments. Women in chick lit experience a profound lack, which the novels, as is characteristic of romance writing, work to resolve (Belsey, 1994). The chick lit heroine's sexual agency is presumed; however, while the novels may assent to the idea that women can be involved in sexual relationships sans an emotional investment, such fleeting encounters are shown to pale insignificantly to that experienced within a monogamous, heterosexual relationship.[6] The dearth of eligible men is a frequent topic within the chick lit narrative, with a number of heroines explicitly ruminating on the man drought.[7] While chick lit narrators may critique men and expose the difficulties of the modern dating world, underscoring the limits of their gendered behaviour, that their presence is desirable is axiomatic. The chick lit novel often does not end in marriage, but commonly implies a stable, heterosexual relationship at the novel's conclusion. Some protagonists explicitly reject marriage, yet nonetheless choose a monogamous heterosexual relationship as a form of narrative closure.[8]

In terms of feminist criticism, the key question around chick lit novels (and indeed their film and television incarnations) seems to have been whether they serve to reinscribe the stereotypical portrayal of the single woman as pitiful and desperate or whether they actively work to destabilize this troublesome discursive construction. As we will see, previous criticism of *Bridget Jones's Diary* is representative of this pattern. That is, Bridget is either seen as progressive, offering a new model of subjectivity for inherently conflicted single young women or, alternately, she is read as further evidence of popular culture's disdain for women and its disingenuous appropriation of (some form of) feminism. In the latter vein, Gill and Herdieckerdorf argue that it 'spawned huge numbers of "copycat" novels centred on the life of a thirtysomething female who was unhappily single, appealingly neurotic, and preoccupied with the shape, size, and look of her body, and with finding a man' (2005, p. 489; see also Maddison & Storr, 2004).[9] Although, at least partially, concurring with this position, I also seek to demonstrate that *Bridget Jones's Diary*'s contribution to (re)figuring women's singleness cannot be so readily dismissed. Since it is commonly seen as the genre's origin text, and given its namesake is still highly visible on the mediascape, I now turn to my critical account of Fielding's novel and its heroine.

Confessions of the original 'Singleton': *Bridget Jones's Diary* (1996)

Bridget Jones's Diary, as its title makes clear, is a novel in diary form, offering a satirical portrayal of a single, young (well, youngish – Bridget is in her early 30s), London professional woman (she works as an editor at a publishing firm and, later, a television production assistant).[10] In its attempts to make sense of women's positioning in a purportedly postfeminist socio-political context, it is effectively a 'bildungsroman of the single girl' (Genz, 2010, p. 100). The plot is commonly recognized to be a modern reworking of Jane Austen's *Pride and Prejudice*, the intertextual debt to which is made obvious in the name of Bridget's seemingly haughty love interest, Mark Darcy, and to which another intertextual layer was added with the casting of Colin Firth – most well-known for his depiction of Darcy in the BBC's 1995 mini-series adaptation of *Pride and Prejudice* – as Mark in both film adaptations.[11] Despite the lack of an economic imperative to marry, the centrality of the project to secure a man in a woman's life appears to have little altered since the appearance of Austen's text. And of course, Bridget Jones – for the majority of her diaries – is not in fact without a man; she has two eligible (if at times dysfunctional) men in her life. In terms of publicly circulating versions of feminism, it is impossible to extricate *Bridget Jones's Diary* from the cultural context of its production, wherein '"girl power" was the most lucid statement of feminist intent available' (Whelehan, 2005, p. 174). Nonetheless, there does appear to be a feminist-informed critique of how single women are positioned in Fielding's novel that cannot entirely be dismissed on the grounds of its heroine's concomitant preoccupation with securing a functional heterosexual relationship.

Popular literary attempts to refigure singleness have not been uncommon, as my brief analysis of *Sex and the Single Girl* in the previous chapter suggested. The 'Single Girl' of Brown's text can in many ways be seen as a precursor to the 'Singleton'.[12] Bridget, bombarded with competing choices (though she rarely actually makes any), came to stand for an entire generation of women, including through attempting to be both feminine and feminist (see Genz, 2009, 2010). As I will demonstrate, her broader cultural resonances yet continue, which speaks not just to the relationship between literary texts and the public sphere but between literary texts and postfeminism. As Sarah Gamble remarks, 'The fact that the generation postfeminism claims to represent is also known as the "Bridget Jones generation" indicates the role literature has played in establishing the salient characteristics of postfeminism in the popular consciousness' (2006, p. 63). Moreover, as I will address, much criticism has centred on the question of its narrator's purported 'authenticity' as a modern, conflicted single woman (Case, 2001; Marsh, 2004), which itself has also been seen as responsible for the book's particular resonance with twenty- and thirty-something women readers. Indicative of its sustained discursive impact, labels such as 'Singleton' and 'smug marrieds' have entered the popular lexicon.

In terms of its market success, the book appeared somewhat of a literary blockbuster; by 2001, it had sold eight million copies worldwide, becoming a bestseller not only in its native UK but also in the US and Europe (Whelehan, 2002, p. 66). Likewise, the film adaptation of the *Diary*, along with its sequel, *Bridget Jones: The Edge of Reason*, were huge box office successes.[13] In 2001, obviously to capitalize on the success of the first movie adaptation and further suggesting a market for all things Bridget, Fielding released a short mock self-help book, *Bridget Jones's Guide to Life*. In 2005, ten years after her original appearance, *The Independent* resurrected the lucrative Bridget in a weekly column by Fielding. As Daphne Merkin argues, '*Bridget Jones's Diary* is the sort of cultural artifact that is recognizably larger than itself' (1998, p. 72). Indeed, its reverberations continue unabated, with reports of a musical adaptation being scored by British pop singer, Lily Allen, for London's West End (Michaels, 2010) as well as plans for a television adaptation (Brown, 2010). Moreover, demonstrating prolonged readerly investment in the novel, it appeared on *The Guardian*'s list of '10 books which the public best felt defined the 20th century', chosen by an online poll of readers (Crown, 2007). That Bridget 'captured the mood' of the 1990s is a claim made repeatedly, and with none of the irony of the text to which such comments refer.

Reading Bridget's Diary

Originally appearing as a series of newspaper columns in the UK's *Independent* newspaper, the novel tracks Bridget's discontentment with various aspects of her life over a year. The novel has, I think aptly, been described as 'a fictional year in the life of a champion muddler' (Arnst, 1998). Bridget commences her diary with a series of New Year's resolutions, divided into two columns 'I WILL NOT' and 'I WILL', through which she proposes to modify her behaviour in a range of ways – emotionally, domestically, administratively, financially, corporeally, ethically, and, perhaps most importantly (for her), romantically. On the first side of the ledger, she includes a number of resolutions relating to men: 'Fall for any of the following: alcoholics, workaholics, commitment phobics, people with girlfriends or wives, misogynists, megalomaniacs, chauvinists, emotional fuckwits or freeloaders, perverts'; 'Get upset over men, but instead be poised and cool ice-queen'; and 'Have crushes on men, but instead form relationships based on mature assessment of character' (1996, p. 2). In the 'I WILL' column she focuses more on the care of the self, which throughout the novel satirizes: 'Be more confident'; 'Be more assertive'; and 'Go to the gym three times a week not merely to buy sandwich' (2).

Bridget's insecurities and extreme self-disclosure in her first-person narrative render her not only unthreatening but endearing. As a subject always in process, and in line with postfeminist neoliberal imperatives, Bridget desires not just a better man but a better self – desires which are thoroughly conjoined in her narrative. Structured by diary entries for each month, the novel deploys a truncated writing style to create the sense of Bridget writing as she experiences, including entries with slurred speech to simulate her drunken-ness (Mabry, 2006, p. 196). Each entry commences by recording her weight (which, much to her horror, fluctuates throughout); the number of alcohol units consumed that day, as well as cigarettes; and her caloric intake. As a self-monitoring and self-disciplining subject (McRobbie, 2009, p. 11), Bridget perpetually diets and invests in fads like an 'intensive detoxification programme' (184). She uses her diary to track and monitor her behaviour (and her many personal and professional failures), and as a space for both self and social critique. As a self-professed 'child of *Cosmopolitan* culture' (59), she may be (at times) interpellated by these texts, and foreground how they come to textually mediate her subjectivity, but her self-reflexivity in relation to the disciplinary practices they advocate, and indeed the way she fails to blindly adhere to them, in many ways often counters the ideological positioning they seek to bring about. In this way, the novel draws attention to how such therapeutic texts seek to promote certain technologies of the self (Rose, 1996, 1999), as well as engendering the subject in particular ways (see Chapter 5 here). Through the multiple self-help manuals and women's magazines consumed by Bridget, the text lampoons the therapeutic rhetoric of self-transformation. To signal the extent to which it critiques such texts, especially those directed towards the single woman, Fielding's narrative and its sequel have even been referred to as 'self-help satire' (Marsh, 2004; Smith, 2008).

In contrast to previous romance narratives, in *Bridget Jones's Diary* 'the mimetic is interspersed with a metafictional self-reflexivity and mixed with mock introspection' (Ebert, 2009, p. 108). As I will show when considering the book's reception, however, its satirical elements and narratorial deployment of irony are largely overlooked (or at least downplayed) in efforts to position the book as a successful act of verisimilitude. Generically, the novel is often seen to be innovative and Fielding's positioning as the so-called 'mother' of the chick lit genre in both critical and popular narratives seems assured. At the time of its production, *Bridget Jones's Diary* is said to have operated 'at the interstices of genre definition': 'Gesturing at both triviality and seriousness, *Bridget Jones's Diary* crosses the borders of genre definition – and assumptions of literary value made of them. *Bridget Jones's Diary*, then, is a paradigm of genre-crossing fiction: a postmodernist and post-feminist publication strategy' (Squires, 2007, p. 161). Furthermore, *Bridget Jones's Diary* is actually unique, in terms of the chick lit for which it is seen to be responsible, in the ways it explicitly foregrounds and attempts to deconstruct the politics of (women's) singleness. Though other chick lit heroines may be jaded or cynical and thereby demystify traditional romance mythologies (Modleski, 2008; Ebert, 2009), Bridget overtly works to 'counter the mythologies of single, abject femininity' (Genz, 2009, p. 149), even if ultimately herself being unable to transcend such abjection.

In Fielding's novel, the binary that constructs subjects as coupled/single is frequently troubled by the narrator and by the novel's other core characters, with varying degrees of success. Offering up the Singleton as a viable form of subjectivity, *Bridget Jones's Diary* performs an important act of resignification; especially given the way this term subsequently came to circulate in popular discourse. But her own relation to, and adoption of this identity (as indeed to feminism), seems rather ambivalent. In this way, and through the place it secured Bridget in the dominant cultural imaginary (in the UK and Australia especially and the US to a lesser extent), the novel makes a significant contribution to the ideologically loaded cultural conversation over women's singleness upon which I focus throughout. It is important, therefore, to track how the discourse around the Singleton operates within Fielding's first Bridget novel, and indeed how it came to subsequently circulate. Before moving on to consider the Singleton as an alternative, 'postfeminized' subject position to that of the 'spinster', it is necessary to take a brief detour via the nineteenth century where this moniker circulated widely.

The Singleton: The Spinster has a postfeminist 'makeover'

In terms of single women in Western public discourse, historically the most prominent – and problematic – characterization has been the spinster. Though this deeply ideological signifier is often said to have fallen out of usage, on the contrary, 'the archetype of the spinster is still alive in our unconscious' (Falk, 2008, p. 43). 'Spinster' is best known as a pejorative label applied to women failing to conform to the dictates of normative femininity, most obviously through remaining manless and especially husbandless. As Laura L. Doan notes, 'The spinster is so enmeshed in cultural stereotyping that it is difficult to extricate her from negative connotations. Yet the label is as ambiguous as it is ambivalent. Society has deliberately deemed her pathetic to mask its fear of the unmarried woman' (1991, p. 1). Spinster, however, in the nineteenth century and beyond has also been conceptualized as an important political identity for women. In *The Spinster and her Enemies*, Sheila Jeffreys comprehensively explores the spinster as a transgressive figure who actively chose not to marry in recognition that it represented 'a form of humiliating slavery and dependence on men' (1997, p. 88). Prominent first-wave feminists argued that spinsterhood could be an ideological choice, made in deliberate response to the sexual demands men made of their wives whom they viewed as subordinates (Jeffreys, 1997, p. 89). In this way, the spinster – like the feminist she invariably came to symbolize in the popular imagination – could be a trouble-some character, working to disrupt the deeply naturalized institution of heterosexuality. As Katie Holmes argues:

> By the early 1900s, however, without giving up on attempts to reform marriage, feminists began to represent singleness as a desirable state. ... Singleness, accompanied by sufficient money, could offer women the opportunity to create a new lifestyle, a new identity; their vision of the single woman involved imagining another self, a self free from the physical, financial and emotional bondage of marriage. Single women could be agents of their own lives.
>
> (1998, p. 74)

In this vein, Jeffreys draws attention to the work of women like Cicely Hamilton, whose tract, *Marriage as a Trade* (1909), was radical in its exhortation that women should remain single due to the dis-advantages they experienced in and through marriage. The spinster provoked anxiety predominantly because, by implication, she was not only unmarried but childless and thereby seen to commit the biggest 'gender crime' (Grant, 1993) imaginable; little wonder that, while her subversive potential was deemed positive within first-wave feminist circles, publicly she became a figure of ridicule and the target of often vitriolic antifeminist rhetoric (Oram, 1992, p. 416). Moreover, the asso-ciation between spinsters and lesbianism served to heighten the threat she posed to the dominant social order; not only did she not have a man, she did not want one. That said, Doan argues that it makes little difference whether the spinster was lesbian or heterosexual; what was important was 'her, deliberate positive choice *not* to define herself in relation to a significant other' (1991, p. 5, original emphasis). Within Fielding's oeuvre, the signifier 'Singleton' appropriates this attempt to positively (re)position an existence without a significant (male) other that marks the identity of the spinster but its politics – and indeed association with feminism – are a little more ambiguous.

Bridget Jones's Diary acknowledges the anxieties that yet exist around women's singleness and which it attempts to address through offering (or rather attempting to offer) an alternative subjectivity for the sin-gle woman. The novel's first invocation of the term 'Singleton' – and it is capitalized – comes not from its confessional narrator but, not insignificantly, from her overtly feminist friend Sharon (or 'Shazzer').[14] After having been confronted at a 'smug marrieds' dinner party about why she remains single, Sharon articulates what becomes in effect a Singleton manifesto (Genz, 2010, p. 112). Shazzer's speech is essentially a critique of what DePaulo, to mark how those not in serious romantic relationships are discriminated against and stereotyped, calls 'singlism' (2006, p. 2):

> You should have said 'I'm not married because I'm a *Singleton*, you smug, prematurely ageing, narrow-minded morons', Shazzer ranted. 'And because there's more than one bloody way to live: one in four households are single, most of the royal family are single, the nation's young men have been proved by surveys to be *completely unmarriageable*, and as a result there's a whole generation of single girls like me with their own incomes and homes who have lots of fun and don't need to wash anyone else's socks. We'd be as happy as sandboys if people like you didn't conspire to make us feel stupid just because you're jealous.' 'Singletons!' I shouted happily. 'Hurrah for the Singletons!'
>
> (Fielding, 1996, p. 42, original emphasis)

Indeed, much of the narrative revolves around Bridget's attempts to internalize this logic, something with which she patently struggles. In line with postfeminist and neoliberal rhetorics, she continuously tries to reinvent herself as the contented Singleton but appears to have difficulty doing so. Characteristically, and indicative of the narrative's central tensions, Bridget's celebration is momentary, quickly replaced by Valentine's Day induced anxiety about the lack of cards, flowers, or a man with whom to share this day of coupledom celebration. Bridget's constant oscillation – one minute, she is writing herself into being as a satisfied Singleton, the next, she is desperate and seemingly man-obsessed – demonstrates the process of a shifting and mobile subjectivity which the diary form allows to be foregrounded. It is Bridget's constant movement between these competing selves and ways of being that make it difficult to argue that the novel performs an overt pathologization – or, conversely, celebration – of singleness in any uncomplicated way.

This politicized discourse around the Singleton also permeates the novel's sequel. In *The Edge of Reason* (1999), in a further challenge to the privilege enjoyed by the coupled, Bridget's other close friend, Jude, makes the following commitment to her Singleton friends at her wedding:

> Today I bade farewell to being a Singleton. But now I am a Married I promise not to be a Smug one. I promise never to torment Singletons

in the world by asking them why they're still not married, or ever say 'How's your love life?' ... I promise never to suggest that Singletondom is a mistake, or that because someone is a Singleton there is anything wrong with them. For, as we all know, Singletondom is a normal state in the modern world, all of us are single at different times in our lives and the state is every bit as worthy of respect as Holy Wedlock.

(401–2)

Here Jude disavows the 'smug married' identity that she and her friends have satirized throughout both novels. Even though she herself participates in that most normative institution, marriage, she seeks to legitimize singleness. Indeed, life as a Singleton is in many senses valorized within the two novels, with alternative models of family seen as preferable to traditional kinship structures (which itself came to be a narrative staple of the chick lit novel as the genre developed). As Bridget's gay male friend, Tom, tells her, '"I know we're all psychotic, single and completely dysfunctional and it's done over the phone," Tom slurred sentimentally, "but it's a bit like a family, isn't it?"' (265). This 'urban family', as I have previously remarked, is a common trope in popular discourses around singles and works to foreground alternative intimacies to those found in coupled relationships.

The novel, therefore, does in many ways attempt to recuperate singleness, especially through often comically drawing attention to societal expectations placed on single women and challenging their denigration in the popular usage of gendered terms like 'spinster'. Although the term Singleton in the novel is ostensibly non-gender specific, it is never directly applied to heterosexual men (and certainly not to toxic bachelors like Daniel Cleaver). Moreover, the way it is subsequently deployed in the public sphere also implies that it is a subject position that is overwhelmingly gendered feminine. In her book on *Bridget Jones's Diary*, Imelda Whelehan argues that the Singleton may function as an oppositional identity with sub-cultural cache:

The coining of the term 'singleton' does suggest a more positive slant than its predecessor 'spinster' ... A stage traditionally seen as transitory for most people becomes, at some of the best moments of the novel, a rebel identity with its own language and attitudes, as if in subcultural rejection of the married state in favour of new models of femininity for the professional woman.

(2002, p. 29)

These so-called 'new models of feminine subjectivity' are perhaps over-stated but these comments do acknowledge the (at times successful) attempt of Bridget and her cohort to refigure singleness. During the reg-ular ritual of debriefing over a glass or two of chardonnay, after reading a patronizing article by a 'Smug Married journalist', Bridget indignantly remarks to her friends: 'Singletons should not have to explain them-selves all the time but should have an accepted status' (Fielding, 1996, p. 245). But again, as is common, the next diary entry commences: 'Oh God, I'm so lonely. An entire weekend ahead with no one to love or have fun with' (246; see also 297).

Nevertheless, the novel offers a self-reflexive critique of the pathologi-zation of singleness in a way other narratives centring on single women (like *Ally McBeal*) do not. Bridget seeks to contest the notion that the only viable self is a coupled one, a widespread assumption she explicitly addresses. Of her 'smug married' friends, Bridget suggests: 'when they are together with their married friends I feel as if I have turned into Miss Havisham' (40). This sense of social exclusion is something of which she is conscious throughout her diary. Invoking the infamous spinster from Charles Dicken's *Great Expectations*, Bridget once again articulates how being single is negatively positioned. As Sarah Thornton argues, 'Miss Havisham has entered that ever evolving textual space which is our cultural heritage: filed away under "weird spinsters, various" we retrieve her periodically' (2010, p. 79). Fielding 'retrieves' this Dickensian figure, much like subsequent writers 'retrieve' Bridget for the same purpose, to create a sense of Bridget's status as outsider in the microcosm of the 'smug married' dinner party (if not more broadly). Of the way she is being discursively positioned by others, she continues: 'Maybe they really do want to patronize us and make us feel like failed human beings' (40). The novel's 'Singleton' discourse and emphasis on the social ostracism experienced by single women especially places it clearly within a feminist discursive realm. At others points the novel's (like Bridget's) relation to this politicization and the feminism it embodies is more ambiguous.

As other critics have pointed out, the young feminine subject of neo-liberalism is thought to no longer need feminist politics, yet is subject to new forms of anxiety – including being single – as a result of this new 'postfeminist condition' (McRobbie, 2009, p. 11). For McRobbie, *Bridget Jones's Diary*, especially in its movie version, exemplifies the reclamation of romance that is integral to postfeminism and to young women's dis-association from second-wave feminism (2009, p. 21). But, whereas the film may be constrained by its location in the romantic comedy genre, the novel is more ambivalent about such retrieval than other examples of single woman centred narratives.[15] Throughout, the novel underlines how Bridget's singleness fails to receive cultural legitimation, from either her parents and their friends or her coupled peers. By the former, she is questioned at the turkey curry buffet: 'How does a woman get to your age without being married?' (Fielding, 1996, p. 11) and by the latter at a smug married dinner party: 'Why aren't you married yet, Bridget?' (40). Such questions, driven by discomfort about Bridget's non-normative status, suggest the residual threat of the woman-without-a-man which the novel seeks, in many ways, to challenge. Moreover, Bridget does not appear beset by the time panic that usually envelops postfeminist heroines (Negra, 2009) but those around her do. As family friend, Una Alconbury, repeatedly warns her, '"You career girls! I don't know! Can't put it off forever, you know. Tick-tock, tick-tock, tick-tock"' (11, 172, 301), as does Cosmo (a smug married): '"You really ought to hurry up and get sprogged up ... Time's running out"' (41).

Despite her own critique of such moments, Bridget herself regularly speaks disparagingly of the 'spinster' and it seems she has internalized the fears that others regularly project onto her. (In terms of such fears, in the film version, she is even seen watching the punishment (i.e. her violent death) of that other iconic single woman, Alex Forrester, in *Fatal Attraction*.) Ending up a 'spinster' continues to represent an unthinkable future, especially as she is acutely conscious of the social liminality of anything other than a temporary hiatus without a man. However, the novel here also winks knowingly at these stereotypes, making clear that Bridget's apparent dread is entirely a culturally constructed one. Bridget voices her fears of remaining what elsewhere in public discourse has been referred to as 'terminally single'. This fear too, as she notes, increases exponentially with age:

> Even the most outrageous minxes lose their nerve, wrestling with the first twinges of existential angst: fears of dying alone and being found three weeks later half eaten by an Alsatian. Stereotypical notions of shelves, spinning wheels and sexual scrapheaps conspire to make you feel stupid, no matter how much time you spend thinking about Joanna Lumley and Susan Sarandon.
>
> (20)

Bridget once again invokes the 'spinster', referring to the spinning wheels after which the term was coined. This trope of being 'eaten by an Alsatian', to connote the loneliness and isolation of being single, recurs throughout (20, 33, 286–7). Her fixation on death 'expresses both the imminent social death for which the single woman is at risk and a sense of the centrality of her abject selfhood' (Negra, 2009, p. 62). The metaphor of singleness as social death has also been evident in other 'Singleton' narratives, including (as I suggested in Chapter 1) *Ally McBeal* and *Sex and the City*.

Although as a Singleton Bridget occupies a non-normative subject position, in other respects she does not transgress the boundaries of hegemonic femininity. Coupled with her obsession for either Daniel or Mark, she is implicated in other normative postfeminist disciplinary practices, such as regimes of bodily improvement and related practices of consumption (Gill 2007; McRobbie, 2009; Negra 2009). Nevertheless, while Bridget does exemplify the 'self-monitoring subject' (McRobbie, 2009, p. 11) of neoliberalism (as well as of postfeminism), she also reflexively critiques restrictive technologies of gender. In particular, offering a feminist critique, Bridget explicitly problematizes the way single women especially must perform various forms of corporeal labour to maintain their capital on the dating market. For example, before her date with Daniel Cleaver she complains:

> 6 p.m. Completely exhausted by entire day of date preparation. Being a woman is worse than being a farmer – there is so much harvesting and crop-spraying to be done; legs to be waxed, under-arms shaved, eyebrows plucked' feet pumiced, skin exfoliated and moisturized, spots cleansed, roots dyed, eyelashes tinted, nails filled, cellulite massaged, stomach muscles exercised ... Is it any wonder girls have no confidence.
>
> (Fielding, 1996, p. 30)

The date is ultimately cancelled, making this time-consuming and excessive regime seem futile (she would not have so transformed herself if not in anticipation of the masculine gaze). While it has been argued that such moments in the novel are indicative of Bridget's refusal to sacrifice her femininity for the sake of her feminism and imply women's pleasure in certain rituals of feminine performativity (Genz, 2010), more interesting is what they suggest about the affective operations of ideology. Bridget is aware of, and critiques, the imperative for women to regulate and produce themselves accordingly to certain somatic norms but she participates nonetheless. This is what many, following Zizek, have seen as enlightened participation in certain social practices and norms that position us subordinately, even while we are conscious of this interpellation (Dorney, 2004, p. 13).[16] As Zizek puts it, reworking the Marxist maxim, 'they know very well what they are doing, but still they are doing it' (1989, p. 29). That is, consciousness is no longer seen to be false (as in the work of earlier theorists of ideology – and indeed feminists) but knowing and self-reflexive although the affective pull of interpellation, especially when it comes to ideologies around romantic love, seems unmitigated (Ebert, 2009). While Bridget is aware that 'love is not the answer to the alienation and frustrations of daily life', her diary reveals that she nonetheless continues to psychically invest in its possibilities (Ebert, 2009, p. 106).

Within *Bridget Jones's Diary*, the apparent public discursive shift – from spinster to Singleton – occurs strategically, permitting the incorporation of feminist assumptions about women, work, independence, and sexuality into a fairly traditional romance frame. Unlike the spinster, the power of the Singleton-as-outsider or counter-hegemonic is marginal. Bridget may 'celebrate the single life' and critique 'the hum-drum world of the smug marrieds' but she also longs 'for resolution to her own romance plot' (Whelehan, 2005, p. 180). In rendering visible such tensions, the Singleton figure exemplifies, perhaps better than any other, the ambivalence towards feminism that continues to mark contemporary popular culture. Informed by feminism, she is sexually empowered, financially independent, seemingly autonomous, but she does little to disrupt the governing hetero-patriarchal imaginary. In fact, she buttresses it, and the Singleton practices 'plastic love' all the while continually searching for, at the very least, a form of 'confluent love' (Giddens, 1992; see also Hanson, 2004). This preoccupation with her lack of a man makes her a much less politically troublesome figure than the nineteenth century feminist spinster who often remained so, but by no means – in *Bridget Jones's Diary* at least – is this figure entirely apolitical.

Fielding's novel engages in a dialogue with feminism, not just through the pro-feminism of the Singleton discourse, but also through its narrator's ambivalent relation to it. As Lisa Guenther puts it, 'a large portion of Bridget's quest for self-definition in the novel surfaces through her struggle to understand her place within feminism as a whole' (2006, p. 91). It is clear her life is indebted to feminism; she takes for granted her ability to move freely about and participate in the public sphere, and to be an active sexual subject. Indeed, she peppers her diary with statements of support for feminism. Although Bridget is a self-identified feminist (54), for her (and indeed for any feminist) this is not a subject position without its contradictions. Her attempt to maintain a feminist consciousness, or at least a feminist-informed celebration of her Singleton status, is itself constantly satirized: 'The only thing a woman in this day and age needs is herself. Hurrah! 2a.m. Why hasn't Mark Darcy rung me? Why? Why? Am going to be eaten by Alsatian despite all efforts to the contrary. Why me, Lord?' (286–7). Within Bridget's diary, feminism and its disavowal exist side by side, a key characteristic of postfeminism. Bridget mobilizes feminist discourses regarding women's autonomy and self-sufficiency throughout which she then, in most cases almost immediately, undercuts with her fixation on male attention and validation. The other key way the text has been seen, not unproblematically, to be consistent with postfeminist logics is in Bridget's efforts to reconcile career and romance (Genz, 2009, 2010).

The single woman's dilemma?

Bridget Jones is by no means the high-achieving, ambitious career woman said to have been produced by feminism and who is single as a consequence. Though part of the generation of which Whitehead speaks in *Why There Are No Good Men Left* (see Chapter 2 here), Bridget has not benefited from the so-called 'girl project' (2003) that channelled much government funding into improving girls' education. Indeed, it is implied that she did not attend a prestigious university due to her poor marks, which is contrasted starkly with Daniel's (and indeed Mark's) Cambridge First; he chides her by calling her an 'intellectual giant' (166). She is embarrassingly ill-informed about current affairs, her ignorance serving as the catalyst for numerous comic moments within both novels (157, 240) and films. Bridget's personal life does not suffer because of her professional life, a charge leveled at successful, single women (see Chapter 2) – she is incompetent in *all* areas; she can't cook (82–4; 270–1); programme a VCR (152–5); and is geographically illiterate (witness her ignorance about the geographical location of Germany in the film adaptation of *The Edge of Reason*). In this way, Bridget's diary 'ultimately serves as an in-house confessional: a private space of self-scrutiny, her diary is where she "puts herself down", simultaneously recording and critiquing the self' (2006, p. 87). As this confessional 'putting down' illustrates, Bridget muddles along and regularly fails, not least in her attempt to convince herself (let alone others) that she is happily single.

While Genz conceptualizes Bridget as deeply longing for both career and romance, rather than being preoccupied with reconciling her desire for a functional heterosexual relationship with her 'public ambitions' (2009, p. 130), she seems to lack any. Indeed, her professional life only serves as a background to her main project of becoming unsingle, as her sexual liaisons with her boss, Daniel Cleaver, indicate. Furthermore,

Bridget appears professionally useless and her faux pas at work provide significant comic moments. After the embarrassing on-camera incident of trying to slide back up the fireman's pole while carrying out her new role on *Good Afternoon!*, Bridget laments: 'I thought I'd found something I was good at once and for all and now it's all ruined ... I'm no good at anything. Not men. Not social skills. Not work. Nothing' (224). Of course, such moments reveal the self-deprecating humour that is the 'dominant register' of the chick lit novel (Whelehan, 2005, p. 219). Indicative of the negligible role her work plays in terms of her identity, Bridget admits that she has a job but not a career (71). In this sense, she does not find any self-fulfilment through the world of work (Radner, 2010, p. 123).[17] Her unsatisfactory personal life therefore is not a product of her professional success; on the contrary, she suggests that she 'career[s] rudderless and boyfriendless through both dysfunctional relationships and professional stagnation' (78). Here, then, the novel implicitly critiques the 'have it all' discourses (public and private success) characteristic of postfeminism, as Bridget does not appear to excel in either sphere. Moreover, Bridget often professes she is depressed, mostly following romantic disappointments; only in moments of romantic success does she feel her life recuperable. Therefore, in *Bridget Jones's Diary* romance, if viewed with some irony and detachment, functions as an escapist fantasy. It appears not that Bridget deeply desires or wants a career but that the realities of consumer capitalism necessitate she be a worker (Ebert, 2009) – at least as a single woman. Presumably, in the future intimated by the novel, given how disinterested she appears to be in work, Mark Darcy's class privilege and considerable wealth would, in a gesture that shows how postfeminism and neoliberalism intersect, enable her to 'opt out' of the workforce once she has children.[18] While Bridget may suggest she is a 'marvellous career woman/girlfriend hybrid' (Fielding, 1999, p. 18), she does not successfully embody such hybridity.[19]

The argument that the 'postfeminist Singleton', which Bridget is said to represent, is fixated on attaining both professional success and romantic fulfilment – and unwilling to compromise on either (Genz, 2009, 2010) – is, therefore, not entirely sustainable. In this vein, presuming that the postfeminist Singleton works to 'negotiate the conflicting demands' of feminism and femininity, career and romance, Genz argues: 'For the twenty-first century woman, "having it all" is a distinct possibility and reality but, simultaneously, an unavoidable dilemma that the PFW has to confront and struggle with' (2009, p. 116). However, these comments do not concede the possibility that a life without a man or a life of prolonged singleness could be a viable option for the so-called 'PFW' ('postfeminist woman'). By positioning this negotiation between career and romance as an 'unavoidable dilemma' Genz helps to universalize and naturalize women's desire to be unsingle and indeed resituates normative heterosexuality as a postfeminist choice. The discourse of 'having it all', through which Genz reads Bridget, further delegitimizes singleness; as I have suggested, 'having it all' means definitely not remaining single. Genz's comments too beg the following question: How did desire for both career and men come to be positioned as *the* central dilemma for women in postfeminism? And how does this delimit the kinds of representations and subjectivities available of/for single women? It has, therefore, particular semiotic and political ramifications for the single woman who, even if temporarily and with some ambivalence (as in Bridget's case), is seeking to resist this dominant life script.

Bridget and the impossibility of satisfied singleness

Bridget repeatedly tells readers that she does 'not need a man in order to be complete' (43), a recurrent trope deployed to suggest that the diary's author remains unconvinced by this self-help maxim; she protests too much. She finds it impossible to fully adopt the identity of the satisfied single that she advocates, as she vacillates between trying exceedingly hard to believe in its viability and lamenting her manlessness. As she attempts to write herself into being, conflicting selves emerge. Bridget's cognitive dissonance about her singleness, especially given the dominant interpretive framework for understanding singleness (i.e. it is aberrant) is resolved, in true postfeminist style, by her embrace of her romantic fantasies and desire to be coupled. The non-normativity of singleness will be replaced by the safety of adhering to the hegemonic life narrative of hetero-patriarchy. The novel's form permits its heroine's psychic turmoil to be satirized as well as foregrounding how these co-existing positions preoccupy her.

After being stood up by Daniel, Bridget appropriates the self-help discourse about which she is ambivalent throughout, noting 'one must not live one's life through men but must be complete in oneself as a woman of substance' (31), followed shortly thereafter by 'What's wrong with me? I'm completely alone' (31). She regularly finds herself consumed by fears about her deficiencies, especially in terms of her prolonged singleness. While she knows she should feel she does not need a man, life without one is deemed inherently undesirable, not least because of societal pressures and expectations. It appears, therefore, she is merely performing as contented Singleton while all the way attempting to fill the sense of lack upon which romance narratives – and desire itself – are predicated (Belsey, 1994). That is, she remains psychically tied to the idea of securing blissful coupledom despite her sporadic, feminist-inspired proclamations of joyful independence.

As these instances illustrate, the novel satirizes her attempts to celebrate her singleness as much as it does her investment in romance mythologies. In her new year's resolution Bridget commits to not 'sulk about having no boyfriend, but develop inner poise and authority and sense of self as woman of substance, complete *without* boyfriend, as best way to obtain boyfriend' (2, original emphasis). She harbours traditionally romantic fantasies, despite her moments of 'feminist ranting' (128): 'Daniel is still being gorgeous. How could everyone have been so wrong about him? Head is full of moony fantasies about living in flats with him and running along beaches together with tiny offspring in manner of Calvin Klein advert, being trendy Smug Married instead of sheepish Singleton' (131; see also 77). This quotation is indicative of the narrator's oscillation between the belief that she should be a contented Singleton (in this instance represented by feminism) and her unstinting quest for a male other. That is not to say the novel engages in any simplistic celebration of institutionalized heterosexuality; on the contrary, its ambivalence on the two opposed states of being it offers up its characters – life as a Singleton or a Smug Married – is patent. In the words of the confessional narrator:

> Talk about the grass is always bloody greener. The number of times I've slumped, depressed, thinking about how useless I am and that I spend every night getting blind drunk and moaning to Jude and Shazzer or Tom about not having a boyfriend; I struggle to make ends meet and am ridiculed as an unmarried freak, whereas Magda lives in a big house with eight different kinds of pasta in jars, and gets to go shopping all day. And yet here she is, so beaten miserable and unconfident and telling me I'm lucky.
>
> (132)

Bridget here identifies the many privileges and forms of capital that accompany marriage, but displays an awareness of the personal dissatisfaction it can engender. That is, marriage is not the 'primary happiness indicator' (Ahmed, 2010, p. 6) it is often seen to be. Moreover, the models of coupledom and marriage further indicate the novel's ambivalence on this subject: Magda's husband is exposed having an affair; Bridget's mother (if temporarily) leaves her father; and Jude is in a constant state of despair over how to interpret the actions of her partner, dubbed 'Vile Richard'. Clearly, Singletons like Bridget appear conflicted about gendered interactions in ways that heroines of previous romance novels are not. The novel sets Bridget and her friends in opposition to the hegemony of coupledom but also reveals its enduring affective pull. Like other texts in which the single woman prominently features, contradictory postfeminist discourses therefore can be seen to coexist within the chick lit novel (and indeed within Bridget herself); discourses of freedom and autonomy operate in tandem with the idea 'that married heterosexual monogamy more truly captures women's real desires' (Gill & Herdieckerdorf, 2006, p. 500).

Bridget's salvation

In her 'January–December: A Summary', with which the narrative concludes, Bridget tells readers: 'Nice boyfriend 1' (310). The closure necessitated by its form (it is still a romance narrative, if reconfigured) is therefore provided. Angela McRobbie sees Fielding's heroine embodying a number of risks that young women in reflexive modernity must face – risks primarily relating to partnership and reproduction and for which Bridget must take responsibility: 'Now there is only the self to blame if the right partner is not found' (2007, p. 37). Despite her pro-single rhetoric, 'the risk that, partnerless, she will be isolated, marginalized from the world of happy couples' (McRobbie, 2007, p. 37) is, in the final instance, too great to take. Although never fully relinquishing the hetero-patriarchal fantasy of coupledom, Bridget has made the effort to consider a non-normative life but it is too 'risky'; she chooses the certainty of a hegemonic way of being (i.e. a coupled existence). While Ebert (2009) argues that this continued investment in romance (albeit cynically) is the heroine's way of managing her sense of alienation as a worker under late capitalism, Bridget implies that there is little alternative. That is, chick lit heroines like Bridget may be disillusioned but ultimately they feel they have no choice but to choose this socially sanctioned coupledom.

She commences the initial narrative with no boyfriend and concludes it with one: 'Bridget Jones is ultimately rewarded for her ineptitude and general lack of capacity; she is "saved" by a supremely accomplished and patient man' (Radner, 2010, p. 121). This notion of the man as saviour has a long history, especially in the romance genre. But in *Bridget Jones's Diary*, there is the sense then that what she is being 'saved' from is herself and, as Suzanne Ferris argues, 'from the complications of life as an independent woman' (2006, p. 81). That is, she may be utterly useless in every other respect but she 'succeeds' in the most significant gendered project for women – securing a man and, by implication, children. Therefore, *The Edge of Reason* commences: '7.15a.m. Hurrah! The wilderness years are over. For four weeks and five days now have been in functional relationship with adult male thereby proving I am not love pariah as previously feared' (3). As Stephanie Genz argues, 'while Bridget is striving to throw off the stigma attached to her single status and resignify it as a novel and rewarding subject position' her anxieties about the social consequences of such a state consumes her (2009, p. 136). She never truly contemplates singleness as a permanent way of being in the world – partially as she recognizes its broader cultural devaluation and the forms of capital that accrue to the coupled (especially married) self. Though she has tried on, and tried to celebrate, the Singleton identity, ultimately it is disavowed. The Singleton was, as we perhaps could have expected, only a transitional, strategic subject position, temporarily invoked to make sense of and help affectively manage life sans partner. Along these lines, some have argued that Bridget's ambivalence towards marriage and questioning of conventional roles for women and the conflicting desires for a loving relationship and 'prolonged, irresponsible youth' evident in the first film is entirely absent from *The Edge of Reason*, in which Bridget is said to be 'downright desperate' (Garrett, 2007, p. 122).[20] And it seems that it is this so-called 'desperation' that has been the aspect of Bridget's contradictory subjectivity upon which most subsequent public engagements with her fixate and which, unfortunately, effectively obscures from public view the novel's (albeit ambivalent) attempt to refigure women's singleness.

Celebritizing the Singleton: How Bridget shapes understandings of women's singleness

Given that my core concern throughout *Single Women in Popular Culture* is to track, and critically interrogate, the broader cultural conversation around women's singleness that has been staged over the past few decades, for the remainder of this chapter I focus on Bridget's broader cultural reverberations. That is, how this fictional figure has been taken up and made to signify in certain ways that illuminate some prevalent, deeply ideological, assumptions about contemporary single women – especially in press coverage from the UK, United States, and Australia. The cultural uses to which she has been put also reveal much about the operations of postfeminist discourse in the journalistic field. Multiple manifestations of Bridget, with often conflicting ideological purposes, have come to circulate in the mediasphere.

In addition to their role in the evolution of a new genre, what perhaps makes Fielding's novels most important is the wider public career upon which their heroine was to embark. As my engagement with her presence in the journalistic field suggested in the previous chapter, Bridget can be seen as a 'figure lodged in the popular consciousness' (Bennett & Woollacott, 1987, p. 160); a figure that has helped circumscribe representations of women's singleness in the public sphere. Rarely do fictional characters come to have the sustained cultural resonances enjoyed by Fielding's creation, and, in terms of the single woman, tellingly the only comparable figure in recent history is *Fatal Attraction*'s Alex Forrester. As infamous celebrity feminist, Germaine Greer, prophetically remarked in 1999, 'Bridget Jones will soon be the world's best known thirty-something female without a boyfriend' (247). Though Bridget does of course conclude both her diaries with a 'boyfriend', it is the hunt for one that repeatedly surfaces in popular narratives about her. To signal Bridget's immense cultural resonances, Imelda Whelehan argues that 'the current era of the single woman might well be described as post-BJ' (2002 p. 12). In 2001, one commentator noted that there had been over 6,600 articles published in Britain and the United States about Bridget since her textual birth in 1995 (Odone in McClanahan, 2003, p. 44).

Public interest in this character has by no means waned in the intervening years since her initial appearance, especially in light of the enormous commercial success of both film adaptations. Following the release of the two films, the image of Renee Zellweger as Bridget came to function as a visual shorthand for a series of assumptions about the single woman and her image is routinely deployed in journalistic engagements with this topic.[21] Indeed, it seems only after the film's release did Bridget, personified by Zellweger, come to circulate so prominently in the public sphere. Especially in the press, it appears mandatory for articles on women's singleness – from various angles and ideological persuasions – to draw upon the experiences of Bridget (despite their fictitiousness). Said to be 'the poster child for the confused woman of the 1990s' (Di Massa, 1998), in both the academy and the popular press Bridget Jones is routinely figured as the zeitgeist's 'everywoman' (Arnst, 1998; Whelehan, 2002; Razer, 2004; Macvarish, 2006). The perceived global resonance of the character is indicated by the title of a *New York Times'* review: 'Bridget Jones? She's Any (Single) Woman, Anywhere' (Hodge, 1998). Her dilemmas, insecurities and neuroses are seen to be those that beset all modern young women; the so-called 'the daughters of the revolution' (Summers, 1994). In this way, Bridget became an important way to semiotically signify how, in the wake of feminism, new forms of subjectivity were apparently being taken up by women.

In early mainstream newspaper reviews, *Bridget Jones's Diary* was judged, not according to any literary regimes of value, but in relation to the degree to which its heroine could be seen to approximate 'real' women readers; and in this regard the novel was deemed incredibly successful. The intimate, confessional tone of the diaries and the apparent insight into Bridget's psyche undoubtedly facilitated such readings. That is, and while aware of its status as fiction, readerly identification is partially secured via Fielding's deployment of first-person narration and its implication of an 'authentic, in-depth account' of Bridget's experiences (Mabry, 2006, pp. 195–6). She came to be viewed as the archetypal single woman, and the book's capacity to 'build empathy' recurs throughout mainstream reviews (Squires, 2007, p. 157). In the *Times Literary Supplement* Nicola Shulman remarks, 'it rings with the unmistakable tone of something that is true to the marrow; it defines what it describes. I know for certain that if I were a young, single, urban woman, I would finish this book crying, Bridget Jones, c'est moi' (1996). In *The Independent*, Peter York remarks that women often approach Fielding 'and claim that they're Bridget Jones, the original; that she's read their thoughts, overheard their dialogue and seen their hidden turbulence' (1997).

When the book was published in America in 1998, reviewers reinscribed the assumptions about Bridget's authenticity that had dogged its initial reception in the UK. Elizabeth Gleick's *New York Times* review is indicative in this regard: 'show me the woman to whom this sort of stream-of-consciousness, self-assessing mental clutter is unfamiliar and I'll show you the person who will not think *Bridget Jones's Diary* is both completely hilarious and spot on' (1998). Another reviewer, in the *Los Angeles Review of Books*, observes: 'But the strengths of *Bridget Jones's Diary* are Bridget and how much of ourselves we can see in her and her parallel universe. She displays – and discusses – the behavior that we try to keep hidden' (Di Massa, 1998). While in *Businessweek*, Catherine Arnst sees the novel exemplifying a broader publishing trend towards 'books that reflect the complexities of their [single women's] lives' (1998). Even the paratexts of *Bridget Jones: The Edge of Reason* helped to buttress this slippage between the real and the fictional. In this vein, Fielding dedicated the book 'To the other Bridgets', a gesture which invokes a community of likeminded single women to whom her character was believed to be speaking in important, timely, and innovative ways. Thus, through the dedication, the book's paratext – made up of those elements outside the narrative (either part of the published text like the title or extrinsic to it like book reviews) that attempt to delimit how it comes to signify (Genette, 1997) – works to buttress these popular interpretations of Bridget's 'authenticity'.

The problem with viewing any text, especially a fictional one, as a transparent reflection of a pre-existing reality should be obvious, especially in the wake of post-structuralism. Nonetheless, this is precisely how Fielding's novel has been positioned. It is a move that has facilitated Bridget's regular appearance in journalistic engagements with the question of contemporary women's singleness (as shown in the previous chapter). Indeed, the way Bridget resonates with audiences – its interpellation of readers through what has been described as the 'That's me!' effect (Maddison & Storr, 2004, p. 4) – has been the subject of much commentary, both popular and academic. It is her 'ordinariness', her myriad failings, which are seen to endear her to other women who encounter similar anxieties. 'Popular media representations', argues Jill Reynolds in her ethnographic study, are a 'critical influence in creating a discursive context for singleness' (2008, p. 149) and this applies to Bridget Jones especially.[22]

Given the role that Bridget has come to play in the mainstream cultural imaginary, Fielding's text provides some salient insights into what David Carter and Kay Ferres refer to as 'the public life of literature' (2001); what happens to a literary work when it comes to widely circulate, the cultural uses to which it is put, and the role of literary texts in precipitating broader debates within the public sphere – including around women and feminism (see Taylor, 2008). Moving beyond the reviews pages of newspapers, Bridget became – and continues to be – newsworthy, because she was seen to exemplify the modern single woman. That a fictional character became emblematic of young women's so-called postfeminist dilemmas suggests much about the ways in which popular narrative operates and comes to signify intertextually (as well as how postfeminist discourse itself circulates). Bridget's 'fictional biography', then, is transformed into a 'quasi real' one, a gesture that is key to what can, following Bennett and Woollacott's work on James Bond, be called 'The Bridget Phenomenon' (1987, p. 45). As Bennett and Woollacott argue in their book on the 'political career' of Ian Fleming's Bond, though popular heroes/heroines:

> usually have their origins in a particular work or body of fiction, they break free from the originating conditions of their existence to achieve a semi-independent existence, functioning as an established

point of cultural reference that is capable of working – of producing meanings – even for those who are not directly familiar with the original texts in which they first made their appearance.

(1987, p. 14)

Bridget, too, has moved well beyond her initial appearance as a fictionalized character in a newspaper column, existing in diverse textual spaces.

Since Bennett and Woollacott's text, theories of celebrity have developed and provide a valuable frame through which to read what happens when fictional characters – like Bond and Bridget – themselves come to operate as figures imbued with celebrity value. While authorial celebrity, as many critics have shown (Gardiner, 2000; Moran, 2000; Turner, 2004), is central to the marketing and promotion of any modern literary work, in the case of *Bridget Jones's Diary* it was its fictional heroine that became most heavily implicated in these processes of celebrification rather than its author. Moreover, in the case of images of Zellweger-as-Bridget consistently used in journalistic engagements with women's singleness, reference to the actor portraying Bridget is rare; and while Zellweger's celebrity may have been buttressed by the circulation of these visual signifiers, I would argue that, in terms of the circuits of fame, Bridget eclipses both the author (who brought her into being in print) and the actor (who brought her into being on film). In this way, the example of Bridget troubles the search for the 'real' subject in celebrity narratives; she is representative, then, of the celebrity as simulacrum.

That Bridget quite literally does not exist outside of signification does not seem to in any way impede the cultural uses to which she is put. However, the celebrification of literary characters is not in itself a modern phenomenon. As Chris Rojek argues, from the eighteenth century fictional characters such as Tristam Shandy and Robinson Crusoe 'began to populate popular discourse, and their fictional lives and opinions inscribed themselves on the public' (2000, p. 104). Such a process of public inscription is applicable to Bridget Jones' presence on the contemporary mediascape; a presence that few modern literary characters have enjoyed. It seems remarkable, however, that a figure incapable of speaking for herself – she was after all a fiction – came to so emphatically *speak for* a generation of women on politically and affectively charged questions such as women's singleness. This is not to suggest that Bridget has not been scrutinized in the popular press; on the contrary, for some critics her hypervisibility has had potentially dire social consequences. The more scathing attacks on the book's heroine have seen some argue that there has been an 'anti-Bridget backlash' (Merkin, 1998). Such a 'backlash' even came to be manifested in British political discourse. In September 2008 (many years after her original public appearance), she became the subject of much debate as Tory politician and Shadow Universities Secretary, David Willetts, laid the demise of the modern family squarely at her feet.

This incident received extensive media coverage and exemplifies the way Bridget has come to be used in the public sphere, so it is worthy of some further analysis here. As *The Telegraph* noted: 'The "Bridget Jones" generation of career women who struggle to settle down and start a family is driving the breakdown of British society, the Tories have said' (Prince, 2008). At the 2008 Conservative Party conference in Brighton, Willetts reportedly remarked: 'Bridget Jones is a real phenomenon, driven partly by the way the pattern of university education is changing' (cited in Chapman, 2008). Once again, Bridget's apparent proximity to the 'real' is mobilized for certain ideological purposes. In terms of these various public uses, 'Bridget functions transtextually as a distinct but malleable image of contemporary womanhood' (Cobb, 2008, p. 283).

According to press reports, Willetts argued at the conference that university educated women, of whom there are now more than men, are depriving men of 'the opportunity of being the breadwinner'. In Willetts' analysis, more public funding is needed to ensure that men have greater educational opportunities and thereby can be thought of as viable marital prospects by women like Bridget: 'The man who can't go out and command a decent wage', he suggests, 'is not going to be able to hold a family together' (in Chapman, 2008). Relying upon retrograde assumptions about men as providers, Willetts situates Bridget and her sisters, and the apparent gendered revolution they exemplify, in a narrative of decline. He sees the fact that Bridget is not married as a profound social and political failure, exemplifying the broader cultural fear of women's singleness that I argue yet exists – especially around the issue of reproduction. His nostalgia for clearly delineated gender boundaries leads him to suggest that the expectations of young post-feminist women, of which Bridget is seen to be one, are having grave social consequences. Willetts, however, constructs a particular version of Bridget for his own political ends. As a journalist in *The Telegraph* makes clear, in presuming her a successful career woman happy with her lot, 'David Willetts misses the angst of Bridget Jones' (Hornby, 20 September, 2008).

While Willetts clearly laments the advances of liberal feminism, including women's enhanced participation in the public sphere through the fields of work and education, much of the press coverage is critical of his comments. For example, *The Guardian* dubs Willetts' comments 'ironic', given that 'there has hardly been a character in popular literature more devoted to finding a man than Bridget Jones' (Cochrane, 2008). This piece shifts the focus to Bridget's desperation to be partnered as a way of challenging Willetts' claims that she has been leading many women by example to reject marriage. Nonetheless, this story in *The Guardian* – 'Did Bridget destroy family life?' – also defends her from such claims and is indicative of how feminist comment and critique is now primarily staged in the media and the press specifically: 'If there's a crisis in the modern family – and I'm not convinced there is – women's academic excellence isn't to blame any more than Bridget Jones is. The true problem is that equality is still a long way off' (Cochrane, 2008).

In terms of the uses to which she has been put in the media, Bridget has also been seen as responsible for a shift *towards* marriage, with contemporary younger women reportedly seeking to avoid the fate of this prominent Singleton. While some newspapers, therefore, sought out the '"real" Bridget Jones' (Gill & Hiedeckerdoff, 2006, p. 489) others shifted the focus to 'real' women who sought to define themselves in opposition to her. As an article in *The Observer* opens (using a term briefly considered in the previous chapter): '"Freemales" – manless women who are happy to remain so for the present at least – are now a force to be reckoned with and are overturning the dated Bridget Jones image of the lonely woman staring despondently at an empty Chardonnay bottle' (Davies, 2008). Becoming Bridget is figured as something women dread. For example, as one *Telegraph* article remarks: 'Four in 10 women in their late 20s fear their private lives resemble *Bridget Jones's Diary*, having already loved and lost Mr Right, according to a study' (Wardrop, 2010).

The study was commissioned by Britain's *More* magazine, whose editor says: '"They don't want to fall into the Bridget Jones syndrome and view their future through an empty wine glass"' (in Wardrop, 2010). Invoking the recurrent trope of the chardonnay-swilling Singleton, the assumption is that Bridget's quotidian existence is inherently undesirable. As another paper suggests of the survey, 'Bridget Jones fear is making women want to wed earlier' (13 April, 2010, *Daily Mail*). Despite its arguably questionable veracity, the study received extensive press coverage, including 'Girls fear Bridget's Single Life' in the tabloid *Sun* newspaper (Hamilton, 2008) and, suggesting the global reach of these debates, the *Times of India* also picked up on its conclusions. It claimed '"Bridget Jones syndrome" makes kids want to marry early' (13 April, 2010), including a further quote from *More*'s editor: 'It's easier to fulfil their "have it all" dream of marriage, parenthood and career while they're still young and full of energy.' Using explicitly postfeminist rhetoric, such comments – like the entire article – attempt to foster the time panic believed to be enveloping the postfeminist single woman. Bridget, then, is here enlisted to help foster the kinds of anxieties discussed by McRobbie (2009) and Negra (2009).

For the women in *More*'s study, *Bridget Jones's Diary* represents a cautionary tale and its heroine is coded as the Other – a modernized spinster – against whom they seek to be defined. It also intersects with fraught discourses about the risk of 'social infertility'. Furthering this theme, one article's title reveals the reproductive consequences of emulating Bridget: 'Bridget Jones generation being urged to freeze eggs' (Johnston, 2006). Similarly in *The Observer*, Louise Carpenter (2007) tells a grim tale about young women and their future, also through invoking our erstwhile heroine: 'For my generation, however, the Bridget Jones generation if you will, a new crisis is presenting itself – infertility. Thirty-something women have spent so much time on their careers that growing numbers are finding they have left it too late to have a baby.' While Bridget herself does not appear to experience such pronounced temporal anxiety in the novels (though others do this for her), the generation to which she has given her name reportedly fear prolonged singleness and the childlessness it implies (despite the fact, especially given reproductive technologies, that singleness itself is no barrier to motherhood). It is, by implication, feminism that has created (and failed to resolve) such circumstances.

Other forms of panic about the so-called 'Bridget Jones Generation' (and this term has been deployed extensively by the press) have been health-related. In this vein, the photographs that accompany such articles usually include stills from the movie, depicting Bridget with a cigarette and/or a glass of wine in her hand. *The Independent* reported on a study that found single women were endangering their lives: 'Being single is as bad for you as smoking – or worse. For the Bridget Jones generation of thirty-something single women, a major study brings the worst possible news – that on top of the cigarettes, wine and anxiety about weight, the very state of being single takes years off your life' (Dobson & Johnson, 2004). Behave like Bridget (i.e. smoke, drink wine, obsess over your weight), it implies, and suffer the myriad consequences – not just a potential lack of offspring (or the partner to help provide them) but premature death. Here, the example of Bridget – coupled with a study of 'real' women imitating her lifestyle – is again invoked as a cautionary tale. Singleness, they make clear, is a health hazard or a disease for women (itself a common trope) and marrying early, which Bridget failed to do, is figured as the antidote. Such articles help to further contest claims that women's singleness is now universally endorsed and even celebrated (see Chapter 2).

The public discourses in which Bridget comes to be enmeshed appear to be contradictory, however. Some articles use Bridget to argue that singleness needs to be recuperated; that is, they seek to revalue women's singleness by defining themselves against what they perceive to be her sad, man-hunting, existence. For example, in the *Daily Mail* – as the article's title puts it – 'One woman shows that the Bridget Jones generation are not all desperate to meet Mr Right' (Mulvey, 1999). Likewise, in 'Aussie Girls Prefer Single Life', accompanied by a photo of Zellweger's Bridget, journalist Michelle Hamer remarks in the *Herald Sun*: 'Single sisters are doing it for themselves. Refusing to buy into a Bridget Jones-style desperation to settle for Mr Average, savvy single girls would rather live it up on their own' (2010). Here, Bridget is reworked as a figure who is 'desperate to settle' in a way that is not borne out in the novels. (Conversely, the heroine's experience with Daniel proves an unwillingness to settle.) Similarly distancing themselves from her, others argue that Bridget's cultural resonances have diminished significantly in the postfeminist twenty-first century. In this vein, a *Guardian* journalist asks: 'Does Bridget still speak for single women?' She argues that, while she may have 'epitomised the condition of the single, early 30s-ish urban female' in the late 1990s, being single has been refigured to a 'positive, life-enhancing affair' and the 2000s is designated the 'era of the power single' (Vernon, 2005). In these articles, Bridget's singleness is seen as comparatively miserable and thereby her own diaristic efforts to recode it are elided.

In contradistinction, for others Bridget is seen to represent all contemporary single women's search for a man, thereby eschewing the character's ambivalence about coupledom and marriage in particular. For example, an article in *The Economist* observes: 'The boyfriend-hunt is a big part of Bridget's life. And so it is with real-life Bridgets, many of whom find the big cities to which they flock lonely places' (22 December, 2001). This invocation of 'real-life Bridgets' is indicative of the broader tendency to take one aspect of the novel and metonymically substitute it for the whole; that is, to conceptualize the narrative primarily as a romance without acknowledging its nuanced critique of both singleness and heterosexual partnerships. It also reveals the inability to recognize that women's singleness could be a desirable, and desired, form of subjectivity and lifestyle of which I have already spoken. It concludes: 'At the end of her day, Bridget is hugely relieved to find that Mark Darcy really loves her. Could that really be what matters most to single women in their 30s?' (22 December, 2001). Therefore, postfeminist women, though they may have full lives in other respects (career, friends, financial independence, interests) are really just in want of a man; the key difference of course is the way this is now figured as a self-conscious choice (see Gill, 2007 and Chapter 1 here).

But while popular fictional heroes like Bond may be seen as 'variable and mobile signifiers' (Bennett & Woollacott, 1987, p. 42), the meanings around Bridget are comparatively static if at times dichotomized. The binary of desperate romantic/contented Singleton – a binary with which the novels themselves struggle and fail to ultimately deconstruct in any meaningful way – continues to structure public engagements with Bridget. Depending on the cultural and ideological purposes of the secondary text in which she is invoked, Bridget is either one or the other, though increasingly it is her figuration as the miserable woman-without-a-man that appears to surface with greater regularity than the satisfied single (especially in public debates around the increased numbers of single women). Thus, in her extra-textual manifestations, the tensions within the text – and indeed within Bridget herself – that some critics have applauded are often sutured. Therefore, in this way, the feminist possibilities of the text – including in terms of offering a counter-hegemonic form of women's singleness – have not been realized by the various forms of paratextuality in which Bridget became implicated. That is, the politicized discourse around singleness that flows throughout Fielding's novel is all but absent in these public engagements with its heroine. Moreover, 'The repeated use of Bridget to function metonymically for that group vitiates the actual difficulties and complexities of contemporary single women' (Cobb, 2008, p. 283).

Taken as an 'authentic' characterization of a modern social phenomenon (implicitly produced by feminism), rather than the largely satirical figure she was, Bridget helped to ensure that certain ways of speaking about single women were publicly foregrounded – in both more overtly factual media forms (such as newspapers) and in fictional forms like television series – at the expense of multiple ways of being, negotiating, and performing singleness. Indeed, she continues to delimit these fraught conversations. That Bridget is a fictional character, and Fielding a novelist rather than a sociologist or interpreter of demographic trends, continues to elude many public commentators on women's singleness. That is, *Bridget Jones's Diary* is overwhelmingly conceptualized as a work of non-fiction, a slippage necessary to enable these public evaluations of Fielding's text to be based not on aesthetic criteria but on the degree to which it approximates the ever elusive 'real'.

The 'Bridget Phenomenon' shows no signs of abating, despite the fact it has been 16 years since she first appeared in ink and ten years since her celluloid debut; whenever single women appear in the journalistic field, inevitably so does Bridget. The example of what has happened to Bridget – that is, how she has made been to signify in public discourse – is instructive in terms of how fictional single women (including, though to a much lesser extent than Bridget, others like Alex Forrester and Carrie Bradshaw) have come to mediate public conversations about women's singleness as well as how postfeminist discourse is mobilized therein. As Roberta Garrett remarks, popular narratives such as *Bridget Jones's Diary* 'did not *invent* the figure of the needy, insecure, single woman, but took up this *pre-existing* misogynist media stereotype and remythologized her as a more sympathetic figure for female audiences' (2007, p. 121, original emphasis). As this section has shown, as anxieties around women's singleness intensify, this sympathy is however rarely evident in mainstream media engagements with Bridget Jones.

Conclusion: From Singleton to Spinster

At the conclusion of *Bridget Jones's Diary* (both book and film) and into *Edge of Reason*, our heroine it seems will be saved from what has been figured as a fate worse than death – her tombstone, as she had dreaded in the film, will not read: 'Here lies the spinster of this parish.' That is, in the final instance she 'gets her Darcy' (Whelehan, 2000, p. 138), thus the narrative closure expected from the romance narrative is predictably delivered. The desirability of, and the centrality of the search for, a heterosexual partnership is ultimately reinscribed. The Singleton is a transient identity; an age and class specific subject position, eliding difference, while – as is common in postfeminist popular narratives – celebrating and universalizing the search for a masculine other as an essential part of all women's lives. Although chick lit and related generic forms may be 'rewriting the romance', they fail to do so 'in ways that allow for complex analyses of power, subjectivity, and desire' but instead reaffirm that 'the arms of a good man' are central to women's 'salvation' (Gill & Herdieckerhoff, 2006, p. 500). What this man 'saves' Bridget from are the uncertainties and risks of living as an autonomous woman in the late twentieth century.

Nonetheless, *Bridget Jones's Diary*'s engagement with, and intervention into, the politics of women's singleness should not be entirely discounted. Bridget's attempt to politicize and embrace singleness as a viable alternative for women itself mirrors the contradictory discourses publicly circulating around singleness. That said, in the media-sphere (and indeed in the novels' film adaptations) the ambivalence of Fielding's heroine towards coupledom, along with her efforts to celebrate singleness, is largely silenced, in favour of popular narratives that (re)constitute her as that which single women fear and should avoid becoming at all costs. In effect, then, in spite of her attempts to escape this identity within the pages of the novel, in the popular imaginary at least, Bridget herself has become a *spinster*. But by no means is she the only single woman whose public discursive constructions should give feminists pause. One of the most troublesome textual sites featuring single women, and which attests to the persistent cultural fears around them, is reality television; it is to programmes focusing on the over-zealous quest to eradicate women's singleness that the next chapter turns.

4
Desperate and Dateless TV: Making Over the Single Woman

Introduction

While much critical attention has been directed towards well-known televised single women, such as those from *Sex and the City*, this chapter instead turns to single women in another form: reality television programmes geared towards single women's purported desperation to be otherwise. To challenge claims that women's singleness now enjoys a widespread form of cultural legitimacy it has not previously, there is no more obvious textual site than that of so-called 'dating' reality television. In this chapter, after commencing with a brief engagement with an Australian version of this style of television, *The Farmer Wants A Wife*, the centrepiece of my discussion is the American series, *Tough Love*, after which I move on to consider the most high profile of this genre, *The Bachelor*.[1] A number of the observations made here about these particular shows and how they work to position single women are generalizable, applicable to this form of reality television as a whole (if not to popular culture more broadly). It is in such programmes that the single woman-as-lack becomes most evident and men, in apparently limited supply, become conceptualized as 'prizes' for which women must quite literally compete. That is, as outlined in previous chapters, a viable postfeminist subjectivity for women is presumed to be contingent on the search for, and attainment, of a man – a desire thoroughly normalized through these narratives.

Rather than simply overtly constructing their women contestants as desperate and deficient due to their lack of a male partner (though this is certainly at times evident), there are a number of complicated ways in which these programmes construct and seek to regulate the single women at their centre. Given this, here I conceptualize 'relationship' reality television as a form of makeover television or 'life intervention television' (Ouellette & Hay, 2008a). These single women, and their life-styles, are presumed to require rectification in much the same way as in more overtly transformatory programmes like *What Not to Wear* or *The Swan*. In the reality genre especially, the single woman is positioned as a figure in dire need of intervention. To varying degrees, relationship real-ity television is involved in advocating behaviour modification for sin-gle women, and thereby makes certain value judgements about them, femininity, and singleness. The sense of 'making over' the single woman operates in two overlapping ways in these shows. Firstly, by making her into a more desirable (competitive) single and, secondly, through quite literally making her *unsingle*. Key to becoming unsingle, these narratives imply, is becoming the kind of woman that men esteem and desire – a pliable, compliant self. In line with the therapeutic rhetorics of neo-liberalism, these women are up for classification, evaluation, and correc-tion (Rose, 1999). Such shows are instructional texts on how this can be done – how single women can be successfully made over, and thereby rewarded with a man. As throughout, these programmes – indicative of the compulsory heterosexuality in which the public single woman is required to invest – can also be read to illuminate how postfeminism is being inscribed in popular culture, especially in its intersections with the rhetoric of neoliberalism, and how certain gendered identities are sanctioned and promoted via this form of reality television.

Relationship reality television

Reality television has been the subject of much critical commentary (Andrejevic, 2004; Biressi & Nunn, 2005; Ouellette & Hay, 2008a; Weber, 2009), with many focusing on the question of the 'reality' to which it lays claim. For Ouellette and Murray, reality television is marked by 'the fusion of popular entertainment with a self-conscious claim to the discourses of the real' (2004, p. 2). They continue, 'reality tv has moved from the fringes of television culture to its lucrative core as networks adopt reality formats to recapture audiences and cable channels for-mulate their own versions of reality formats geared to audience niches' (2004, p. 4). One such niche, as this chapter explores, is the single woman demographic, with programmes buttressing – and purporting to resolve – claims common in popular discourse about the 'man drought'. As previous chapters have suggested, constructed as a straw figure delim-iting women's agency, feminism is often blamed for women 'mistakenly' focusing on career over love, leaving many, in their 30s in particular, sadly un-partnered. Not to fear; this is where reality television has stepped in. Tapping into such discourses around women's personal dissatisfaction with men (there aren't enough emotionally available catches on the overly crowded dating scene) and feminism (a career won't keep you warm at night), dating reality television thus purports to provide a creditable form of social service. Of course, such texts presume that for love-starved women any man will do, while men are constructed as the more discerning sex; indeed, these narratives are structured around such an assumption, with men overwhelmingly being the ones doing the choosing. Agency in (televised) love, then, is predominantly gendered masculine. At times in quite extreme ways, the dating reality programme aims to *fix* single women both as in delimiting viable subject positions and as a problem to be solved. That is, the presumption of the illegitimacy of women's singleness is fundamental to these texts.

In his study on reality television and/as surveillance, Mark Andrejevic argues that 'Reality shows are becoming the latest and most self-conscious in a string of transparently staged spectacles' (2004, p. 3). His comments allude to the very constructed-ness of such 'realities', something Rachel Dubrofsky has extensively taken up specifically in relation to *The Bachelor*, emphasizing that we need to understand that the narratives offered in such shows are constructed by television workers, using only a small portion of the footage shot, and whose careful editing works to constitute a certain version of non-scripted reality (2007, pp. 265–6) and indeed certain 'versions' of their participants. In a similar vein, Wood and Skeggs instructively put it like this: 'Whilst the staging of events on "reality" television complicates any ontological claim to the "real", it can make a claim to the "actual" – the camera tells us this "actually" happened as a response to an unscripted, if contrived, actual situation' (2008, p. 559). With this caveat in mind, we can presume then that these are the actions – and most importantly for these programmes, the emotions – of actual women. Moreover, drawing upon J. L. Austin's work on the performative utterance, Misha Kavka argues 'by creating a setting where intimacy must be "done with words" as well as bodily actions' dating reality television shows rely upon and facilitate a form of emotional performativity, thereby making the vexed question of authentic versus 'false' emotions redundant (2008, pp. 123–4).

Since the 1990s, reality television has insinuated itself into all facets of modern life – there are makeover shows (both of self and home), social experiment style programmes as exemplified by the genre's earliest manifestations, *Big Brother* and *Survivor*, and cooking series as well as those focusing on health and weight-loss: 'Their rapid proliferation has irrevocably altered our mediascape and, to the extent that our interactions with mass-mediated cultural forms shape our identities, they are in the process of altering us' (Morreale, 2007, p. 93). That is, they foreground the kinds of selves that are inhabitable, especially through assiduously policing the boundaries of those which are not (Ringrose & Walkerdine, 2008). However, it is not just identities that such programmes are working to mediate but relationships and gendered intimacies. As the audience for reality television has continued to grow so too have series centred on interpersonal, and especially romantic, interactions. The reality dating programme is now 'a major entity on the televisual landscape' (Gray, 2004, p. 262), which – in addition to those analyzed here – has included *Joe Millionaire, The Age of Love, Flavor of Love, Rock of Love, Average Joe, Momma's Boy,* and *The Cougar.* Celebrities have also been highly visible in this genre. For example, *Rock of Love* tracks Poison's Brett Michels in his search for love while *Age of Love,* starring Australian tennis champion Mark Philippoussis, pits women in their 20s (kittens) and women in their 40s (cougars) against each other in a battle for his affection. As instances of relationship reality television, and given the heteronormativity of mainstream media culture, it is not surprising that all of these programmes revolve around, and help to further normalize, heterosexuality (not to mention certain assumptions about gender, class, and race and their intersections).[2]

Television – like other media technologies such as the internet – now routinely mediate romantic relationships.[3] Through this type of programme, it has become thoroughly implicated in the process of partner procurement. In addition, as private life comes more thoroughly under surveillance, and affect comes to be performed in and through the mediasphere, the staging of interpersonal conflict, desire, and emotional excess in television shows like those examined here becomes more pronounced. Moreover, given that gender is not innate or natural but performative (Butler, 1990), such programmes contribute to a complicated process of legitimizing certain femininities over others. Unsurprisingly, critics have emphasized the political limitations of these programmes in terms of how they code women especially (Kingston, 2004; Maher, 2004; DePaulo, 2006; McClanahan, 2007; Negra, 2009; Douglas, 2010; Pozner, 2010). As Annette Hill argues, '*The Bachelor,* and other reality formats such as *Joe Millionaire,* constructs negative representations of single women, as it is the job of the single man to find the honest woman amongst many dishonest women' (2005, pp. 119–20). Women, then, are ordered according to the degree of their dissembling; those exhibiting the most 'authentic' traits and emotions are positioned on a hierarchy above the women whose performances are exposed, mostly through their interactions with their 'competition' (i.e. the other single women), as rather more calculating. Although I am not dismissing the potential of audience creativity or multiple viewing positions, it is difficult to ignore the sexual politics of such shows, especially their nostalgic naturalization of a masculine (active)/feminine (passive) binary. And while programmes like *The Bachelor* also spawned 'gender-flipping variants' such as *The Bachelorette*, they 'often made the single female appear more desperate than the cool and collected men, and they allowed the men considerably more power and agency in the process' (Gray, 2004, p. 264). In these inverted narratives, it is still the woman who is most deeply invested in this mediated process of becoming unsingle.

While reality television enables 'ordinary' women to become media objects (Turner, 2010) – that is, to be celebritized – to do so the single woman must invest in and reaffirm her own lack. That is, she must acknowledge that being single renders her fundamentally deficient, something that relationship reality television both relies on and purports to rectify. Such programmes are important not only in terms of how single women are positioned but in demonstrating the immense force with which heteronormative romance mythologies continue to operate – and indeed manifest in new ways. For Ingraham, such reality shows are part of a broader televisual strategy of 'hyper-heterosexual programming', working therefore to buttress the heterosexual imaginary (2005, p. 6) and, in particular, the institution of marriage. In addition to the overt displays of sexuality required from women participants, conflict within such programmes intensifies their prurience; the promise of a 'cat-fight' between women looms large. Simultaneously, and paradoxically, the contestants are shown to bond over their common quest for a man, a bond which is easily frayed when one contestant comes to be favoured over another – which is, after all, the very raison d'etre of relationship reality TV and which provides the shows with narrative closure.

Making over the single woman: The transformative promise of relationship television

More than just the promise of a man, relationship reality television programmes promise a new self, and in this way they are consistent with the makeover logics that are central to postfeminism. That the self can be made and remade is the premise underpinning, and the process that is staged within, makeover and life transformation television. The 'life intervention' performed by such shows follows the 'diagnosis' of participants' problems, transforming the '"needy" individual into functioning citizens' (Ouellette & Hay, 2008a, p. 6). As I have shown throughout, such a 'diagnostic gaze' is being directed towards the single woman in various sites of postfeminist media culture (Negra, 2009, p. 61). Quite clearly, in the examples I look at here, the 'diagnosis' for single women is that what they 'need' is a man. In their analysis of reality television, drawing upon Foucauldian ideas about governmentality, Ouellette and Hay argue: 'Life interventions circulate techniques for a government of the self that complement the value now being placed on choice, personal accountability and self-empowerment as ethics of neoliberal citizenship' (2008b, p. 476). In this way, they complement postfeminism, which also appropriates discourses around self-governance, taking charge of one's life, as a form of self-empowerment (see Chapter 1 here). The ultimate purpose of the mobilization of such discourses, in *Tough Love* especially, is not only an improved but a coupled self.

As a genre, makeover television builds 'upon an existing training regime that has historically offered women techniques to bolster their value in the heterosexual dating market' (Ouellette & Hay, 2008a, p. 7). It is perhaps no surprise, then, that assisting women in this process has produced a series like *Tough Love*, which both seeks to transform the individual, as per makeover logics, and to transform her life, as per the broader project of 'life intervention'. Further, although neither *The Farmer Wants A Wife* nor *The Bachelor* seek to transform women via an authoritative intermediary (as does *Tough Love*), as programmes reliant on both the surveillance and elimination of women contestants they do work to govern their behaviour (Dubrofsky, 2005) and seek to transform their lives through the provision of a life partner in a way that makes them entirely consonant with the 'makeover' process more explicitly enacted on *Tough Love*.

Like other forms of popular culture centring on the figure of the single woman, relationship reality television can be seen to offer more or less reactionary narratives – from those that explicitly render single women pathological to those which are less blatantly offensive in how they work to code them. One of the seemingly more innocuous examples of this style of television is *The Farmer Wants A Wife*, so I will briefly consider it as an introduction to this genre before moving on to consider one of the most extreme forms in *Tough Love*. This series has not received much critical attention, so I have chosen to place it at the centre of my analysis as a way to tease out some broader concerns about reality television, postfeminism, and gender. In contrast, *The Bachelor* has been subject to extensive feminist analysis; nonetheless, it is impossible to ignore one of the most well-known, longest running, and most watched of this reality subgenre. Therefore, I conclude this chapter by engaging with *The Bachelor*.

The Farmer Wants A Wife: 'How far will you go for love?'

In terms of cultural flow, reality television programmes have a high degree of 'transnational mobility and saleability, as they are amenable to being readily indigenized' (Lewis, 2008, p. 20), and *The Farmer Wants a Wife* exemplifies this process. *The Farmer Wants A Wife* was developed in the UK in 2001 and has since been adapted multiple times for a variety of countries, including Australia where the version produced by Fremantle Media premiered in 2007 and has continued each year since. The format was modified for Australian audiences in ways that enabled it to tap into certain culturally specific discourses used to define the urban and the rural, each reliant upon certain assumptions about the role of women in these apparently conflicting spaces. In this section, I briefly consider its fifth season which aired in 2010. The programme, as its title implies, dubbed 'Australia's greatest search for love', centres on finding a mate for six isolated Australian farmers. The season featured five men and one woman farmer, who is unsurprisingly defined by her maternal status: 'Five handsome boys and an outback mum'. Moreover, in this season, the participants are not told where they will be going, a gesture serving to underscore the trope of how far one is prepared to go for love – both into the geographical and the affective 'unknown'. This is the competitors' first test and reveals the women's level of commitment to becoming unsingle. Rather than the romanticized 'largely idyllic version of rurality' of the countryside in British programmes of this nature (Little, 2007, p. 855), the Australian outback connotes a harsher, less hospitable landscape, signalling a more extreme and intense form of sacrifice on the part of these single women. In terms of the so-called career/romance dilemma often seen to be at the heart of postfeminist media culture, *The Farmer Wants A Wife* is the most interesting of these shows as it necessitates that the successful participant be willing to relinquish not just her career but her entire world in favour of becoming a farmer's wife. She is required, if successful, to leave her friends and family and move to the remotest corners of the country to be with her farmer.

After choosing six women from applications received when the farmers' posted their profiles online, and following a five minute speed date, the farmers invite three women back to their regional home. Once there, the women have to work on the farm to prove that they can handle life on the land. It is expected that they familiarize themselves, and be sympathetic to, the various commitments of rural life. The programme relies upon the city/country binary, which also comes to be figured as a gendered binary. The city, traditionally seen in opposition to the 'nature' of the country, must be relinquished in order for the relationship to flourish (Little, 2007); city girls need to be *made over* into country ones. Moreover, the implication is that in 'returning' to nature, and therefore 'natural' gender roles, the women's new occupation will not only be wife but mother. In this way, the programme also functions nostalgically, invoking a prefeminist world where women did not participate in the public sphere and were relegated to the domestic. Accordingly, these shows facilitate the performance of, and help construct, certain rural heterosexualities; they also romanticize rural relationships over city ones (Little, 2007).

While the voiceover tells viewers that one of the farmers is 'a prize worth fighting for' (Episode 2), conflict and competition between women is not foregrounded – perhaps because the competition is on a much smaller scale than in other programmes of this ilk; with a one-in-three chance, the women each have decent odds at securing their farmer's heart. The women are shown to become friends and viewers hoping for the 'cat-fight' common to other examples of this format are routinely disappointed. Moreover, the women appear more heterogenous than those on other dating shows. They do not conform to a uniform standard of conventional beauty and are not put – or required to put themselves – on sexual display, with fairly innocent kissing and hugging being the only form of intimacy depicted as opposed to the requisite steamy hot tub scenes of *The Bachelor*. Indeed, 'a particularly powerful aspect of the distancing of the rural from urban is the associated portrayal of rural relationships as innocent' (Little, 2007, p. 860). The emphasis on women's corporeality and appearance, as well as mechanisms of governance, is much less overt in this series than the two examined subsequently. An implicitly 'natural' femininity – as in requiring less overt performativity – is staged on this programme; indeed, a more 'high maintenance' or stylized femininity is seen as an impediment to transforming these city women into farmers' wives.[4] The farmers themselves, unlike the slick players of *The Bachelor*, are not especially polished and are quite bashful (witness the young Farmer Charlie), contributing to the sense of 'authenticity' that is also created by the programme's emphasis on nature.

Farmers in the outback, the narrative suggests, have especial difficulties in accessing not just true love but women in general. Here, then, nature 'is seen as responsible for the plight of the bachelors, denying them potential partners' (Little & Panelli, 2007, p. 179). In this way, the programme positions itself as proffering a social service, including – as a number of the farmers mention – through ensuring population growth via the wife and the children that will by implication follow (see Little, 2007). As Devon emphasizes, 'there isn't a lot of women left in our town' (4). Here, the gendered narratives of man drought are inverted and it is women who are in short supply. In *The Farmer Wants a Wife*, the rhetoric of finding 'true love' dominates, as it does throughout the genre: 'Everyone wants the fairytale ending' (Becky, 4) and, once eliminated by farmer Nathan, Jemma confesses she has always wanted a 'fairytale' and she hopes that 'Prince Charming could turn up next week, and knock on my door, and I could live happily ever after then'.

Given that there is much less happening on the farm, in terms of competition and melodrama, the narration, unlike in the other programmes, is central, interpreting and summarizing the action for viewers: 'Over the next few hours, our hopefuls must do everything they can to win their farmer's heart or risk leaving the farmer forever' (4). However, the agency of the women in this series appears more pronounced than in other examples of dating reality television, especially as a number actively remove themselves from the process. In episode three, one woman (Michelle) chooses to leave early as she confesses she is not ready to 'settle down' with her farmer (Shaun). And again, in episode four, immediately before the farmer is to make his choice about who will leave, Christina tells Devon that she does not feel she could live in a small town and would rather make the choice to leave. To camera, she commends all women married to farmers for their sacrifices – sacrifices she is implicitly unwilling to make. Both the women challenge the supremacy of masculine agency in this process, disrupting the programme's logic and assumption of feminine passivity (i.e. that the women simply wait to be chosen). Though the farmers express disappointment, the women are not criticized but nor is their decision sanctioned, either by the farmer or by the omnipresent voiceover of Natalie Gruszelski. Such moments, however, also serve to underscore the other women's commitment as well as the authenticity of their desire to be in the competition. Nonetheless, it is significant that these particular women enact their (postfeminist) agency to *not* choose a man.

In the fourth episode, the farmer has to choose which of the three women will be sent home. The women each make a short plea – which highlights the gendered power dynamics – before the eliminated candidate is chosen. Predominantly, in these monologues, the women suggest they would like more time to get to know the farmer but rarely are they as effusive or their expressions of affect as hyperbolic as their counterparts on programmes like *The Bachelor*. Convincing the farmer they would be prepared to move to the farm is largely how the women come to be differentiated. As Little and Panelli argue of a similar series (*Desperately Seeking Sheila*), 'it is the women's ability to adjust to a country way of life and forgo the comforts of the city that largely determines their potential as wives or partners' (2007, p. 184). For example, one of Charlie's three choices, Sophie, exhibits a lack of proficiency in farm chores and she tells him she fears he thinks she is incompetent. While Charlie reassures her that he is looking for a wife not a worker, a comment which itself reveals certain ideological assumptions about women and the invisibility of gendered labour, she is nonetheless eliminated shortly thereafter.

Although the moments of emotional excess that characterize other shows seem absent, the women are shown to 'authentically' articulate their emotions, especially on elimination. After being eliminated by Jamie, Lynn cries and concludes that she will 'just keep looking, I guess' (4). The women frequently tell the farmer how much they 'love' his farm, which comes to stand for the farmer himself who emphasizes that his future wife must commit not just to him but to his lifestyle, including the quotidian drudgery of farm life. In these conversations, there is no reference to the women's jobs or studies (a number of them are students). As is characteristic of this genre, it is clear that, if successful, 'life will unfold on his terms' (Pozner, 2010, p. 244). While this is certainly the case in programmes like *The Bachelor*, this relocation is often to another urban centre. In contrast, on *The Farmer Wants a Wife* the chosen women must move to a remote and often isolated place. And although there have been versions of this programme in the other countries (including a short-lived version in the US), in Australia the successful candidate must traverse vast geographic spaces in order to secure her man who lives on the land. Despite the fact that the series lacks many of the other troublesome elements of relationship television discussed later in this chapter, in its core assumption it inscribes the notion that women's lives (and especially their careers) are worth less (indeed worth nothing) compared to the potential validation of securing a husband. The trope of being prepared to 'go anywhere for love' is starkly literalized, given the vastness of the Australian landscape, in this programme in a way it is not in the others.

During the course of the series, both the farmers and their potential 'wives' speak about falling in love as something that may happen in the future, so the narrative closure and over the top performance of affect characteristic of other dating programmes is also absent. That said, there was one proposal during the last season's finale, as Farmer Nathan (who, not insignificantly, was the most remote of all the farmers) asked Amanda to marry him. Although of course its premise is the same as others in this genre, arguably *The Farmer Wants A Wife* is less offensive than its counterparts and does not rely upon overt moments of humiliation or shame and the 'behind the scenes' surveillance of women's daily lives characteristic of other programmes of this nature (Andrejevic, 2004, p. 64) is kept to a minimum; competition is less visible (given the pool is almost immediately narrowed to three women); and women's agency seems to be enacted more readily and visibly on this programme than others. Nonetheless, in its very premise, it yet valorizes marriage and unabashedly reinscribes hetero-patriarchal romance mythologies, not to mention fairly traditional gender boundaries and roles. Moreover, there is scant recognition of the enormous sacrifices these women will be required to make for the transformation to farmer's wife or the gendered inequities of such a process. To sum up, while politically I do find *The Farmer Wants A Wife* to be troublesome like others in this category, the women are not as overtly coded as deficient (or indeed desperate) as in some of the other examples of this genre, the most extreme of which is undoubtedly America's *Tough Love*.

Tough Love: Disciplining the single woman

Tough Love is a reality television series which aired on VH1 in the US in 2009 and 2010, but – like most of these programmes – has also been screened internationally (including in Australia on the Fox cable network). Eight women, in their 20s and 30s, are sent to a singles' 'boot camp', hosted by matchmaker, Steve Ward, wherein they will be taught how to overcome the personal inadequacies keeping them single. In this way, the immense undesirability of women's singleness is taken for granted. Although *Tough Love* is the most extreme example of the way single women are constituted as deficient in this form of cultural production, it is not atypical in the kinds of narrative it offers about single women as exemplars of an abject form of femininity (Negra, 2009) that must be 'made over'. On its website, *Tough Love* brands itself thus:

> The series revolves around his 'Tough Love Bootcamp' where Steve works with a group of eight single women to change their dating ways. Steve guarantees that if they follow his rules, by the end of eight weeks, they will be ready for love.
> (http://www.vh1.com/shows/tough_love/season_1/series.jhtml)

The show, then, is explicitly predicated on rendering the women pathological; there is something deeply *wrong* with the eight women participating in the programme that has led to their prolonged singleness and
that can be fixed by its male host – whose own claim to authority, apart
from his masculinity and thereby apparent epistemological 'insight'
into the male psyche, is that he is a matchmaker by profession. Perhaps
because the idea of men being in short supply that governs other relationship television shows is not part of the narrative constructed by
Tough Love, the element of competition is missing but conflict between
women is not. Nonetheless, the boot camp participants are shown to
form close bonds over their shared search for a man (but not, as in *The
Farmer Wants a Wife* or *The Bachelor*, the *same* man).

Given that 'non-normativity invites policing' (Weber, 2009, p. 133), it
is perhaps unsurprising that a programme like *Tough Love*, which works
to 'police' single women and relies upon tropes of singleness as disease,
exists. (Others, like *The Bachelor*, focus on the potentialities and desirability of being partnered without so blatantly pathologizing its single
participants.) But its very existence does challenge more celebratory
arguments about how reality television can function to provide models
of alternative subjectivities and facilitate the performance of gender
fluidity and subversion.[5] Consistent with self-help books like *The Rules*
(1995) and *The Surrendered Single* (2002) analyzed in my next chapter,
the single woman can be seen as a personal and social ill that requires
various, carefully orchestrated, remedies.

Presenter Steve Ward, appropriating authoritative 'psy' discourses, tells
the women he will 'condition them' to find the man they are looking
for (201). In the militaristic language of 'boot camp' he acknowledges he
will be attempting to 'break' these women as the first stage in helping
them overcome the 'bad' dating habits that have led to their lamentable
singleness. In this way, as I have suggested, *Tough Love* operates as a form
of makeover reality television, though the site for this transformation is
not primarily corporeal, as in many other televized instances, but psychological: 'Over the course of the eight episodes, we'll see our love-lorn
ladies be put through the paces – and come out the other side transformed.' Accordingly, such a programme is consistent with the postfeminist logic discussed throughout that envisions women – including
single women – via the postfeminist 'makeover paradigm' (Gill, 2007).
Although in the second episode of each season the women are also
physically made over, given new hair, makeup and clothes, the most
important 'makeover' single women can be seen to undergo is to be
made into a viable girlfriend, fiancé, or wife. In this episode, Steve makes

explicit that they need an attitudinal and behavioural makeover too: 'Each one of you could be doing something differently to attract men' (202). This quotation articulates the show's very premise – single women need to take responsibility for their own limitations in this area before Steve helps to 'solve' and, in the process, 'save' them. In this way, such a programme reveals much, not simply about television's role in 'making subjects', but about 'unmaking' them, 'cultivating new sensibilities and engagements, in enabling different micropolitics of the self' (Hawkins, 2001, p. 414). In *Tough Love*, a man is seen as both reason and reward for such mediated self-transformation.

Tough Love and/as makeover television

Tough Love is part of a broader televisual context, in the US especially but also in other Western countries, wherein viewers are inundated 'with imperatives about self-appraisal, self-critique, and self-improvement' (Weber, 2009, p. 2). Makeover narratives depict 'failed or imperiled self hood' (Weber, 2009, p. 5); and in terms of *Tough Love*, these women are deemed to have such 'failed selfhoods' due to the lack of a consistent male other in their lives. Perhaps contradictorily, neoliberal rhetorics regarding the need to work upon the self are enlisted in the service of shoring up the hegemony of heteronormative coupledom. That is, the feminine self must be shown to have been *bettered* in order to constitute her both ready and worthy of the reward of a functional romantic relationship. 'Scare tactics', argues Weber, 'function as rationales to bring the subjects into line' (2009, p. 69). In the case of *Tough Love*, it is the fear of being – or, more appositely, remaining – alone that is mobilized and fostered in order to secure contestants' conformity and compliance. Steve describes himself as the 'pied piper', assuring the women that if they follow him they will have success in life and, most importantly the show tells us, love (204).

The programme's opening credits feature its 'match maker' host proclaiming: 'Nobody knows single women like I do – the lonely, the clueless, the needy. I can tell just by looking at you.' He frames these single women as deficient and in dire need of masculine intervention (both his own and that of a future partner). The show tracks a pseudo-therapeutic process, mediated by the male 'expert' who both identifies (and indeed constructs) the flaws and proffers the solution to them. In their introductions, the women position Steve's 'boot camp' as their last resort, despite the fact that the majority of the women are only in their 20s. Indicative of the time-panic that I have, following Negra, shown to mark these postfeminist constructions of women's singleness, the participants in this series repeatedly invoke the idea that time is of the essence (by implication this panic is tied to their reproductive capacities). The televised boot camp, like other forms of reality television, proffers 'the fantasy of remodeling a dysfunctional self' (Biressi & Nunn, 2005, p. 105), a process that requires firstly that singleness be constituted as a form of dysfunction (which *Tough Love* does in abundance) and secondly that the behaviours that are sustaining such dysfunction be modified. One of the key 'problems' identified within *Tough Love* is women's inability to recognize what men want, and more importantly, what men *see*.

In the first episode of each season, Steve surveys the group of eight women, working through them all to identify what he believes to be the individual flaw that is ensuring they remain without a man. These women, therefore, are seen to embody various forms of singleness. In the first episode, 'What men really think' (indeed this could be the subtitle of the entire series, given that each episode has at least one component wherein the participants are judged by men), Steve – often quite offensively – defines each of the women (101). He includes 'Miss Bridezilla' (Jaclyn), who is 22 and desperate to be married by 25 and thereby scares men away; 'Miss Lone Ranger' (Jody), who is 38, has been a bridesmaid 18 times, and claims to be 'freaking out' about being alone. To camera, she confesses to 'experiencing panic and anxiety attacks like you've never seen ... I'm running out of time'. She concludes that if Steve cannot help her, she 'just might end up alone'; a fate the programme teaches the women to dread. Angel (Miss Closed Off) tells viewers 'I need Steve to break down my walls' (201). Others include: 'Miss Fatal Attraction' (Jessa), who, as the name suggests, turns men off by coming on too strong; 'Miss Picky' (Abiola); 'Miss Ball Buster' (Tasha); 'Mis-Guided' (Natasha), who is told she has a 'nurse curse', dating men who need to be looked after; and 'Miss Gold Digger' (Taylor). Tina (Miss Career Obsessed) too confesses to camera that despite a successful career: 'At the end of the day, you're still sad and alone at home ... what's wrong with me? This is one of my last options because I feel like I'm on the path to not find someone. I'm ready for Steve to control my fate' (201). Kanisha too, allegedly a 'gold digger', suggests in the show's promotional material: 'I believe Steve Ward can put me in my place' (cited in Pozner, 2010, p. 244). As Pozner notes, it is especially problematic that two African American women, Tina and Kanisha, are shown to ask the 'patriarchal white man' to '"control" their fates' (2010, p. 244).

All women concede that they 'really need Steve's help' and their agency in constituting their own singleness as a problem to be solved, albeit via a male authority figure, should not be overlooked. Of women's complicity in such shows, McRobbie notes: 'These programmes would not work if the victim did not come forward and offer herself as someone in need of expert help' (2009, p. 140). Nonetheless, a series like *Tough Love* suggests that women's singleness is perceived to be so abject that the sacrifice, shame, and humiliation to be endured during boot camp is not only worthwhile but imperative. Locating them in this relationship with a paternalistic figure, *Tough Love* also restages the infantilization of single women I have shown to be evident elsewhere in postfeminist media culture. Within the show's frame, a future without a man is simply inconceivable and represents a fear that Steve fosters. After sending boot-camp participants to a staged 'Single Women Anonymous' group, where older women lament their singleness as a form of cautionary tale, he says: 'I don't want the girls to be afraid of growing old but I do want them to be afraid of growing old alone' (209).

In line with the surveillance that marks the entire series Steve tells them: 'I know everything about you; I've studied each of you very carefully,' including speaking to friends and family (Season 2, premiere). At the end of each episode, the women undergo group therapy sessions, so they can 'learn from each other's mistakes' (Steve, 102). This form of 'pseudo-authoritarianism' – or 'tough love' – is justified within the logics of the show; humiliation and surveillance are seen to be enlisted in the 'creation of a self-governing [neoliberal] subject' (Ouellette & Hay, 2008a, p. 110). That women are responsible for the gendered labour of securing and maintaining a relationship is thoroughly naturalized, as it has been historically (Hochschild, 1994; Gill, 2007). Rather than a singular revelatory moment as is common in makeover TV (Weber, 2009, p. 31), there are multiple small victories (or, conversely, defeats) in *Tough Love* where the women are shown to have successfully implemented Steve's rules; being designated the 'winner' in group therapy is one of these micro moments of 'reveal'.

Fixing the single woman: Shame, group therapy, and the disciplinary 'hot seat'

These programmes can be seen as just one in a number of technologies of gender exhorting women to self-transformation. Although conceding that this focus on women's bodies and psyches as the site for transformation is certainly not new, in line with the 'neo-liberal ethos of continuously maximizing, bettering, and reinventing the self', Ringrose and Walkerdine conclude that the current 'methods of intense psychical and psychological scrutiny and the calling upon the subject to enact self-regulatory methods to accomplish an ever-adaptive self ... indicates a discursive shift' (2008, p. 236). This discursive shift is also coterminous with, or operationalized in and through, postfeminism, with its increased emphasis on self-surveillance, discipline, and self-transformation (Gill, 2007). However, in reality television, the self is not simply left to its own devices to perform this transformation but enlists, or is enlisted by, various intermediaries (McRobbie, 2009) – in this case, a matchmaker posing as a therapist. As the resident bad girl of season one (and indeed season two where she makes a dramatic reappearance), Taylor tells viewers: 'I hate him [Steve] because he makes me fix myself' (202) – and 'fix' them he indeed does.

In the context of group therapy, and within the entire boot camp, the women must confront their fears and take personal responsibility for the singleness that is shown to be causing them such deep dissatisfaction and that has driven them to the extremes of Steve's 'tough love'. Indeed, the programme presumes that the very definition of unhappiness for women is to be man-less. He warns them that if they fail to heed his advice they 'may very well end up alone' (101). In keeping with the overt pathologization of women that marks this series, he suggests that the women involved in the camp have a 'dating disease' (101). In each episode, Steve articulates a number of rules, usually following tape of the women's behaviour; they include: 'Don't bring wedding plans up on the first date or a guy is going to think your biological clock is more like a stopwatch' (101) and 'When you're around a guy you're attracted to, you never want to whine and complain' (101). The women are seen to provide an example, for each other but also for the audience, of how *not* to behave. Unsurprisingly, within relationship programmes like *Tough Love*, gendered imbalances of power are, as Pozner argues, both 'codified and glorified' (2010, p. 246).

Steve's tone is aggressive and frequently patronizing; pushing these women to breaking point – one of his explicitly identified aims. Like much reality television, the show thrives on the melodrama of these moments of emotional excess. Forcing them to watch themselves (mostly during their interactions with men) on film, via the 'telestrator', Steve shames the women at the weekly group therapy sessions with which each episode concludes. In order to attain 'real' love, the women must be capable of enduring 'tough love', a key part of which are these moments of harsh criticism and public shaming. As Weber argues of reality makeover television shows like *What Not To Wear*, 'It is only after her shaming and capitulation that she can be praised' (2007, p. 89) and this is a process that can be tracked in *Tough Love*, especially during group therapy sessions: 'Unique to the makeover narrative is the way that experts point out flaws in a combined gesture of humiliation and care, what I call affective domination' (Weber, 2009, p. 30). On *Tough Love*, Steve is certainly adept at such 'affective domination' and the pseudo-therapeutic discourse of 'tough love' itself invokes harshness coupled with care. Being placed in the 'hot seat' is a form of caution and the woman is told she can – and must – amend her behaviour. The hot seat is also a form of confessional, where women can explain their behaviour via narratives of a troubled past. For example, Taylor, initially deemed a gold digger, breaks down and confesses that it is the memory of having to give up her child for adoption due to financial difficulties that drives her search for a man with a substantial income.

The behavioural transgressions for which the women can be relegated to the 'hot seat', a bar stool at the front of the room, positioned next to the television on which they are forced to watch these surveilled transgressions, include not being attentive enough to a man or, conversely, being too attentive. For example, in one episode Tina is in the hot seat; she is punished for her lack of sexiness (203), while Liz's place there is secured by virtue of her being 'too hungry' for a man (207). She scared her date away; this charge is a serious one within the *Tough Love* boot camp and once again emphasizes the programme's positioning of the women as deficient. At other times, the hot seat serves its therapeutic purpose. For example, Jaclyn is the 'winner' in episode 7 for managing the potential tensions between an ex-partner and the one she met while in boot camp: 'You managed to keep both of these guys feeling good about themselves' (Steve, 107). Through such positive reinforcement, the women learn how they can obtain Steve's – and by implication, other men's – approval and admiration. Commending Tina for her successful flirting (when her usual behaviour is to treat men like 'buddies'), Steve suggests 'when you act like a woman it makes all the difference in the world to a man' (208). He validates the women, telling him he is proud of them when they demonstrably follow these rules. As in other forms of makeover television, the show therefore tracks the process of the women 'unlearning what is considered unacceptable and unattractive about them' (McRobbie, 2009, p. 144). But it is not only during group therapy that the women are made to endure humiliation in Steve's efforts to 'correct' their behaviour. The boot camp women are encouraged 'to objectify their lives in order to pursue the care of the self. Through television, the self becomes something that can be studied, reflected upon, surveilled and therefore recalibrated' (Ouellette & Hay, 2008a, p. 97). However, in *Tough Love*, it is not simply their lives that the women are taught to objectify but their bodies as well.

'Men are, women appear'[6]: Women watching men watching women

As part of the boot camp process, Steve sends the women on filmed dates, after which he interviews the men for an evaluation of their date, questioning them as to whether they would see the woman again. If the response is a definitive 'yes', the women appear validated, signified most obviously as the others smile and congratulate her. Moreover, they often cry joyfully when hearing that a man would consent to see them again, suggesting they have internalized one of Steve's key mantras: that what men think is paramount. Conversely, if the men do not wish to pursue the relationship, it is positioned as a reflection on the inadequacies of the woman's actions, not that Steve has failed professionally as a matchmaker. At other times, Steve deprives the women of agency as he dictates whether a particular 'match' will develop. He judges them on whether they have adhered to what is cast, and normalized, as appropriate gendered behaviour; they need to perform the right kind of femininity to escape censure.

In terms of the series' governing logic, the desires and authority of men are paramount throughout, but not just via the host's analysis, and evaluation, of the women and their actions. In each episode Steve draws upon the authority of other men to quite literally pass judgement on the women. The masculine word, and interpretive framework, is privileged throughout. As a genre then reliant upon surveillance (Andrejevic, 2004), it is perhaps not surprising that the male gaze – which, as many feminists and others have shown (Berger, 1972; Bartky, 1990; Tseelon, 1999), has long been directed at women – is active/activated the way it is in these programmes. The women contestants, like those in other forms of postfeminist media culture, function as spectacle, but the idea that women must learn to internalize the disciplinary male gaze is explicit in *Tough Love*; this is the show's central pedagogical imperative. For example, in the first episode, the participants are forced to parade in front of a judging panel of three unknown men, and are then made to watch a tape of the men's (often extremely harsh) assessments. In this way, for the duration of the boot camp the women exist in what, following Foucault, has been called a 'panoptic spectatorial environment' (Weber, 2007, p. 91; Foucault, 1977). While a number of the women are deemed to have 'a lot of potential', others are subject to critique for their overtly sexual appearance. One male surveyor offensively suggests (of Arian): 'I'd love to do her, I'm not going to date her' and, equally obnoxious, another observes of Taylor: 'I'd be pissed off if I woke up next to her.' Such opinions, however, are valorized and Steve urges the women to take note and consider the kinds of selves they are projecting; they are single, he implies, because of the way they are being read. He reminds them that the '[male] gaze is always present' and that 'shame falls on those who do not work hard enough to be pleasing to the gazer' (Weber, 2009, p. 85). He exhorts the women to make themselves aware of the way their bodies come to mean in a patriarchal signifying economy, something the show seeks to achieve in a number of ways.

As in season one, in the premiere of season two the women find themselves projected onto a large screen in public, and must submit to the same evaluative process. The men form an assessment not only of the women's level of sexual desirability but of their character through looking at them, and are asked to pronounce each woman 'dateable' or 'undateable'. In contrast to the idea often mobilized in postfeminist discourses about women's own willingness to subject themselves to the male gaze, ironically, knowingly or playfully, in *Tough Love* women unwittingly find themselves called upon to perform what Projansky (obviously indebted to Laura Mulvey) has called a 'to be looked at postfeminism', for the pleasure it provides to men (2001, p. 80). Furthermore, when they cause displeasure – not being deemed attractive or date-worthy – they are told they must transform to become more appealing. When the women initially react against this form of objectification (as they do in each season), Steve tells them he is only showing them what men *see*, providing a valuable insight that will help them increase their currency on the dating market. His sporadic assertions regarding the importance of 'inner beauty' are persistently undercut by the show's simultaneous emphasis on watching, and evaluating, women's bodies throughout.

In 'Sex and the Male Brain' (103), this focus on the gaze becomes even more extreme, as the women endure a photo shoot and a lingerie party to which Steve invites a date for each of them. Likewise, in the third episode (203) of season two where each woman has to partake in a supposedly 'sexy' photo shoot in an episode about what men find attractive. The lingerie photo shoots gauge the women's capacities to make themselves into sexual objects capable of eliciting male approbation. In each season, the photos are 'assessed' by a panel of men, who provide a verdict on whether the women have succeeded at performing sexy; the women then watch these assessments during group therapy. Some evaluations are scathing, disparagingly comparing the women to porn stars or failing to find any redeemable attributes. Being designated 'undateable' means the women are of no value in a homosocial economy predicated on their exchange (Irigaray, 1985). As in other makeover programmes, *Tough Love* presumes 'that sexual attention from men functions as the most significant form of female power' (Weber, 2009, p. 164). Such televised makeovers advocate 'salvation through submission' (Weber, 2009, p. 6), and in terms of *Tough Love*, it is submission not just to the patriarchal authority of its presenter but to that of the panel of men called upon throughout to literally pronounce judgement upon its participants.

In *Ways of Seeing* John Berger underscores how men are positioned as 'being' while women are merely 'seen': 'A woman must continually watch herself. She is almost continually accompanied by her own image of herself ... She has to survey everything she is and everything she does because how she appears to others, and ultimately how she appears to men, is of crucial importance' (1972, p. 46). But what Steve works to promote is not the women's 'own image of themselves' but the perspective of the men he employs to judge the boot camp women and who are seen to represent *all* men. Within the *Tough Love* frame, the women are made to watch men watching them and modify their behaviour accordingly. Moreover, the disciplinary role of the camera itself cannot be overestimated. In addition to Steve's various sanctions and punishments, 'The fact that their every move can be recorded by a camera works to control the activities of participants, to transform them in some sense: they know they are being watched and that they are there to be watched, which serves to regulate their behaviour' (Dubrofsky, 2007, p. 273). In this way, the transformation promised by makeover rhetoric occurs, at least in part, through the process of surveillance itself. Furthermore, during group therapy the participants themselves take up the position of 'watcher' (Dubrofsky, 2007, p. 273), as they watch themselves – and each other – via the 'telestrator', as Steve and eventually viewers do.

The process of 'disciplining' women, not just through the male gaze, becomes intensified in *Tough Love* as it extends into the area of corporeal punishment. In a bizarre adaptation of a Skinnerian inspired behaviourist experiment, the women are trained on how to maximize their chances of becoming unsingle. They each have to wear an electronic device dubbed 'The Zapper' on a 'training date': 'If I catch any of you reverting to your old behavior, I'm going to shock you.' He warns them immediately prior to these dates: 'Ok ladies, don't scare these guys off' (102). Steve watches the women, who are being filmed, and activates the zapper when they veer into topics of conversation repellent to men. The women then are monitored and physically punished (via electronic shock) for a number of dating 'crimes', such as talking about their career. This means of behaviour modification is extreme but indicative of the programme's governing logic – that these single women need, by any means, to be recalibrated. A similar form of 'punishment' is enacted in the next season (202), where the women are sent on filmed dates at a theme park and are subsequently quizzed about how much they listened to the information the men imparted about themselves. To demonstrate how attentive they have been, each woman is then made to sit in a 'dunk tank'; if their answers to his questions are wrong, Steve dunks them in cold water. This act of public shame – it is performed in the middle of a theme park – is just one of a number of disciplinary tactics mobilized within the show. In either of these instances, the punishment is not the 'zapping' or the dunking but rather the humiliation endured by the victims, a kind of humiliation that is integral to reality TV – and especially the makeover show.

The series' emphasis on discipline and punishment is once again made explicit through the use of a mock court, in which boot camp women appear as defendants, with an all male juror and Steve's mother, Joanne Ward, as judge (206). They will, Steve explains, be charged with either 'a dating felony, crime of love or just inappropriate behaviour'. (However, the 'crime' for which they have already been convicted, and 'sentenced' to boot camp, is their singleness.) Again, the all male jury will pronounce them either 'dateable or undateable'. Whether it is cheating on a fiancé, 'keying' an ex-boyfriend's car, or being a 'tease', the women are put on the stand and made to explain their past behaviour to the anonymous men who will convict or exonerate them. Of public judgements on reality television, Weber notes 'Through these moments of public displays and assessment, the show plays out a public referendum' (2009, p. 71). In *Tough Love*, this 'public' (represented by the mock jury) is solely gendered masculine. (That said, it is important to remember that women viewers who enjoy the programme and its humiliation of women may also be performing such acts of evaluation and judgement from their living rooms.) Furthermore, moments like the court scene – where the women arrive with trepidation, unaware of what awaits them – remind us that, within the boot camp, they are effectively within Steve's custody, subjected to a series of exercises and challenges which he has set. Weber sees such programmes creating 'mediated environments that are benevolent dictatorships in which the demands of certain authorities must be adhered to' (2009, p. 40). Steve disavows his own authority and instead attempts to position himself as a benevolent agent of change, helping to facilitate a self-transformation desired by the single subject – whether or not he is involved: 'I don't want to change anything about you that you wouldn't want to change yourself' (Steve to Arian, 101).

'Unruly femininity': Class and the spectacular failure of transformation

Consistent with the self-fashioning that is part of a broader therapeutic culture, Steve implores the women participating in the boot camp to 'do the work' on themselves, heavily castigating them when they appear unwilling to do so. For example, he swears, telling one of the women (Jenna) she is starting to 'piss him the fuck off' when it appears she is not taking his 'lessons' seriously (205). Likewise, he tells another: 'If you don't want to do the work, get the fuck out of my boot camp' (Steve to Taylor, 203). In addition to the liberally doled out expletives, Steve's language is inflected with a missionary zeal: 'As god is my witness, you are going to walk out of this boot camp a changed woman' (to Jenna, 206). Steve expresses his frustration at Jenna, whom he dubs 'addicted to negativity', something jeopardizing not only her chances with men but her place within the boot camp. While Jenna is shown to offer partial, though apparently not wilful, resistance to Steve and his wisdom in season two, in the first season another woman is depicted as less pliable.

One of the women in the boot camp, Arian, is shown to be disruptive and especially troublesome, challenging Steve's authority from the initial episode. A dancer in a nightclub, who professes to having a two week limit on relationships, her overt sexuality also renders her problematic and there are class dimensions which position her as incapable of transformation. On her date at the trivia night, Arian is shown to be having sexually explicit conversations that the show, via Steve's subsequent analysis of her behaviour after replaying it during group therapy, deems to be inappropriate. She repeatedly expresses concerns about not having 'been laid' for a few weeks; her excessive sexuality is deemed to be out of control, both by Steve and the other women (104). In this episode, Arian's 'raunchy behavior' is deemed 'pathological', and Steve offensively tells her it could lead to her being raped (104). While she (justifiably) storms off after such an obnoxious comment, the programme cuts to interviews showing the other women supporting Steve's assertion. She is represented as crude and crass – Jody rhetorically asks to camera: 'What rock did you crawl from under?' (107). When footage of Arian's hyper-sexualized antics is played back to her mother (107), she fails to display the outrage expected of her and instead defends and normalizes her daughter's behaviour, therefore implying it is bad mothering (not a distant father as she claims) that is the source of Arian's dysfunction and hence singleness.

Arian begins to hyperventilate during group therapy, fearing she will be placed in the 'hot seat' (107). Her attempt to defer the impending judgement is also an attempt to resist moral evaluation. As Ringrose and Walkerdine argue, 'most make-over shows are premised on the possibility of the transformation of a specifically abject subject (working class, wrong femininity) into something else' (2008, p. 236). This of course is nothing new; working class women have long been seen as 'as threats to the moral order who must be monitored, controlled, and reformed' (Ringrose & Walkerdine, 2008, p. 233).While there are indeed other women on *Tough Love* who are coded as working class (such as Taylor), they stand in opposition to Arian in their willingness to be positioned in the role of willing makeover subject. The working class woman is not always already a failure, then, but through her crude and vulgar antics, Arian is situated outside of the bounds of respectable femininity. As Wood and Skeggs note, 'In opposition to the ethical self that can transform, tell and show its moral worth, is the self that does not know how to tell or display itself correctly and cannot claim or profess propriety' (2004, p. 207). That Arian does not know how to display this propriety reveals much, as Wood and Skeggs have argued, about the restaging of 'traditional narratives of gender and class' in the world of reality television (2004, p. 205). If the single woman is abject, then it seems the most abject of them all (at least in this narrative) is the working class single.

Throughout *Tough Love*, Arian's resistance to Steve's (masculine) wisdom is punished with expulsion; she cannot be redeemed in and through the boot camp experience: 'Throughout her stay at boot camp, Arian's displayed an unwillingness to change and dangerous behavior' (107). Such moments, however, have been seen to be central to the makeover narratives proffered by reality television, with 'resistance' providing vital narrative tension in the shows (Weber, 2009, p. 74). Moreover, 'recalcitrant subjects introduce the possibility that makeover might fail' – that there might not be a 'new self' (Weber, 2009, p. 113) and therefore, perhaps worse in the logic of this show, no man. In this way, underscoring the precarious nature of this transformation, they function pedagogically, telling the other women that their own potentially new selfhood – and therefore potentially coupled self – may itself be jeopardized. As punishment, Arian departs untransformed and unpartnered.

The 'dateable' subject

At the end of each season, a number of the women are shown to be pursuing relationships with the men that Steve, the professional match-maker, has found them; therefore, his goal of making the boot camp attendees 'dateable' has been achieved. In their exit interviews, most of the women deploy self-help style rhetoric about loving oneself as key preparation for a loving relationship and in this way they echo their paternalistic mentor: 'Boot camp put these women on a better path to finding love ... In order to find Mr Right, you have to be able to take a long, hard look at yourself' (Steve, 108). In the final group therapy, all the women break down (though to varying degrees) and thank their boot camp mentor (108). Steve provides his final assessment of each of the women; for example: 'When Jody came to boot camp, she was single and hiding behind her career; now she's approachable and willing to take chances' (108). Implicitly the product of feminism, Jody's 'problem' was the centrality of her career in her life; by the end of the season she has reprioritized and decided she wants to marry and have children. As she observes, 'Success and money and career: if you don't have anyone to share them with, then what's the point?' (108). Though viewers are told the relationship she began on the series ultimately failed, she was suffi-ciently 'recalibrated' to ensure that she will be able to find another, more suitable, partner. These women now inhabit '"new and improved" selves that they can parlay into social capital' (Morreale, 2007, p. 97) – including becoming partnered. Others are not so successful, demonstrating the con-sequences of their failure to heed Steve's advice. For example, rather than continuing to pursue the blossoming romance begun on the show with Steve's match, Brock, viewers are told that after filming Jaclyn returned to her commitment-phobic boyfriend, reassured by his proclamations of change and an engagement ring, but the relationship once again fizzled. Unlike Jody, Jaclyn did not appear to have been successfully retrained and, away from Steve's disciplinary gaze and punishments, reverted to her old habits and suffered accordingly.

If we see the televised makeover as a triangulated process, from abjec-tion through suffering and concluding with redemption (Weber, 2009, p. 137), in *Tough Love* redemption for a woman is being successfully 'made over' into a desirable, hopefully partnered, heterosexual sub-ject. She is socially redeemed; value accrues to her in ways it did not and could not when she was pronounced, by the show's male judges, 'undateable': 'All of you have put my rules into practice, and you're hav-ing success' (Steve, 108). Some of the women do not leave the series with their perfect match (or indeed any match) but the overarching narrative in the programme's finale is that they have, through adopting Steve's various mantras and lessons, exponentially increased their chances of doing so beyond the scope of the show. In particular, if the boot camp (and Steve) has done its work, the women have learnt to internalize the male gaze and thereby are now cognizant of what men are (quite literally) *looking* for in a woman. That excessive energy is expended on such a task, and that being partnered comes to be tethered to these televised discourses of self-empowerment (i.e. a new self leads to a new man), and thus to postfeminism, suggests that the man-less woman remains a threat requiring intense management. Such management, while explicit in *Tough Love*, is more subtle in other variants of the relationship programme including the most well-known example of the genre: *The Bachelor*.

The Bachelor: Single women and competitive heterosexuality

The Bachelor is one of the earliest, and longest running, forms of relationship reality television. Like other examples in this chapter, it is predicated on the inherent undesirability of life without a man. Although of a very different tenor to *Tough Love*, and less explicit in terms of its advocacy of behaviour modification, *The Bachelor* also inscribes makeover logics as it seeks to transform single women into wives or at the very least to sanction particular ways of performing single femininity which will facilitate this outcome (either on the show or beyond). That is, as Dubrofsky emphasizes, it does indeed work to *govern* the women in what she calls 'The Bachelor Industry' (2005), so the process of judging single women's behaviour that is so blatantly enacted in *Tough Love* also underwrites this programme. The first series of *The Bachelor* aired in the United States in 2002; and given that a 15th series aired in early 2011, audience investment in the programme does not appear to be waning.

Produced by the ABC, prior to filming 25 women are chosen to meet that season's Bachelor. In pitting these women against each other, *The Bachelor* is predicated on the notion that men are at a premium and drastic measures must be taken to secure one. As host Chris Harrison tells viewers in the series' premiere: 'Twenty five women trying to prove they're the One.' This idea of surplus single women is embedded in the show's very structure and is most blatantly enacted via the 'rose ceremonies' or what have been called 'ritualised expulsion ceremonies' (Kavka, 2008, p. 124). As part of this ritual, the Bachelor gives the women he wishes to stay on a long-stemmed red rose, which they can choose to accept or refuse (rarely of course is this 'gift' rejected). An explicitly staged part of the programme, the ceremony is constructed to mirror a marriage proposal (McClanahan, 2007), thereby foregrounding the show's teleological outcome. There is seldom a question of whether any of the 25 beauties want the man for whom they are competing[7]; it is their desirability, not his, that is being called into question and indeed 'tested' in each instalment of the programme. Narratively, *The Bachelor* is 'about failed love' (Dubrofsky, 2009, p. 355) and, most importantly here, is about the 24 single women who thus come to be deemed failures. The Bachelor always 'wins' – unless he decides *not* to choose any of the available women, as was the case with Brad Womack whose refusal in Season 11 to propose to the two finalists caused outrage among fans; given a second chance, he was the featured bachelor in Season 15.[8]

To say that *The Bachelor* works to buttress the heterosexual imaginary is perhaps stating the obvious (McClanahan, 2007); however, that such a programme, based on fairly retrograde assumptions about gender, emerged during a time of comparative gender equality is in itself remarkable. Opposition to the sexism of the show's very premise – that women are so desperate to find 'the One' that they will compete with each other; willingly place themselves and their daily lives (at least during the course of the competition) under 'comprehensive surveillance' (Andrejevic, 2004, p. 64); consent to a deprivation of civil liberties and their own effective imprisonment in the programme's house (albeit a mansion); and participate in what is effectively a polyamorous relationship – would have undoubtedly been fierce during feminism's second-wave. What makes it possible, or at least harder to critique, are attendant arguments about women's agency in the process alongside the idea that heterosexuality, and institutionalized partnerships through marriage, can now be freely embraced by agentic women as an ostensibly postfeminist choice. More than just a glorification or valorization of heteronormative romantic relationships however, *The Bachelor* works in a number of intersecting ways to 'regulate women's behaviour' (Dubrofsky, 2005, p. 119), and I argue it is in this sense (as well as how it intervenes to remedy women's lack of a man) that it can also be seen as a form of 'life intervention' television.

In recognition of its deeply troublesome gender politics, reality television has been dubbed 'the ground zero of enlightened sexism' (Douglas, 2010, p. 189), and programmes like *The Bachelor* suggest that such claims are not hyperbolic.[9] In terms of gender, the series reinscribes the masculine/feminine binary, especially in assumptions about men as active agents and women as passive objects. It is clearly, as Caryn James has suggested, 'an exercise in nostalgia': 'And like all nostalgia, it speaks to the longing for an idealized past. We're in an age where sexual roles are fluid, and 'The Bachelor' offers an escape from ambiguity, a temporary and knowingly false return to an era in which male and female roles were clear – stereotypical but clear' (in Stephens, 2004, p. 207). *The Bachelor* may seek to embrace prefeminist figurations of gender but, in its reclamation of romance and celebration of heterosexuality by seemingly independent women, it is quintessentially postfeminist.

To continue to be constituted 'eligible', the women are shown to draw upon various forms of capital – especially corporeal – to render themselves, in the eyes of the coveted Bachelor, rose-worthy. Moreover, through the mise-en-scene, audience sympathies are directed in a particular fashion, towards certain types of women. Over eight weeks, contestants live in a mansion, dress up in evening wear, are ferried around in limousines, and go on a number of fantasy-style dates (either as part of a group or the coveted 'one on one' dates). For one 'lucky' woman, the so-called prize bestowed during the series' finale is not just the Bachelor but, and perhaps even more importantly in these narratives, the ultimate public symbol of the defiance of singleness: the engagement ring. Given the pervasiveness of the 'matrimonial fetish', for women especially such rings (particularly wedding rings) are 'still the primary indispensable symbol of external validation' (Geller, 2001, pp. 11–12). During the season finale, the Bachelor has two spectacular diamond rings, one for each of the finalists, and the rings are fetishized throughout the episode as he routinely gazes at them while discussing his (often fluctuating) feelings in regard to each of the remaining women.

In the field of reality television, 'media imagery can offer pseudo communities of ordinary people temporarily bonding in competition' (Biressi & Nunn, 2005, p. 107); however, there is nothing 'ordinary' about the women in *The Bachelor* mansion. As Dubrofsky underscores, most of the women in the competition have the appearance of 'starlets', and not only must they be of a particular size and weight 'as a precondition to access the competition to win a husband', they must be willing to place their bodies on display in certain ways (2005, pp. 128–9). The women are all conventionally attractive, exhibiting a normative femininity, and the majority are in their 20s. Female participants are overwhelmingly white, with perhaps one African American or Asian woman per season who is often eliminated early in the competition. Moreover, the show's troublesome racial politics also manifest in the way it is based upon a Westernized appropriation of a harem (Dubrofsky, 2006).

Hierarchizing the single woman

Here, drawing upon Rachel Dubrofsky's extensive feminist scholarship on *The Bachelor* and looking at *The Bachelor 12: London Calling* and *The Bachelor 14: On the Wings of Love*, I consider a number of ways in which the women are positioned as incapable of being made over from single to married (or at least affianced). Much of the debate staged around reality television invokes the question of 'authenticity' and, in terms of relationship television, it is the apparent authenticity of participants' emotions upon which the programmes pivot. The refrain of 'being in this for the right reasons', which signifies genuineness, surfaces throughout (Cloud, 2010). Being able to convince the Bachelor of their deep desire to be married is central to their ability to remain on the show and to be seen as a viable fiancé. In *The Bachelor*, there appear to be a number of ways in which these single women come to be judged, by other women and by the Bachelor himself. The first of these relates to particular gendered performances of affect – or its lack. That is, excessive emotionality *or* a failure to adequately express one's emotions both become constituted as forms of behaviour that are to be commented on and regulated in various ways (Dubrofsky, 2005, 2006, 2007, 2009). The 'narrative in the series is built around how well or poorly participants confess themselves under surveillance' (Dubrofsky, 2007, p. 272). While there is an obvious disciplinarian in *Tough Love*, in *The Bachelor* threat of elimination acts with the same purpose as does the camera. They come to be evaluated, not just by the Bachelor and their competitors, but by the viewers who witness their interaction with each other and how they conduct themselves beyond his gaze. On *The Bachelor*, certain behaviours are sanctioned or rewarded over others, representing a key way in which these participants are disciplined; these single women thus 'police' themselves (as well as each other) and adhere to certain 'successful practices' and technologies of the self to receive this reward, including through adequate confessional practices (Dubrofsky, 2005, p. 45). In doing so, it works to transform the women in ways that are similar, if less blatant, than *Tough Love*.

To signal these moments of excessive affect, Dubrofsky appropriates the idea of the 'money shot' from pornography. As she notes, the 'problem' is not with the women displaying emotion – indeed the programmes rely on this – but when this emotion is seen to be excessive and out of the contestant's control (2009, p. 356). The women are shown to be deeply affectively invested in the process, but in these moments the implication is that it is *too* much. As a strategy for becoming visible within the narrative and to the Bachelor, however, this is dangerous as it more often than not leads to their expulsion, as Dubrofsky emphasizes

(2009, p. 357). There is, of course, a complex production apparatus that ensures such ruptures come to be centre stage. As Aslama and Pantti argue, these programmes are edited in such a way as to 'foreground moments in which self-control is lost' and how feelings are either 'managed' or 'unmanaged' is central to reality television (2006, p. 179). Such moments of mismanagement provide the melodrama upon which relationship television thrives; like Alex Forrester, the single woman who appears to be *too* heavily invested evokes profound anxiety and must be controlled. In the case of *The Bachelor*, her removal from the house, and thus her opportunity to become unsingle, is her particular punishment.

These moments of excessive affect represent one of the programme's key methodologies not only for constituting single women as aberrant but for simulating a hierarchy of single women; that is, as in the other instances of postfeminist media culture to which I have turned my attention, some types of single women are permitted while others are, in this instance quite literally, expelled. As Dubrofsky argues, like in melodrama, 'In *The Bachelor*, the "good" women vs. "bad" women dynamic is key' (2009, p. 359) and this goodness or badness is tied to particular performances of affect that are either sanctioned within the narrative or rendered inadequate or inappropriate. At all times in *The Bachelor*, women are expected to be in control of their self-presentation but too much control means that these women are not displaying enough of their 'real' selves (Dubrofsky, 2009, p. 360).

The women must be explicit about their feelings or face the consequences. But, the Bachelor attempts to convince each woman 'that she could still be "the one"' ... Thus, women's role is that of supplicant, waiting passively for the redemption of romance' (Cloud, 2010, p. 420). In series 12, as early as the second episode, as is common, many of the women profess their growing feelings for the Bachelor (12.2): 'Matt and I have a really great connection' (Robin, to camera) and 'You can't feel how my heart beats when I'm around you' (Marshana, to Matt); and 'I don't feel like this for anyone' (Shayne, to another woman). These examples reveal how these confessions occur to a number of addressees – to camera, thereby the audience; to the Bachelor; and to other competitors. In terms of the discursive construction of single women, these moments operate as a way of naturalizing and normalizing single women's intense desire to be *otherwise*. On the hierarchy of women singles constructed within this narrative, these effusive women feature at its peak. Women are punished for failing to perform this 'compulsory confession of [their] feelings' (Cloud, 2010, p. 424) or indeed compulsory vulnerability, while those who do are rewarded. Rhetoric about women being guarded and 'putting up walls' is commonly deployed both by *The Bachelor* and by the women about themselves: 'I don't think I got a rose tonight because I have a hard time opening up, it's a big problem for me, being able to open up, taking down that wall' (Kristine, 12.3). Unlike the other women, she felt unable to be 'upfront' with the Bachelor about the depth of her feelings for him, thereby failing to secure her place in the house (and, by implication, the Bachelor's heart). In her analysis, she did not receive a rose – and thus departs the mansion still single – because of her 'big problem'. She recognizes her flaw but has not engaged in self-transformation; that is, she has not made herself over into the kind of single celebrated within the series. In this way, she is seen to be diverging from the type of normative femininity upon which the Bachelor fantasy is predicated and therefore her eligibility – to be on the show and to be a successful wife – is compromised.

On their home town dates (where the Bachelor meets finalists' parents and friends), both Chelsea (12.3) and Noelle, two of the four finalists on Season 12, exhibit a consciousness that their emotional reservation may jeopardize their chances of success: 'I really need to work on opening up on this date. It's very important that I just let down all the guards and just be me' (Noelle, 12.5). Matt also positions Noelle's fate in her own hands: 'She just needs to show me her true colours and she could be a serious contender' (of Noelle, 12.5). After she is eliminated she tells him, 'I take the blame for not opening up sooner' (12.6). In her exit interview in the limousine she continues this theme of accepting responsibility for her expulsion; there is something wrong with her, not just in this instance, but with other men: 'It's not the first time that having walls up has gotten me here, happens a lot … I have a hard time letting people in. I'm terrified, all my life, that's what I do, I don't let people in, I don't let guys in' (Noelle, 12.6) Here, she participates in her own evaluation and pathologization.

Given assumptions about women's innate emotional literacy that I will explore further in the next chapter, these women are seen to embody a form of deficient femininity which will (and does on this show) function as an impediment to winning their man. To be constituted an eligible single, 'she has to be willing to open up to a man in a manner that suggests she is not, in fact, in a harem, under surveillance or in a constructed environment' (Dubrofsky, 2005, p. 239). Like in *Tough Love*, such women are positioned as responsible for their singleness; these emotionally reserved women, the narrative implies, need to amend their behaviour or risk remaining alone. In contrast, ironically but perhaps unsurprisingly, the actress, Shayne, seems adept at the kind of 'authentic' self-presentation which is valued on *The Bachelor* and through which she effectively communicates her desire for marriage. Confessing on the penultimate episode in Barbados that she is falling in love with Matt, she revels in the fact that she has opened herself up: 'I put myself out there for a man first, and I couldn't be happier' (12.7). For this performance of affect, in the finale she receives the ultimate reward: the proposal. Another form of judgement to which the women are subjected revolves around the performance of sexuality; through its punishment of overtly sexual contestants, the narrative warns other singles how *not* to behave.

Sexual excess; or why bad girls finish last

While emotionally 'holding back' is coded as undesirable, and indeed unfeminine, sexually 'holding back' (to a degree) is expected. Sexual excess is also punished, at least once, in each season. In Season 14 there was a scandal when it was revealed that one of the women, Rozlyn, had been 'intimate' with a *Bachelor* staff member, who was consequently fired. Overwhelmingly, it was her disingenuousness that was seen to be her transgression – her actions were seen as proof that she was an illegitimate potential partner (at least within *The Bachelor* narrative); she was deemed unworthy of the Bachelor's attention/affection and the show's host tells her she is being removed (14.2). In another incidence of apparent sexual impropriety, in the first episode of season 12, one woman – Stacey – is drunk, slurs her words and swears, rubs the Bachelor's leg, and places her underwear in his pocket. The programme includes interviews with the other women who judge her behaviour: 'I don't want to say anything negative, but Stacey's a bitch ... She's loud, tacky, tasteless' (Marshana). Another woman pronounces her a 'whore', suggesting that 'twenty-four other women here think so' (Erin H.). In this way, '*The Bachelor* recruits women into the job of governing the bad behaviour of other women' (Dubrofsky, 2009, p. 366). And indeed, the way the other women are shown to react to Stacey suggests that such governance is a task they take very seriously. Unsurprisingly, Stacey is not granted a rose. As in the case of Arian in *Tough Love*, such abject or 'unruly femininities' are positioned against other idealized forms of femininity, with the former being seen as beyond the bounds of what is acceptable and that which must be cast off (Ringrose & Walkerdine, 2008, p. 233). In *The Bachelor*, this quite literally occurs through banishment from its constructed universe. For some critics the presence of such an 'unruly woman', and the comic effects her performance generates, is subversive and indicative of the show's carnivalesque elements (Gray, 2004, p. 270). While perhaps some viewers may read it this way, it is also clear that on *The Bachelor* the so-called 'good girl' wins by exhibiting 'moral superiority' over the other women on offer (Johnston, 2006, p. 124).

Later in the season, in a 'one on one' conversation with Kelly, the Bachelor seeks reassurance from her that she is interested in him; the episode then cuts to her monologue to camera, where she notes that she is not the type of woman to desperately say 'like please pick me, Matt' (12.4). But this is precisely what the women are supposed to do to remain in the game. The next shot returns to Matt and Kelly, when suddenly she opens the front of her dress to reveal her breasts; she almost falls off the chair, suggesting she may be drunk. Predictably, in the rose ceremony almost immediately after Kelly fails to receive a rose. The women in the programme are expected to be sexy, but not to excess as in such moments of overt sexual display. That is, within the show, there are significant 'prohibitions on women's sexual agency' (Cloud, 2010, p. 421). So, while postfeminism presumes women are active sexual agents, in the way it positions women like Kelly *The Bachelor* reveals that certain kinds of performances remain subject to value-judgement and moralizing, something we also saw at work in *Tough Love*. It seems that girls can 'go wild' (the title of another American reality television programme) but potential wives (or perhaps, more appropriately, fiancés) may not. Furthermore, the women are expected to appear sexy but not to practice their sexuality in ways that demonstrate any control: 'Looking the part of the *femme fatale* is expected; *acting* the part will earn them the scarlet letter' (Pozner, 2010, p. 258, original emphasis), and most definitely not a rose. One of the other key ways the women (though not necessarily the Bachelor) judge each other, and via which this hierarchy of single women is established, is through their attitude to competition.

Singleness and competition

In terms of competition, the entire premise of programmes such as *The Bachelor*, *The Farmer Wants a Wife*, *Age of Love*, or *Joe Millionaire* is that the women have voluntarily enlisted in a 'battle' for highly coveted and limited spoils: an eligible single man.[10] Naturally, competition between women is shown to intensify as the show progresses and the roses on offer become fewer, enabling the trope of the 'cat-fight' to be mobilized. Media interest in – and indeed manufacture of – cat-fights between women provides both the sense of conflict and melodrama upon which the media industries commonly rely (Douglas, 1994). Moreover, the prurience signalled by such potential cat-fights also helps attract and secure audiences. That said, there is yet an expectation that this element of competition be masked somewhat, and participants exhibit contempt for overt competitiveness and manipulation by other women in the house. In one episode of *The Bachelor 12*, a woman having much coveted 'one on one' time with the Bachelor is interrupted by one of her competitors, Robin, who 'steals him' from her. This leads to a heated group discussion in the house about the ethics of such behaviour. Robin, to camera, explicitly addresses the question of competition, reflecting on the rest of the women's aggravation that she had 'stolen' Matt from another contestant: 'This whole idea that we're not going to take Matt from each other – are you serious?' (12.3). All the other women are shown to harshly judge Robin for her overtly competitive stance, and she is warned she 'may get slapped in the face doing it' (Chelsea, 12.3). While eradicating singleness may be figured as (women's) work, the contestants' labour (including competing), as in much reality television, is expected to be invisible (Andrejevic, 2004).

As they make clear, invoking the authentic/contrived opposition, contestants want the Bachelor to recognize when the other women are being disingenuous; that is, when they are *performing* or 'playing the game' (as opposed to being their 'real' selves). On *The Bachelor 14* conflict between the two obvious front-runners, Ali and Vienna, intensifies as the series progresses (see 14.5). Each of them expresses the hope that Jake, the season's Bachelor, will 'see through' the other. Such conflict and cattiness has been naturalized as 'what girls do', including on *The Bachelor* itself. As Amanda predicts, 'One man and a bunch of girls, it's definitely going to get ugly' (12.1). In this vein, on *The Bachelor 12* tension arises between Robin and Chelsea who express diametrically opposed positions on the nature of the competition: 'You can't compete for somebody else's love' (Chelsea), contrasted with Robin's 'It IS a competition – I will fight for what I want' and 'I'm not here to play fair' (12.4). Such dating programmes are, of course, a game and contestants must be strategic, 'navigat[ing] the sexual marketplace as highly calculating and self-enterprising individuals' (Ouellette & Hay, 2008, p. 125). But such strategizing must be masked as part of establishing genuineness, for both the Bachelor and the other women if not for the viewer.

This element of competition functions to highlight the entire premise of the show: that men are at a premium, requiring women to take drastic action (such as putting themselves under surveillance on a reality television programme) to secure one. As Robin suggests: 'I'm willing to do whatever it takes to get that rose'; a common refrain by at least one woman in each series. On the group tennis date, she is therefore punished with ostracism by the other women and ultimately with elimination from the competition. For these women (and the Bachelor who ultimately rejects her), Robin's 'failure' is that she refuses to hide her desperation – or agency, limited though it may be. But these moments reinforce the show's premise: that the single woman is desperate and will go to extreme lengths to be otherwise. On *The Women Tell All* special, where all the contestants self-reflexively analyze their own performance and especially its ethics, in a discussion about her views on *The Bachelor* as a form of competition, the other women judge Robin for not having 'the right intentions … we thought she was there to win and not for Matt' (Amanda). Exhibiting this desire to win in a competition of this nature is seen to exist in conflict with a genuine desire for love and to undermine its authenticity, provoking a strong reaction from the other women seeking to uphold this patriarchal fantasy. The final expectation placed on single women in this narrative is that they must be prepared to relinquish their own life for the fuller one apparently promised by connubiality.

Articulating the postfeminist dilemma; the case of Ali

One of the other ways single women can effectively disqualify themselves from the competition is by a failure to prioritize love over career and, indeed, so deeply normalized/naturalized has this sacrificial gesture been that there has only been one instance of this in the show's history – in 2010's season 14. Rarely, if ever, do the women on *The Bachelor* discuss their professional lives, though it is presumed they have one (especially as when they speak, text appears with their age, their home town, and their occupation). Indeed, from the programme's editing, the most important thing for these women is finding a husband (and this particular husband). It seems, not that they are 'negotiating' the apparent tensions between life as independent professionals alongside their desire for a functional heteronormative relationship, but that the latter is prioritized to such an extent as to render the former entirely invisible. While fictionalized postfeminist singletons may want to 'have it all', the women on relationship television want just one thing: a man. Part of being deemed eligible is reassuring the Bachelor that she will relinquish her own life, giving up her job and home to be with him. On a joint with season 12's offering, Matt, Marshana and Holly are both embarrassingly effusive about their desire to be anywhere he is; Marshana telling him that there is nothing 'keeping her in New York' and Holly, likewise, follows up by emphasizing that she wants to be anywhere he is, even his hometown of London. As Cloud argues, 'the programme resolves in favour of those women who are the most compliant, who seem to achieve their heartfelt ambitions by abnegating their autonomy' (2010, p. 422). Within the Bachelor universe, therefore, agency exercised by women is tacitly condemned – unless it is 'choosing' to do anything to be with the Bachelor.

In Season 14, competition frontrunner, Ali Fedotowsky, made the apparently fraught decision to leave *The Bachelor* mansion for her career, which was under threat due to her absence. She tells Jake: 'I have to choose between staying here or going back to work.' As she leaves, she sobs, 'I hope I made the right choice' (14.6). What happens to Ali becomes a cautionary tale but also represents a very deliberate staging within the programme of the so-called 'postfeminist singleton's' dilemma theorized by Genz (2009, 2010). This incident with Ali is remarkable, especially as it has been argued that – in its 'postfeminist nirvana' – *The Bachelor* does not engage in any meaningful way with the career/family tension: 'Simply put, in the "Bachelor Industry", unlike in other postfeminist texts, women's desires are no longer in competition, but rather, exist together quite amicably' (Dubrofsky, 2005, p. 148).[11] However, I would suggest not that these desires have been thoroughly reconciled (as Dubrofsky suggests) but that there is no tension for these women for the implication is that – through their willingness to participate in a programme of this nature – they have already chosen a man at all costs; this is what makes the foregrounding of Ali's 'dilemma' especially interesting.

Although women can, and sometimes (though rarely), do remove themselves from the competition, Ali's exercise of agency is noteworthy given she explicitly – and very publicly – chooses career over potential husband. Ali melodramatically confesses to the Bachelor: 'I didn't know that I would fall in love and I'd have to choose between a guy I love and a job I love ... It's like the two loves of my life I feel like I have to choose between.' She tells Jake prior to the rose ceremony: 'I came into this with everything I wanted in life except for you and there's a chance I could leave it with nothing.' Weeks after her departure from the show, she is seen to be begging Jake to take her back, telling him she had made a horrible mistake; that is, with temporal distance from the programme she constructs an alternative narrative. By making the decision to leave to return to work, Ali merely shows that she was not the 'right woman' for Jake as she put herself (via her career) ahead of her man.[12] Ali rendered visible a choice that *The Bachelor* frame had obscured. This aporia offers an alternative possibility in the supposed ubiquitous postfeminist career/love dilemma; women can, and do, prioritize career and thereby their autonomous subjectivities in ways that such programmes usually work to obscure. On *The Women Tell All* special, when questioned if she would make the same decision, Ali partially accedes to the host's clear desire for an affective performance of regret but her response is also a cautious one. She notes that if she knew then what she knows now she may have made a different decision. She adds, however, 'but I would fight like hell to get my job back'. In this way, she refuses to entirely reinscribe the privileging of heterosexual romance at all costs as well as challenging the show's efforts to regulate her gendered behaviour as a single.[13]

Conclusion

Makeover and 'life intervention' programmes like those analyzed here clearly exhibit what Weber calls 'ideological opportunism' in the way they use feminist-informed rhetoric while also being in many ways hostile towards feminist practices (2009, p. 26). In this way, however, they are consonant with broader postfeminist logics and its complex process of 'double entanglement' (McRobbie, 2009) that I have show to be in operation throughout. As an exemplification of the postfeminist single woman, deeply invested in the (re)embrace of heterosexual romance mythologies, participants on relationship reality television programmes are regulated, and in some cases made over, in very specific ways. In *Tough Love*, this regulation is explicit, through – for example – the presenter's literal adoption of the role of disciplinarian. Not only does he seek to regulate the women's behaviour through privileging certain ways of acting over others in his faux 'therapy' sessions, he deploys technologies that physically punish them (such as 'The Zapper') in an effort to help eradicate their singleness. Should they unlearn their 'bad' behaviour as single women, they will enjoy the ultimate reward: a man. Likewise, in *The Bachelor*, certain ways of being are shown to be rewarded, initially with a rose and, for one of the women, ultimately with an engagement ring. On *The Bachelor*, women are instructed through watching other women being punished (i.e. expelled from the house) for what comes to constitute inappropriate behaviour; the most obvious of which includes being affectively excessive or, conversely, not being emotionally open at all, or being too sexually available. Similarly, in *The Farmer Wants a Wife*, the single women are required to exhibit, not only their intense desire to be partnered, but a willingness to relinquish their own lives, including their careers, for married farm life.

In their heteronormativity and the promotion of its ultimate manifestation, marriage, as well naturalizing the desire for a family, such programmes can be seen to in part do the work of the State, an argument

Ouellette and Hay (2008a, 2008b) have made about how reality makeover television functions in a neoliberal political climate. In this way, while there is little to suggest shows like *The Bachelor* have 'an explicit agenda of promulgating marriage for an overt political motive, it is interesting that the show corresponds to a larger governmental push to encourage marriage' (Stephens, 2004, p. 199). That is, the work of promoting institutionalized heterosexuality can be seen to have, at least in part, been taken over by relationship reality television; a genre which further suggests the nexus between postfeminism and neoliberalism. As I have made clear throughout, the celebration of women's active investment in heterosexuality and romance is central to the logics of postfeminism, and these texts certainly perform this promotion. These shows also buttress Ingraham's (1999) and McRobbie's arguments (2009), discussed here in Chapter 1, regarding the new forms of symbolic labour continually required to shore up the heterosexual imaginary.

In conclusion, it is important to pose a series of questions around audience investment in these narratives and the cultural work they do in regards to the pathologization of single women: what appeals to the audience in such narratives? Is there a degree of schadenfreude here, where those safely ensconced in a couple can revel gleefully in the trials, especially in *Tough Love*, of their as yet single sisters? As Cloud puts it, 'How can we explain such investment of millions of viewers in the outcome of what is a transparently staged and gender-disciplining process?' (2010, p. 414). Further analysis of textual sites such as fan discussion boards could, at least partially, provide answers to such questions.[14] But far from being isolated instances, this ideologically suspect work of 'making over' the single woman, through either changes in interiority or through providing her with a man (or indeed both), is also visible in the self-help manuals examined in the following chapter. However, in addition, there is also important symbolic work being done in self-help manuals to recode women's singleness in ways that contradict prevalent narratives of pathology.

5
Self-Help and the Single Girl: From Salvation to Validation

Introduction

In line with the previous chapter, my focus here is on how another set of popular texts seek to transform and regulate – in often conflicting ways and for different ideological purposes – the single woman. Here I consider a number of self-help and conduct style manuals directed towards single women produced in the 1990s and 2000s. This subgenre of self-help writing, corresponding with increased numbers of singles, appears to have experienced a boom over this period. Self-help can lead readers, as Micki McGee argues, 'into a cycle where the self is not improved but endlessly belaboured' (2005, p. 12). This chapter asks if such manuals simply promote such labour on the single self as a means to secure the other; that is, it examines the degree to which they participate in constituting the single woman as a problem (either individual or social) that needs to be remedied. If self-help's purpose is apparent self-correction, as a number of critics have emphasized (Kaminer, 1992; Rimke, 2000; McGee, 2005), what is it about the single woman that needs 'fixing'? Within these therapeutic discourses, what kinds of single selves are considered 'healthy', or indeed 'unhealthy' (Hazleden, 2003)? That is, what type of (postfeminist) selfhood is permissible for the single woman? What kinds of behaviours require modification, how and why? Through their prescriptions, such texts seek to bring into being particular gendered single subjects and it is the discursive processes, and the politics underpinning them, through which this is achieved that concern me. However, rather than simply acting as a form of governmentality, seeking to discipline citizens, as many have argued (following Foucault) is self-help's *raison detre* (Rose, 1996; Rimke, 2000), I suggest there is something much more complicated being staged. This includes – in some instances – an attempt to refigure and revalue women's singleness. Moreover, a number of these manuals reveal how postfeminism works to shape the public stories in circulation around women's singleness, stories which help delimit how it is possible to *be* (or, in some cases, *not* be) a single woman in the contemporary West.

Exemplifying the meta-commentary that regularly characterizes the voice of self-help books in general, in *If I'm So Wonderful, Why Am I Still Single?* Susan Page identifies a polarity in these publications: 'Most books and articles directed at singles tell you either that there is something wrong with you for wanting a relationship and that you ought to be basking in the joys of singlehood, or that there is some pathological reason why you are still single' (2003, p. 34). However, while there are indeed many textual examples that adhere to both these extremes, there are also self-help narratives that fall in between these two poles. Accordingly, in sketching out a taxonomy of this genre, this chapter demonstrates that modern self-help books and advice manuals written for single women operate along a broad spectrum. This stretches from those that conceptualize singleness for women as a complete aberration that must be remedied at any cost, through to those that genuinely celebrate all the pleasures and benefits of living without a significant male other (for such books are invariably addressed to heterosexual women). Given they are the most high profile, I begin with a longer analysis of the most extreme in terms of how they attempt to 'cure' single women, and move through to (perhaps lesser known) texts which contest dominant ways of figuring singleness. These variations within the genre draw on precisely the contradictory, competing discourses around women's singleness identified in previous chapters.

To summarize, there appear to be at least four (at times overlapping) categories of self-help books for single women: single women need to be taught, at all costs, how to become unsingle; single women will not find a partner until they turn their gazes inward and work on themselves; single women need to personally challenge the denigration of singleness to feel empowered; and the 'Single Girl' should celebrate her singleness, including through various practices of consumption. In the following analysis, I ask if all these singles' self-help books necessarily offer what has been called 'an archetypal narrative of female experience as disease' (Schrager, 1993, p. 188); and correlatively, whether the so-called cure is taken to be the presence of a man or is instead to be found elsewhere (such as within the self). As Lisa Blackman notes of self-help genres, 'the issue of what dilemmas are created, for whom, and how these are resolved and made intelligible is an important part of understanding how popular discourse functions in relation to identities and subjectivities' (2010, p. 22). The single self comes to be seen as a troublesome self in many of these manuals, and self-help is central to both the creation of such dilemmas and the proffering of deeply ideological solutions to them. Accordingly, the following readings centre on the key tropes and metaphors deployed by authors; laying bare the books' assumptions about gender; exploring the forms of subjectivity they constitute as 'legitimate'; how writers work to authorize their accounts; and the degree to which they engage in political and cultural critique (as opposed to simply finding fault with an individual). As 'commercially-based advice givers', the authors of such books 'act as emotional investment counselors' (Hochschild, 1994, p. 2), and it is the varying degrees of investment they recommend in both self and other that can be seen to differentiate them.

Myriad experts now 'make their living out of the single woman' (Dux & Simic, 2008, p. 76): 'These are experts who have a vested interest in promoting and spreading the anxieties they are purporting to diagnose.' They work, as Nikolas Rose (1999) would suggest, to help 'govern the [single woman's] soul'. Although there are different addressees, these books are largely marketed towards thirty-something women who have never been married (a whole other industry, which I do not address here, has been built around divorced and/or widowed readers). These are the women for whom questions around partnership and reproduction are presumed to be central. All of the books analyzed in this chapter are written by women; and although a few are therapists and psychologists, most authors claim personal experience as a single woman as the basis for their authority. Notwithstanding the focus on the individual experience of the authors, Schilling and Fuehrer (1993, p. 419) argue that in self-help writing women are approached as 'an undifferentiated group', with differences in race, class, age, and sexuality elided (though in the manuals considered here the presumption of heterosexuality is clear).

Self-help, feminism, and women

As a form of popular non-fiction, the genre of self-help is undoubtedly one of the most successful (in market terms at least) types of modern writing. The cultural impact of self-help literature in the West simply cannot be overestimated, especially in terms of its mediation of gendered subjectivities. Historically, the genre has been overwhelmingly directed towards, and consumed by, women. As Negra notes, 'When it comes to popular perceptions of gender, perhaps the most voluminous body of contemporary textual material is to be found in the various forms of self-help literature that have driven American publishing over the last twenty years' (2009, p. 136). In terms of self-help books that are what she describes as 'intensively postfeminist', Negra singles out dating conduct literature and the panic-driven literature relating to marriage and reproduction (2009, p. 137). The single woman's self-help manual, though at times fitting into both these categories, offers a more compli-cated picture, as I will show. Indeed, their relationship to feminism helps determine how they 'treat' (in both senses) the single woman and the dissatisfaction that has driven her to purchase such a self-help book.

Self-help books are 'part of an extensive web of psycho-media', includ-ing women's magazines, fiction, and talk shows that all seek to advise women on how life should be lived (Simonds, 1992, p. 133). Such books have been viewed as a core component in a broader 'culture of recovery' and are commonly seen to offer apolitical 'solutions' to what are funda-mentally political problems (such as gender inequality) (Rapping, 1996). However, Eva Illouz argues that it is not enough to insist that the 'thera-peutic lexicon "depoliticizes" problems that are social and collective'. This, she suggests, has resulted in problematic assertions about readerly 'false consciousness' or located forms of therapeutic discourse as part of a broader, modern network of surveillance (2008, p. 19). Such strategies, she argues, have made it difficult for some critics to grasp why women and the so-called 'new middle classes' have 'enthusiastically endorsed the therapeutic discourse' (2008, p. 19). It is important, therefore, to not simply condemn these texts as vehicles for regressive ideologies, bearing strategies women passively imbibe or which they are 'duped' into fol-lowing. As Simonds argues, critics have tended to 'label them [self-help manuals] as politically backward, narrow, and even potentially damaging to the more gullible readers' (1992, p. 174). However, as she puts it, 'the fact remains that these books do appeal, do sell, and do tell a fascinating story about womanhood' (1992, p. 134). Like any textual product, it is impossible to be aware of the cultural and individual uses to which they can be put, and indeed how they can be contested by readers. But the recognition that they may play an important interpretive role in some women's lives need not preclude an analysis of how their assumptions can, at times, position women in ways that are politically troubling from a feminist perspective (Simonds, 1992, p. 140, Rapping, 1996). On the other hand, later in this chapter I demonstrate that an *a priori* condem-nation of the genre as politically reactionary is not possible given the way some authors have appropriated the form to revalue women's sin-gleness in innovative ways. Furthermore, as Illouz argues, the affective work of such texts should also not be downplayed. Self-help books, like other popular narratives, work not just as 'hermeneutic devices helping us to make sense of our world but also as cultural devices that tap into, elicit, and channel complex emotional apparatuses (such as indignation, compassion, longing for love, fear, and anxiety)' (2008, p. 18).

The analysis of these self-help books provides particular kinds of insights into how feminist and anti-feminist (and, more recently, post-feminist) ideologies are disseminated through popular culture (Simonds, 1992, p. 7). They act as important textual spaces for the construction of certain ideologically loaded ways of figuring gender. Such books also work, as Simonds emphasizes, as important frameworks through which readers come to interpret themselves and their relationships (1992, p. 47). Revealing a debt to feminist discourses of women's empower-ment, the rhetoric in these books is overwhelmingly that of gaining control; getting the life one seeks, whether through a man or enjoying singleness. In this way, self-help books can operate as a form of popular feminism (Simonds, 1992, p. 34). However, as is common with popu-lar feminism more generally, critics have emphasized its limitations, especially in how self-help authors advocate micro level shifts by the individual as opposed to broader socio-political change. This privileg-ing of the transformation of the self over that of the social dates back to popular feminists such as Betty Friedan and Helen Gurley Brown (Whelehan, 2005, p. 31); the latter who produced one of the most well-known modern self-help books for single women (see Chapter 2 here). In such texts, Schilling and Fuehrer argue, 'the solutions for individual women's problems lie in their ability to reframe and recreate their own thoughts, behaviours, and relationships, rather than in the restructur-ing of social arrangements' (1993, p. 418; see also Hochschild, 1994). In this way, self-help rhetorics are coterminous with neoliberal discourses of self-governance and self-discipline explored in Chapter 1. As Rimke argues, self-help is 'an individualized voluntary enterprise, an under-taking to alter, reform or transform the self, or some "intrinsic" aspect of it, which is contingent upon a person's seeking some external form of authoritative assistance' (2000, p. 62). If popular culture provides the narratives through which the single woman is regulated (as I have argued it does), then the self-help genre is a key part of this broader disciplinary project and indeed postfeminist neoliberalism.

Of the implied reader of self-help manuals directed towards single women, Cynthia Schrager observes:

> Economically independent, professionally successful, and desper-ately in need of a man, this 'contemporary woman' is what might

be called the tragic heroine of feminism. Self-help books promise to empower her to make healthier relationship choices at a time when, by all accounts, satisfying intimate relationships between the sexes are increasingly imperiled.

(1993, p. 178)

This idea of the miserable single woman being the 'tragic heroine of feminism' informs books such as Whitehead's *Why There Are No Good Men Left* (2002) and Gottlieb's *Marry Him* (2010), discussed here in Chapter 2. In these texts, feminism is accused of 'imperilling' these gendered intimacies. Nonetheless, self-help writing has appropriated feminist discourses in ways that are consonant with the broader cultural logics of postfeminism outlined previously. As Schrager argues of relationship guides, they offer '"solutions" to women's problems that often borrow from the discourse of feminism even as they work against feminism's fundamental tenets' (1993, p. 177). The degree to which self-help literature for single women can be seen to operate in opposition to feminism (or 'work against its fundamental tenets') varies, but the first subgenre I examine – which includes its most well-known examples – exhibits an incredibly hostile relationship to feminist reconceptualizations of gender.

'Saving' the single girl: The rules of surrendering

While they have undoubtedly proliferated over the past few decades, especially in light of the increasing numbers of single women, self-help and conduct advice manuals were marketed towards the woman without a man throughout the twentieth century (and indeed even earlier).[1] In *Bachelor Girl: The Secret History of Single Women*, Betsy Israel sardonically underscores the variety of approaches in the contemporary subgenre of self-help for single women:

Nonexpert advice and guide books for single women could fill a New Age college catalogue – finding soul mates; learning to love yourself first; identifying obstacles and creatively crashing through them; and how to drag him back using every part of your body as an arsenal.

(2002, p. 8)

Although she fails to include those that seek to legitimize singleness, her comments are apposite to the first set of books I consider in this chapter; what I am calling the 'retro' self-help narrative. The books I examine in this section – including Elaine Fein and Cindy Schneider's *The Rules* (1995) and Laura Doyle's *The Surrendered Single* (2002) – are those that presume no woman would ever wish to remain, or enjoy being, without a male significant other; their readers simply need guidance on how to bring about and effectively maintain the relationship they are thought to invariably crave. That women are the gendered subjects who should undertake this 'work' is taken for granted.

In addition to those considered in detail in this section, there are many books on how women can make themselves more attractive to men and thereby avoid spinsterhood; titles such as *Man Magnet: How to be the best woman you can be in order to get the best man* (Miller, 2009), *Make Every Man Want You* (Forleo, 2008), and *Sexy and Confident: How to Be the Dreamgirl Men Want, Have a Better Life and Improve Your Self-esteem* (Green, 2009). As in *Tough Love*, the onus is on women to transform themselves into objects that men will find desirable. There is also a surfeit of books by male authors on how to 'think like a man' which purport to unlock the secrets of the male mind in order to achieve romantic success. In addition to *He's Just Not That Into You* (Bernherdt & Cucillo, 2004), there are titles such as *Every Man Sees You Naked: An Insider's Guide to How Men Think* (Matthews, 2008) and *Men Are Like Fish: What Every Woman Needs to Know about Catching a Man* (Nakomoto, 2002). The fundamental assumption underpinning these publications is that being single is an illegitimate, unhealthy, and 'unnatural' subjectivity for women.

According to these books, then, women who remain single can be seen to perform a type of 'improper womanhood' (Simonds, 1992, p. 7) and thus such publications function as pedagogical narratives demonstrating how to unlearn this so-called un-womanliness. These books, therefore, tap into and help create a panic around being a single woman that I have shown to especially mark the 1990s and 2000s. Although more complicated than simple backlash narratives, the type of subjectivity they advocate for women is in many senses a reaction against feminism, while the type of men they invoke appear to have been damaged by it: they lack the cultural competencies to understand the new women (and their expectations) feminism apparently created (see McMahon, 1999). These texts are often immensely popular in terms of sales and public profile, and their authors are celebritized through these often provocative narratives. They are also undoubtedly some of the most potent in fostering, and normalizing, single women's sense of liminality. As McGee emphasizes, such books routinely work to instill the sense of inadequacy which they purport to remedy. Although readers 'turn to self-improvement literature for inspiration in times of despair, for specific advice on how to conduct their lives, and for assurance in the face of enormous social, political, and economic changes, paradoxically this literature may foster, rather than quell, their anxieties' (McGee, 2005, p. 17). Such texts, she continues, do not merely offer advice; they serve to 'impugn the individual' (2005, p. 18). The individual most commonly so 'impugned' is overwhelmingly the single woman, despite nods here and there to 'emotionally unavailable men'.

Given that the 'literature of self-improvement defines its readers as insufficient' (McGee, 2005, p. 18), it stands to reason that within these texts single women are seen to be lacking and their behaviours targeted as in need of modification. Therefore, such books patently undermine optimistic assertions that singleness has been largely, and irrevocably, refigured as a valid form of feminine subjectivity. Further, they argue that singleness, like any other state from which readers of self-help are taught they can 'recover', is transcendable – with the right book to assist, of course. Perhaps the most well-known modern relationship manual is John Gray's *Men are from Mars, Women are from Venus* (1990); while not specifically written for the single woman, the cultural reverberations of his book are evident in the way it, and its ideological investment in a series of fixed gender binaries, informs a number of texts directed at 'solving' the problem that is the single woman. In this way, books like this reveal a tendency within self-help to view women as 'mutable' and 'correctable' while men's identities are seen to be fixed and unchangeable (Simonds, 1992, p. 224). Thus, as in relationship reality television, it is the single woman's responsibility to change herself if she wishes to change her singleness.

While it is difficult to know the degree to which such books succeed in textually-mediating the actions of single women readers, their immense cultural visibility and the sheer fact that they each sold in the millions more than hints at the perceived value of their strategies.[2] In terms of gender, 'Difference is naturalized and deemed "healthy", making it difficult to dispute or reject claims about its extent or even to see them as mere claims' (Crawford, 2004, p. 69). Through such naturalization, books like Gray's have been seen to entirely depoliticize heterosexual relations (Crawford, 2004, p. 68; Potts, 2002), a gesture replicated by the antecedents considered in this section. Such publications are based on essentialist ideas (and ideals) about femininity and masculinity that feminism has sought to destabilize. All of these authors focus on how to make the single woman otherwise; they take it as axiomatic that their women readers – for books of the same tenor addressed to men are few and far between – feel incomplete without a (male) partner. The assumption underpinning books like *The Rules, The Surrendered Single*, and *He's Just Not That Into You*, as Cristina Nehring points out (2002), 'is that its audience is not pleasure-seeking but desperate; not confident, adventuresome, and looking for tips on how to have a good time, but frightened and looking for hints on how to avoid disaster – how to avoid further time as a single girl'. Next, I consider these publications in detail to identify some discursive, rhetorical, and most significantly, ideological commonalities.

Essentialism and accepting 'natural' gender difference

Elaine Fein and Cynthia Schneider's *The Rules: Time Tested Secrets for Capturing the Heart of Mr Right*, originally published in 1995, reportedly sold two million copies and was translated into 27 languages (Whitehead, 2003, p. 171). Despite pockets of public opprobrium, 'Its appeal was impossible to ignore, or to wave off as a mere backlash. Too many smart women were intrigued by its promise of success in finding a husband' (Whitehead, 2003, p. 172). Whitehead argues that *The Rules* was the first book to recognize that educated, so-called 'new single women' were a key market segment in terms of dating advice (2003, p. 172). Since its appearance, this market – as the evolving subgenres suggest – has continued to grow and prove incredibly lucrative for publishers. The enduring market appeal of Fein and Schneider's approach is also evident in the appearance of various follow-up books: *The Rules II: More Rules to Live and Love By* (1997), *The Rules for Marriage: Time Tested Secrets for Making Your Marriage Work* (2002), and, in an acknowledgement of how new technologies are mediating intimacy, *The Rules for Online Dating: Capturing the Heart of Mr Right in Cyberspace* (2002).

In keeping with the valorization of heterosexual coupledom and romance that marks postfeminist media culture, Fein and Schneider position this search at the centre of women's lives. While *The Rules* has been described as a 'man-hunting manifesto' (Salerno, 2005, p. 169), such a description is not entirely accurate as hunting implies an agency which the book's authors deplore. The authors of *The Rules*, however, are brazenly confident of their formulaic approach. In total, there are 35 rules to which women must strictly adhere: 'The purpose of *The Rules* is to make Mr Right obsessed with having you as his by making yourself seem unattainable. In plain language, we're talking about playing hard to get! Follow *The Rules*, and he will not just marry you, but feel crazy about you, forever!' (Fein & Schneider, 1995, p.8) Invoking Gray, Fein and Schneider entreat women to recognize:

> *Men are different from women.* Women who call men, ask them out, conveniently have two tickets to a show, or who offer sex on a first

date destroy male ambition and animal drive. Men are born to respond to challenge. Take away challenge and their interest wanes. That, in a nutshell, is the principle of *The Rules*.

(pp. 9–10, original emphasis)

Deploying pseudo-scientific rhetoric and biologically reductionist assumptions about gender, they note: 'In a relationship, the man must take charge. He must propose. We're not making this up – biologically, he's the aggressor' (12). Their approach, they argue, is scientifically proven, not just 'made up', and therefore epistemologically legitimate. In making such claims, they seek to disavow the inherently limited (and limiting) politics on which such 'rules' are predicated. A series of orchestrated gendered behaviours are advocated on the basis of these biological 'facts' while, conversely, other forms of agency, like approaching a man, initiating a conversation, or the greatest sin, asking for sex, are not only 'unnatural' (and therefore unfeminine) but are seen as the impediments to finding, securing, and keeping 'the One' firmly within your grasp.

Essentialism is also central to Laura Doyle's *The Surrendered Single*, which argues that women who approach and pursue men necessarily drive them away. Accordingly, she offers a guide on how relinquishing control will lead the reader's soul-mate right to her. Such women need to become more 'feminine' – code, in Doyle's retro narrative, for passive. She addresses her audience as those single women who had read her earlier book, *The Surrendered Wife* (2001), and wondered how they could find a husband to whom they too could surrender: 'These women, like me, recognized their tendencies to dominate and manipulate, and they identified with my message: Control is the enemy of intimacy' (16). The single woman finds herself in this position because she has attempted to exercise a form of control that is simply, and profoundly, at odds with her gender. Her singleness is, then, her own fault. We can see echoes of this rhetoric in *Tough Love*, which also places the responsibility for women's singleness (as well as the personal transformation that would alter it) firmly at their own feet. For Doyle, a woman's 'feminine side' is 'soft, tender, vulnerable, and receptive', which she sees as 'undeniable feminine qualities' (17). The key, therefore, to remedying this situation is to rediscover this naturally 'feminine' way of being. In her 'Men will never be good women' section, it is clear Doyle relies upon the incommensurability of the sexes on which Gray's internationally successful work also pivots: 'It's easy to forget that men come from a different culture. In the male culture, talking about feelings is not a common or comfortable practice ... Think of the male culture the way you would any foreign culture – not bad, just different' (53).

According to *The Surrendered Single*, the best way to manage this incommensurability is simply to relinquish all control. Mobilizing an ostensibly pro-woman discourse, Doyle argues: 'Since femininity is what men are fundamentally drawn to, those are the qualities that will attract a man who's right for you. Surrendering means acknowledging that you are a woman, with a feminine mind, body, and spirit' (17–8). Men, she suggests, are attracted to vulnerable women (itself seen as an essentially feminine trait) and so the single woman's primary project should be to become such a subject. 'Surrendering', she argues, allows a woman to 'become the best version of herself' (32), which will lead to the best version of life: a partnered one. She offers up surrendering as a form of subjectivity; by adopting the subject position of 'surrendered single', readers will effectively be positioning themselves in ways that will ensure they get their man – and, most importantly, their husband. The direct control that women are implored to exercise is over the self not the other. In this way, texts such as *The Surrendered Single* are consistent with the broader logics of self-help discourse that presume self-governance leads to empowerment (Rimke, 2000). Correlatively, through this exercise of *self*-control, a woman will – if indirectly – be able to manipulate the behaviour of the man she covets.

The paradox of performing an essential feminine self

While the idea of femininity as masquerade dates back at least to Joan Riviere's work (1929), and the notion of gendered performativity has been developed by Judith Butler (1990), in *The Rules* such assumptions are oddly coupled with essentialist ideas about femininity. If passivity is a fundamentally feminine trait, as its authors (and indeed Doyle) assume, why does so much energy need to be expended and labour undertaken to perform this ostensibly natural feminine self? This is the inherent paradox of the culture of self-help. As Simonds argues, 'this contradiction between a makeable self and an innate one' recurs through-out self-help writing and has particular implications for women (1996, p. 16). In its emphasis on performing a natural femininity, *The Rules* embodies the deeply ideological inconsistency critiqued by Simonds. *The Rules*, as its authors make explicit, is all about performance – '*You act as if!*' (25, original emphasis); as if you're fabulous and oozing with self-confidence; as if you have so many other options; as if you are quiet and lack opinion; as you are 'feminine', demure, malleable etc. Readers are urged to, in true performative style, bring themselves into being as subjects within *The Rules'* discursive framework. For more circumspect readers who may be concerned about this masquerade and its ethics, the authors advise that eventually – once the man has been secured – readers can gradually reveal aspects of their 'real' personality. In contrast, such a self must be strategically hidden until readers have achieved their goal: commitment, preferably culminating in an engagement ring. Similarly, in Doyle's narrative, the ultimate goal of marriage remains unquestioned; even co-habitation is frowned upon, seen as detrimental to readers' chances of metamorphosing from a surrendered single to a surrendered wife (267–75).

As a single, the *Rules'* girl invests all her time and energy in becoming *otherwise*. As is common, the undesirability of singleness is a taken-for-granted assumption that underpins the text. The Rules codified in the book are anachronistic and arbitrary, however (Salerno, 2005, p. 169). As Wendy Kaminer argues in *I'm Dysfunctional, You're Dysfunctional*, 'The self-help tradition has always been covertly authoritarian and conformist, relying as it does on a mystique of expertise, encouraging people to look outside themselves for standardized instructions on how to be' (1992, p. 6). In addition to outlining the 35, to greater or less degree, reactionary rules, the book consists of warnings about what has happened to various women who have failed to religiously follow *The Rules* and have misguidedly approached men in whom they were interested or foolishly 'given up' sex too early. The consequences for such women are exposed as dire: their boyfriends broke up with them or their dates were never heard from again. Fein and Schneider regularly commence these cautionary tales with 'Our friend Marcy' or 'Our good friend, Candy' etc. These 'everywoman' figures (if of the Stepford variety) are invoked throughout to help legitimize the authors' advice. Such storytelling within the self-help manual, whether the stories are 'based on the lives of patients in an author's psychotherapeutic practice, interviewees or the author's own life', tend 'to be either exemplary or cautionary' (Hochschild, 1994, p. 4). Arlie Hochschild continues: 'Stories contain magnified moments, episodes of heightened importance, either epiphanies, moments of intense glee or unusual insight, or moments in which things go intensely but meaningfully wrong.'

The Rules routinely employs both these types of stories, narrating alternately moments of triumph and utter despair in lonely women's lives. In the case of the latter, the authors assert that readers break the rules at their own peril:

> When you break *The Rules*, you automatically take away the pleasure men get from pursuing you, and they end up resenting you for it.

Then they treat you badly and you're left wondering if it was something you said, did, didn't say, or didn't do that caused the problem.
The answer is simple: you broke *The Rules*.

(139)

Here, as throughout, the reader's sense of personal responsibility is
invoked; the self-determining neo-liberal self has the capacity to control
her (and, through this textually-sanctioned manipulation, his) destiny.
To illustrate the efficacy of Rule #2: 'Don't talk to a man first', the
authors warn of the consequences of breaking it:

> Our dentist friend Pam initiated a friendship with Robert when they
> met in dental school several years ago by asking him out to lunch.
> *She spoke to him first.* Although they later became lovers and even
> lived together, he never seemed really 'in love' ... He recently broke
> up with her over something trivial ... Had Pam followed *The Rules*
> she never would have spoken to Robert or initiated anything in the
> first place. Had she followed *The Rules* she might have met someone
> who truly wanted her.
>
> (31, original emphasis)

Due to this fundamental mistake, Pam finds herself in the worst
situation imaginable: she is, once again, single. The authors affectively
appeal to their readers' deep-seated fears about remaining alone (which
they themselves fuel). Conversely, when the Rules are unfalteringly
adhered to, readers will be rewarded in spades:

> Our friend Jody felt she was 'losing' Jeff, her boyfriend of three
> months, when after a Saturday night date he said good-bye to her very
> casually and told her, 'I'll call ya. I'll let you know what's a good night
> for *me* next week.' Jody felt the tables turning and took an extreme
> Rules action. She didn't answer her phone the night he usually called.
> She just listened to it ring and ring. When he finally reached her the
> next day at work, he was a little less cocky and somewhat nervous.
> He asked her what night would be good for *her*! The phone strategy
> worked – he never pulled another stunt like that again.
>
> (50, original emphasis)

Such behaviour modification is central to achieving the success promised
by *The Rules*. In addition to wearing skirts and keeping hair long, because
men prefer it, 'when you're with a man you like, be quiet and mysterious,

act ladylike, cross your legs and smile. Don't talk so much' (22). Keeping quiet is, apparently, an intensely desirable quality in a woman, with readers being told that 'most men find chatty women annoying' (37). Likewise, according to Doyle's logic of 'surrendered dating', women should talk as little as possible on dates, which will make them appear more 'feminine': 'We're softer when we're simply smiling and responding than we would be if we were trying to direct the conversation' (156). Being quiet, she argues, allows you to 'listen to your heart messages' (158). Moreover, both texts argue women should maintain other interests, but only so they appear unavailable to men (which in turn is believed to enhance their attractiveness). In *The Surrendered Single*, maintaining friendships with women is important, because men do not want to hear about women's fears, anxieties, and insecurities: 'Casting aside friends and hobbies that you once enjoyed in favour of total immersion with a man could make you cranky and miserable, which is not attractive' (254). In order to achieve this attractiveness, both books advocate what seems like an oxymoronic strategy – a kind of performative passivity.

Embracing passivity or how not to be an emasculator

In terms of dating, for a Rules girl, a paradoxically cultivated feminine passivity is key: 'Dating is like slow dancing. The man must take the lead or you fall over your feet' (85). Likewise, women must curtail their sexual desire or risk their date's 'emasculation': 'Don't initiate sex, even if you want it badly. Let him be the man, the aggressor in the bedroom. Biologically, the man must pursue the woman. If you bring up sex all the time, you will emasculate him' (119–20).[3] The trope of emasculation resurfaces throughout *The Rules*; for example, Rule #16, 'Don't Tell Him What to Do', is justified on the following grounds: 'You will end up emasculating him and he will come to see you as a domineering shrew' (84). This use of the figure of the emasculating shrew is a clear invocation of popular representations of the feminist; the Rules girl, then, is defined in opposition to such a caricature.[4] The spectre of the aggressive feminist also haunts Doyle's reactionary narrative. Throughout the book, as in *The Rules*, certain actions are advocated to avoid 'emasculating' your man (Doyle, 2002, pp. 264, 289). In these retro narratives, the personal must be seen to be *a*political. As has been argued of *Men are From Mars, Women are From Venus*, a woman must shift from the competent, autonomous subject she has become in the public sphere and return to being a 'feminine female'; that is, 'she must allow herself to stop doing (like a subject), and start being (like an object), "being special" and "being cared for"' (Cowlishaw, 2001, p. 180).

Despite being published seven years later, Doyle's approach differs little from that of *The Rules* (and indeed *He's Just Not That Into You*); women should not 'aggressively hunt for a husband ... because he will find you' (2002, p. 37). Doyle also argues that a woman should never approach a man in whom they are interested, as such a gesture undermines her very femininity and thus what makes her attractive to men (69). As in *The Rules*, women should learn to cultivate their innate passivity and concomitantly their femininity. This rhetoric around the reclamation of femininity is common in such books; women's alienation from their essential feminine selves has had a detrimental effect not only on women but, more importantly for these narratives, on men. Gendering agency masculine, Doyle argues: 'The essence of feminine behaviour is receiving' (112). In contrast, 'to demonstrate an ability to provide, please, and protect is masculine' (124). Here, men are the *doers* and women are the *done to*: 'If your goal is to be attractive to the right man, then make a habit of taking a feminine approach by receiving as much as you can' (122). Women, therefore, remain the agents in the solution of their (relationship) problem, even when attributable to men. Not only does such a gesture reinscribe the idea that women are emotional labourers (Hochschild, 1994) it also reinforces essentialist notions about masculinity and men's alleged emotional illiteracy. Men, such authors presume, must be 'coaxed, coddled, finessed, handled, or outright tricked' into marriage (Geller, 2001, p. 40) – and they possess the inside knowledge on just how this should be done.

Conversion and salvation

The rhetoric of *The Rules* is overtly evangelical and commitment to its key tenets mirrors a religious conversion, with authors warning readers not to 'be surprised if the people around you don't support your new philosophy' (122). In fact, they even profess that it *is* a religion; women who break their rules 'don't realize that *The Rules* way is not a hobby, but a religion. We keep doing *The Rules* until the ring is on our finger' (137). *The Rules* is not simply about maximizing women readers' chances of finding a partner, it is about increasing their chances of finding (and keeping) a husband. However, in a cult-like rhetoric they advise against discussing this new belief-system with potentially unsympathetic friends, family, or even therapists. For example, Rule #31 warns 'Don't discuss The Rules with your therapist' because he/she will mount arguments against this quasi-religion: 'It's hard enough to do *The Rules* when you believe in them, it's even harder when you talk to people who are downright against them. You should also not read any books that go counter to this philosophy or preach another method' (135). Readers should, however, ignore such reactions and ill-informed opposition and seek out other Rules' girls as a support network. Apart from being entirely patronizing to women readers, who cannot be exposed to conflicting ideas, they dangerously advocate isolationism and detachment from loved ones on the basis that they may be 'non-believers'. *The Rules*, therefore, is what Steven Starker calls a 'closed system' self-help narrative, in that it 'presents a self-contained philosophy, complete unto itself, which resists and discourages interaction with other perspectives' (1989, p. 9). Furthermore, this correlation with religion is even more problematic as it positions *The Rules* as a form of salvation for the single woman, whose deep need and desire to be saved (from singleness? from themselves?) drives the entire narrative.

Books such as *The Rules* and *The Surrendered Single* (and others in this vein such as *He's Just Not That Into You*) in their exhortation to not approach a man in whom you are interested, reconstitute feminine passivity as agency; doing nothing, which is actually seen as an embrace of an innate, naturalized 'femininity', becomes the ultimate act of regaining control. In the logic of such texts, it is this self-consciousness and self-reflexivity that marks out the current valorization of feminine passivity from earlier forms of subordination. In this way, they are consonant with other forms of postfeminist cultural practices that are predicated on the assumption that a simple consciousness of one's adoption of a less than empowered position has the effect of mitigating its potentially subordinating effects. As Gill argues, 'the notion that all our practices are freely chosen is central to postfeminist discourses, which present women as autonomous agents no longer constrained by any inequalities or power imbalances whatsoever' (2007, p. 153). Thus, deliberately choosing a position of subordination bizarrely becomes empowerment, a logic which relies upon the mobilization of feminist notions of agency and neoliberal rhetorics of the control of the self for politically questionable ends. This, of course, begs the question – for which sort of women is this 'choice' not only desirable but viable?

These retro narratives and their bestselling status are a testament to what Suzanne Leonard (referring to Lori Gottlieb's rhetoric on 'settling') identifies as 'the symbolic power that the marital economy still yields over women' (2009, p. 112). Moreover, the widespread circulation of such narratives demonstrates 'the continued popularity of conversations that frame unmarried women as deficient, positing them as a class that must rouse to action – and do so before it is too late – if they have any hopes of securing for themselves a connubial future' (Leonard, 2009, p. 112).

While there have been several books of this ilk published in the 1990s and 2000s, alongside them on the bookshelves have been those focused less on readers obtaining happiness through investment in a romantic relationship than on celebrating the pleasures and freedoms of living as a single woman. The rhetoric is, however, complicated. For some, accepting one's single self and the possibilities it offers is key to securing love; for others, the often overlooked benefits are emphasized and singleness revalued as an alternative, entirely viable way of living as a woman. However, while the remainder of this chapter attends to some of these texts, it is important to note that none of the books considered in the preceding sections appear to have had the same immense cultural reverberations as self-help 'blockbuster' texts like *The Rules* and *The Surrendered Single* (or indeed other popular cultural texts considered here). This is an important point, especially when it comes to the final two sets of texts, which offer a more positive take on women's singleness. Though they undoubtedly attempt to rewrite dominant scripts, how many single women are actually consuming these alternatives? First, however, I consider some texts that appear initially to be refiguring singleness but which ultimately serve to reinscribe the pathologization of singleness evident in the more overtly 'retro' narratives.

Men will love you if you love yourself

The books I engage with in this section – such as Amanda Ford's *Kiss Me, I'm Single* (2007) and Jennifer Bawden's *Get a Life, Then Get a Man* (2002) – are generally ideologically in line, if rhetorically taking a different approach, with those already analyzed. While these books purport to focus on the single self, and encourage an acceptance of women's singleness, the underlying goal for readers is patent: work on the self in order to secure the other. In terms of intimate relationships, such books urge women, as Lisa Blackman notes, to engage in an 'emotional and/or psychological transformation in order to achieve certain desired ends'; that is, to increase their chances of success with 'an intimate other' (2004, p. 230).[5] Even in *Sex and the Single Girl*, Brown encouraged her single women readers to focus on and value themselves while always being on the lookout for eligible bachelors (2003, p. 120). By turning inward, these books argue, the feminine self will achieve success on multiple levels and, most importantly, in the realm of affect. As Blackman notes, single 'women are encouraged to work on themselves so that they remain open to relationships and do not become "defensive"' (2004, p. 228). For women, of course, whose emotional literacy or competency is believed to exceed that of men and which is thought to be inherently 'feminine', this charge of 'defensiveness' is particularly loaded as it suggests a gendered being at odds with her femininity.

In this sub-section of the genre, readers are urged, initially, to cultivate a relationship with the self. These writers, including Jennifer Bawden (2002), Amanda Ford (2007) and Jennifer Schefft (2007), presume that an over-zealous focus on the other means that the self 'has become separated from, or been forgotten by, itself' (Hazleden, 2003, p. 416). This self, therefore, believed to be entirely in control of the direction in which her life is heading, is encouraged to undertake various forms of self-labour to help cultivate a more 'healthy' relationship with itself (Hazleden, 2003). It is such 'unhealthiness', then, that these books seek to remedy. In *Kiss Me, I'm Single: An Ode to the Single Life* (2007), full of anecdotes and mantras celebrating the single life, Amanda Ford routinely utters platitudes such as: 'Believe that the most important relationship you will ever have in your life is with yourself. Believe it down to your bones: The search for another person must never preclude the search for yourself' (19) and 'Create an existence that is full of joy regardless of your relationship status. Vow to enter a lifelong love affair with yourself. This is the first priority' (26). Similarly, in *Better Single Than Sorry: A No Regrets Guide to Loving Yourself and Never Settling* (2007), Jennifer Schefft remarks: 'No woman (or man) should feel incomplete because they are not in a relationship. Complete yourself' (p. 20).[6] As Ford's and Schefft's comments suggest, this subgenre deploys characteristic self-help discourse – the self as agent of change; downplaying, or rather eliding altogether, the socio-political context in which that self operates and that works to delimit the types of subjectivities available. It is the neoliberal self, free to create the circumstances in which this self will thrive, to which these texts speak. Such books must also be read in the context of self-help's focus on the 'disease' of co-dependence, signalling a neglect of self which must be combated: 'Defined as a dysfunction (a disease and/or addiction, depending on the author) co-dependency designates a person's extensive and unhealthy focus on the other rather than on where the experts claim a person's attention needs to be – on one's self' (Rimke, 2000, p. 65). Redirecting the focus from other to self, therefore, is seen as the way for a 'healthy, normal and functional self to emerge and prosper' (Rimke, 2000, p. 66), to in turn establish the conditions for a 'healthy, normal and functional' relationship to come into being.

Paradoxically, the self upon which these manuals urge readers to lavish attention and self-acceptance must also be transformed into an object worthy of heterosexual romantic love. That is, implicit here is the idea that women's relationships with themselves are the source of their 'failure' in romantic relationships. These authors, therefore, proffer ways in which readers can bring themselves into being as loveable, and concomitantly *unsingle*, selves. As in reality television, singleness is seen as a fundamentally feminine problem, the solutions to which are also gendered feminine. Seeking to claim a high moral ground against the superficial elements of self-transformation, these authors position their approach against (and hierarchically above) makeover culture especially – it is the inner self that must be the site of this labour. As Ford notes: 'Dare to grow. No amount of perfume, clothing, plastic surgery or guidance on how to find and keep a man will do you any good, unless you're prepared to make yourself whole on the inside. [...] Refining rough edges may be all that lies between you and "the one"' (2001, p. 32). The final sentence here is telling, and indicative of the type of slippage that recurs through these 'work on the self in order to gain the other' books. Its authors make clear that the creation of a contented, man-less life has its ultimate purpose: 'No man can wave a magic wand and provide you with a magical life; it's up to you to create a magical life for yourself. There is nothing more exciting to a man than a confident, independent woman with a life of her own. Allow yourself to shine and don't let anyone (including yourself) hold you back' (Ford, 2001, p. 244). As this quotation suggests, a postfeminist rhetoric centring on the individual's autonomy and capacity for self-actualization suffuses Ford's text. Moreover, that the time readers have to work on the self is limited is taken for granted; that is, readers are urged to enjoy their singleness, but they are assured it will eventually come to a welcome end. Singleness, as is common in public discourse, is seen as just a transitory stage along the life course. Rather than 'an end in itself' singleness is a temporarily inhabitable space where self-development can take precedence over the cultivation of a relationship (Macvarish, 2008, p. 6). This compulsory self-work will have its interpersonal rewards, however – a male partner.

Such manuals can be seen as entirely consistent with the broader, and pervasive, logics of postfeminism. For Gill, the current 'postfeminist moment' entails a 'focus upon the psychological – upon the requirements to transform oneself and remodel one's interior life' (2008, p. 441). However, while positioning the self as central, such books – like those in the previous section – advocate a form of 'intimate self-surveillance' within which it is not only one's own 'feelings, desires and attitudes' that a woman must monitor, but also those of a current or future partner (Gill, 2009, p. 365). Indeed, that the emotional work in interpersonal, and especially romantic, relationships, has been historically – and indeed continues to be – gendered feminine has been explored by feminist critics (Hochschild, 1983; Gill, 2009). Linking such affective 'work' to neoliberalism, Gill identifies this discursive repertoire as 'intimate entrepreneurship', where the focus is not just on relationships as work but as *women's* work. In such a context, 'women are enjoined to self-monitor and monitor others, to work on and transform the intimate self, to regulate every aspect of their conduct, and to present every action – however constrained or normatively demanded – as the outcome of individual choice and a deliberative personal biography' (Gill, 2009, p. 366). In this way, she argues, texts that so enjoin women are indicative of the 'marriage (heteronormative metaphor intended!) of postfeminism and neoliberalism' (Gill, 2009, p. 366). Within this articulation of postfeminism and neoliberalism, women are believed to perform this kind of self-regulatory work, then, because they now *choose* to do so, rather than having it required of them as innately feminine work. As I have argued throughout, the deployment of the loaded rhetoric of 'choice', even when reinscribing fairly tradition models of femininity and gendered interaction, is a constitutive element of postfeminism – and, as exemplars of postfeminist media culture, these figurations of the single woman are no exception.

Another book which couples this rhetoric of self-love with assumptions about women's universal desire for a man is Jennifer Bawden's *Get a Life, Then Get a Man* (2002). Its title, which foregrounds the two-step process constitutive of this subgenre, clearly invokes such postfeminist rhetoric to challenge the passivity advocated by the authors of *The Surrendered Single* and *The Rules*, against which she explicitly positions her own text. It commences: 'Have you read rule books that promote dating as a game and passivity as the winning strategy? [...] Are you – or would you like to be – a strong, independent, confident woman in charge of her own life, one who isn't afraid to go after what she wants?' If so, she tells readers, 'someone has finally written a book for *you*!' (1, original emphasis). In the governing neoliberal rhetoric of self-help, and indeed of postfeminism, she argues:

> Attractive, intelligent women are sitting at home right now waiting for the phone to ring. I believe you deserve to go out and get what you want. Not just a man, but whatever it is you want. Being proactive in your life means reaching your highest potential. Women who follow the old rules are looking for men to save them. Unsure how to reach their goals, afraid of hard work or even success, they will never reach their goals or develop their own strong life.

(4)

Nonetheless, even in texts which explicitly disavow the man-as-saviour trope such as Ford's and Bawden's, it is presumed that 'once a woman achieves emotional enlightenment ... she will find her optimal male partner, or, rather, he will find her' (Geller, 2001, p. 33). In this sense, these manuals valorize heterosexual coupledom in much the same way as the more overtly reactionary texts analyzed in the previous section. Their authors, therefore, have been described as 'faux singles advocates' (*Onely*, 8 December 2009).

In these books, as Rose argues of therapeutic culture more broadly, the 'expert' positions herself as offering the promise of, and techniques for, self-transformation by the 'autonomous, choosing, psychological self' (1996, p. 157). Accordingly, 'Contemporary individuals are incited to live as if making a *project* of themselves: they are to *work* on their emotional world, their domestic and conjugal arrangements' (Rose, 1996, p. 157, original emphasis). For the single woman addressed by these books, a calculated self-fashioning will help produce 'a better and healthier life' through following the 'expert's advice' (Rose, 1996, p. 157). This knowledge, ultimately, is enlisted in the service of the goal the authors purport to deprioritize: securing a man. Indicative of such contradictory rhetoric, Bawden makes it very clear that the kinds of self-labour she advocates will have the desired result: 'Work on yourself and your goals first, and the right man will follow. I guarantee it' (5). As in *Kiss me, I'm Single*, platitudes about self-love abound, such as 'Happiness doesn't come from acquiring something or someone, it comes from within you' and 'Being single is a valid and valuable life stage that can provide you with some of the most enriching moments of your life. Don't waste your time crying and wishing you were in a relationship' (100). While such comments emphasize agency and the value of single life, they are juxtaposed with those that make explicit reader's investment in a partnered future: 'Your goal is to get good at being single, to enjoy it as much as you will someday enjoy being with a wonderful man in a committed relationship' (100). In this way, the familiar view of singleness as merely a temporary state appears to drive her narrative.

While Bawden's disavowal of previous texts that endorse women's passivity is certainly laudable, and singleness is viewed not as better but as simply different to being partnered, the book's very structure functions to undermine this rhetoric: Part I: Get a Life; Part 2: Get a Man; Part 3: Dating; Part 4: The Relationship. Only a quarter of the book, then, attends to life without a man while the remainder is preoccupied with the various strategies, and stages, of securing one. Again, like Ford, the by-product of this self-work will be the production of a more desirable heterosexual subject: 'Your happiness is not on hold until you find "the one" and that elusive ring is on your finger. If you're busy and fulfilled, enjoying the present, you'll be the type of woman men want to meet' (100; see also 43). These actions will help her become more alluring – and thus, most importantly, unsingle. This quotation evidences the inherent contradictions of the manuals examined in this section; being happy, contented, and personally fulfilled as a single person is endorsed but the benefits of such an approach are not simply for the self – they will help readers attract men and provide the grounds for successful intimacies. In such narratives, as is characteristic of self-help in general, techniques are advocated and legitimized that enable the self/self and self/other relation to be remodeled (Blackman, 2010, p. 36) but in ways that will ultimately prioritize blissful coupledom.

To conclude her book, of the role of men in women's lives Bawden says: 'We must develop ourselves and be content with our own lives before merging it with someone else's. A man is an added bonus to your own success. He's the frosting, but you're the cake' (223). However, as mentioned, three-quarters of her book focuses on how to attain this 'bonus' and the possibility, to take up her metaphor, of a cake sans frosting, for any length of time, seems un-representable. In this type of book, there is no sense that remaining single is a viable option or that some women may not wish to co-habit or indeed marry and may choose singleness as a permanent, desirable way of being in the world. In contrast, another series of self-help books works to destabilize this pervasive, deeply problematic, hetero-patriarchal narrative and focus less on readers obtaining happiness through investment in a romantic relationship than on celebrating the pleasures and freedoms of living as a single woman and challenging its devaluation. Foregrounding some of these counter-narratives, I conclude this chapter by engaging with two different types of publications that both nonetheless work to revalue singleness for women.

Satisfied Singles: 'Professional' advice

The singles' manuals, such as Florence Falk's *On My Own: The Art of Being A Woman Alone* (2008), Judy Ford's *Single: The Art of Being Satisfied, Fulfilled and Independent* (2004), and Karen Lewis' *With or Without A Man: Single Women Taking Control of Their Lives* (2001), considered in this section share a key assumption about the single woman within Western culture: she has been taught to disdain her state, to view alone-ness entirely as a tragedy – as books like *The Rules* and *The Surrendered*

Single exemplify. Their initial, unifying goal is to validate women who, for whatever reason, remain without a heteronormative romantic partnership. Their implied reader has been damaged, they argue, by the insistent cultural denigration of single women, and such damage must be repaired if she is to obtain happiness, either alone or with an other. That is, they seek to trouble those discursive constructions of single women as aberrant and socially liminal which continue to circulate in mainstream media culture. In this way, the 'problem' identified in these publications is not the single women herself but the way she is being conceptualized – including by herself. They provide practical advice on how to negotiate the quotidian aspects of singleness as well as how to manage its psychic dimensions.

These texts appear to be addressed towards single women in their 30s and beyond who have found themselves, for overdetermined reasons (there are women referred to within the texts who are divorcees, widows, and those who simply prefer to live on their own), without a partner. The writers of these texts are largely single women who are therapists and/or psychologists; their authority is therefore not only professional but personal. Authors seek to identify the source of single women's sense of inadequacy as an integral part of mounting a challenge against it. Generically, these texts are hybrid forms, combining biography, autobiography, social commentary, and, at times, polemic. Using stories based on their interactions with patients and interviews with diverse groups of single women, the evidence of other practitioners and theorists as well as their own experiences, they position their texts as counter-narratives, disrupting how women's singleness is figured in public discourse.

In terms of the work they encourage readers to undertake, chapters conclude with 'self-assessment' exercises (Lewis) or 'Try This' (Ford) sections that encourage readerly introspection and creative activities to reimagine their singleness. These 'authorities', therefore, as is characteristic of therapeutic discourse, proffer techniques through which readers can examine and evaluate the self, such as writing exercises to help bring a certain self into being (Rose, 1999, p. 251). Central to this subgenre is a pronounced revaluation of the single self: 'We don't have to be in a relationship to be content. We're not insignificant if we don't have a significant other' (Ford, 2004, p. 199). In addition to encouraging such revaluing work at the level of the self, these writers seek to politicize women's singleness, reinscribing the second-wave feminist axiom that 'the personal is political'; this is contra the previous manuals examined, wherein the personal is figured as entirely apolitical and women's yearning for a masculine other seen as universal.

Therefore, even if not explicitly identifying themselves as feminist or invoking the signifier, these books are clearly informed by feminist discourses and can be seen to represent a feminist (re)appropriation of the single women self-help genre. In so doing, they challenge not just limited stories of women's singleness but the postfeminism that has produced and keeps them in circulation. Such books are instructive in terms of how feminist discourses operate in the realm of popular publishing, even if not overtly named as such.

The fact that there is a market for this type of affirmative text suggests much about the construction of single women within hegemonic discourses. Such narratives work to validate women's singleness and problematize its status as a marginalized identity. They focus on women's agency in creating a life, a home, a career, and a friendship network through which they can achieve fulfilment, 'with or without a man' (Lewis, 2001, Chapter 4). Lewis, a practicing psychologist dealing predominantly with single women, tells readers: 'Hopefully, some of these ideas will strike a resonating cord, confirm your own values, validate your confusion, help you challenge the internalized messages, and re-educate yourself and your loved ones' (2004, p. 4). Her therapeutic project therefore is pedagogical. Similarly, Judy Ford identifies the constitutive elements of her narrative and what she hopes it might achieve for single readers: '*Single: The Art of Being Satisfied, Fulfilled and Independent* is a peek into the everyday life of ordinary singles – part memoir, part self-help, part inspiration – the message of *Single* is a clear one. *Single* is about being satisfied and happy as an individual, whether you end up in a relationship or not' (2004, p. ix). Drawing upon interviews with groups of women (Lewis) or offering auto/biographical vignettes (Ford) helps underscore the sense of a community of women negotiating and coming to terms with their singleness (especially how they are being positioned by others). These books tell the reader she is not alone and, most importantly, not diseased.

Deconstructing the myths

It has been common to critique self-help discourses on the grounds that they work to implicate the individual in her own subjection, and help her become a compliant (neo)liberal citizen (Rimke, 2000). However, these authors insist that while the individual may need to re-negotiate her own relationship to her singleness (i.e. to rethink it as a positive way of being in the world), it is the social context making her feel aberrant that comes under scrutiny. The women writing these sorts of texts (for they are invariably women) make explicit their desire to challenge the myths that single women may have internalized. These books are quite polemical, positioned as they are against hegemonic assumptions about gender and relationships, and the authors are deeply ideologically invested in the reassessments they proffer. In *With or Without a Man*, Lewis devotes a number of chapters to deconstructing what she identifies as the nine key 'messages' about being a single woman (such as 'You'll find a man but only after you stop looking' and 'You should always look good, just in case you bump into your future husband'). Likewise, for Florence Falk, in *On My Own: The Art of Being Alone* (2008), single women harbour feelings of shame and guilt about singleness which need to be unpacked:

> When we take into consideration the many cultural messages that encourage a woman to think of herself as less than – to not accept herself as she is – together with the many assaults to the self that are personal and individual, we can begin to understand why the uncomfortable feelings we carry make us veer away from aloneness. The challenge to women alone is to confront these feelings so that we can enjoy the creative rewards of solitude.
>
> (2008, p. 62)

Overwhelmingly, these texts position singleness as an unrecognized source of potential self-empowerment (Ford, 2004, p. 86). They also engage with the affective dimensions of singleness, especially in their acknowledgement that it is a way of being about which women may be ambivalent; in this way, they do not fall into the trap of simply installing singleness as a 'compulsory sociability' (Riley, 2002)[7] and provide a more nuanced approach than unreserved celebration. And although their narratives presume readers are open to the possibility of coupledom, it is clearly not their central preoccupation.

While acknowledging that readers may feel discontentment at times, the books in this subgenre underline the potentially liberatory aspects of singleness. The single self, they argue, is a self to be actively embraced: 'A satisfied single, like a poet, a musician, or a dancer, is committed to celebrating all existence. They see beauty it in all. Such a single stands on her own, apart from the crowd. She dances to the beat of her own drum' (Ford, 2004, p. 38). The self-determining subject of neoliberalism is evident here, whose agency is unfettered. However, Ford's rhetoric is in many respects strategic, as she attempts to intervene and challenge the dominant discourses around singleness. And unlike the books in the previous section, for Ford this 'self discovery' is not intimately linked to a two-step process where developing the self will lead to a successful relationship. Rather, such self-work is an end in itself, and therefore in these narratives a single self is conceptualized as permissible in ways that it is not in other forms of popular discourse. Although Rimke argues that 'self-help encourages some ways of life and living over others' (2000, p. 73), the books in this section suggest that this process need not be politically reactionary. That is, in offering singleness as a viable subject position, these texts do not necessarily call into being hegemonic selves, or those that adhere to normative models of femininity, but act counter-discursively, contradicting dominant narratives of pathology and abjection. The political (and indeed personal) import of such strategic acts of resignification should not be under-estimated. As Falk remarks, 'The act of reimagining aloneness will make it possible for us to incorporate it into our lives in a new and integral way, because we have finally realized that to be a single woman is a prerogative not a plight' (2008, p. 19). These authors therefore attempt to alter the cultural vocabulary, both at the level of the reader's self and at a broader social level, that delimits how singleness is experienced.

Like many examples of self-help, these books are littered with authorial self-revelations, offered to secure and retain the reader's trust (Simonds, 1992, p. 120). Such insights have been called 'authenticating anecdotes', common in popular feminist non-fiction, where the narrative 'I' self-reflexively foregrounds her relationship to the material she is discussing (Pearce, 2004). In these single women guides, it is the author's experiences of singleness – as well as their status as 'professionals' in the field of the affective – that provide the grounds for their authority. As Dolby notes, writers of self-help often narrate their own conversion or transformation to help augment their authority. They commonly narrate an incident, or series of incidents, that 'captures the essence of their conversion to the idea presented in the book but also a recurring tone of earnestness and zeal that conveys the authenticity of their emotional involvement with the topic at hand' (2005, p. 48). In this vein, Ford recounts numerous personal moments where she was forced to rethink her own attitude to singleness. While the narrative voice may at times confide her own anxieties and ambivalence about her singleness, the dominant tone is one of optimism, despite the lack of external validation for her life choice. For Ford, singleness is indeed a legitimate lifestyle but her following comments here exemplify how it is continually disavowed and seen as inherently undesirable: 'When people ask me, "Judy, do you like being single?" I'm careful about my answer. It's really hard for people to believe that a single person could like being single. I do like' (2004, p. 220). She highlights here the sheer unrepresentability of a permanent, pleasurable singleness – something she works throughout to contest.

In terms of how they address relationships, these books do consider the search for an other but in significantly different ways to those in the previous sections. Being part of a couple is not hierarchized over single-ness. Sexual fulfilment is an important area explored in these texts, as it is in the 'Single Girl' manuals examined subsequently. The recognition of women's desire, even though not as part of a heterosexual couple, is a recurrent theme; for example, Lewis (2001) includes a chapter on how single women can 'face [their] sexual feelings'. However, she and other writers in this subgenre also seek to underscore non-romantic relation-ships and the kinds of fulfilment they offer single women. In this way, they challenge the idea that the only legitimate forms of cathexis and affective bonds for women are those relating to men and children, as critiqued here in Chapter 1. In so doing, they seek to deprioritize the coupled relationship as the most important and most coveted. They highlight that being alone is not necessarily a state of loneliness, and thereby challenge the still prevalent assumption that happiness is con-tingent upon romantic partnership.

Although critics have argued that 'therapeutic culture' merely entails the 'recasting of social problems as individual ones' (Furedi, 2004, p. 24; Reynolds, 2008; Dubrofsky, 2009), the self-help manuals in this subgenre clearly do seek to repoliticize women's singleness. In this vein, Lewis contests the hierarchal binary of couples/singles: 'We live in a society that values marriage as the "norm". If that value judgement were removed, being married and being single would be two equally viable paths through adulthood. There would be no need for women to blame themselves for being single' (2004, p. 1). As part of the socio-political critique proffered throughout, she proposes a new 'life-stage model' that 'allows Single Adulthood to be recognized as both a jour-ney toward marriage as well as a destination in its own right' (Lewis, 2004, p. 37). Indicative of her politicization of singleness, Lewis views the public reconceptualization of singleness as key to combating the prejudices against it and in challenging the continued normativity of marriage. Moreover, further indicative of her text's politicization of sin-gleness, she argues for a 'cultural revolution' led by single women (2004, p. 227), thereby emphasizing the need for more than just a 'revolution from within'[8].

These books, in shifting the focus from the strategies women need to deploy to remedy their singleness to exploring its potentialities, clearly participate in a dialogue with feminism in a way that the books considered previously do not. Their authors rely upon feminist vocabularies, suggesting the distillation of which I have previously spoken, but without the repudiation of politics that often mark postfeminist narratives about gender and singleness. Rather than presuming that heterosexual coupledom is a universal feminine desire from which women (because of feminism) have been alienated, these authors posit singleness as a viable mode of being. As with those considered in the next section, it is not a man these women readers are presumed to lack but the 'correct' attitude towards their singleness; this is what these manuals hope to 'fix'. In the final series of books analyzed here, the 'Single Girl' conduct manual, I consider how its authors work to validate women's singleness in ways that can be seen to simultaneously tap into and problematize the broader cultural logics of postfeminism.

Celebrating the 'Single Girl'

These books overlap in many pertinent ways with those in the previous section; however, there are some key differences that warrant some deeper critical attention. As Caroline Smith argues (2008), chick lit books like *Bridget Jones's Diary* engage in critical commentary about the efficacy of self-help manuals. Heroines are commonly reading various manuals, and identify a disjuncture between their own lives and the book's prescriptions on how it should be lived. The 'Single Girl' conduct manual examined in this final section – including *The Single Girl's Guide to Life* (Lloyd Weber, 2007) and *The Single Girl's Manifesta* (Stewart, 2005) – likewise exhibits a debt to the chick lit novel that in many ways helped create the consumer for this type of book. Such texts appear more like conduct manuals than authoritative guides offering ways to change cognitive behaviour (as in those considered previously). In terms of packaging, many of these books give an intertextual nod to the bright pinks and cartoonish figures of chick lit book-covers. In so doing, they seek to appeal to a pre-constituted audience, with a firmly established grammar and vocabulary around women's singleness. But rather than simply acting as the non-fictional equivalent of chick lit, these texts do not place the search for the male partner at their centre. Instead, as with those examined in the previous section, they presume that the meaning-making network in which the figure of the single woman is enmeshed requires destabilization. Their authors likewise refuse to conceptualize women's singleness as a pathology. These books, and their publishers, recognize that women are seeking counter-narratives.

They are indebted to feminism and, in particular, discourses about women's empowerment, agency, and autonomy. In this way, they exemplify how feminism is being taken up within popular cultural realms such as non-fiction publishing (as in some of the other textual sites upon which I have focused). They deploy a comic tone and the self-reflexive narrative 'I' often appears to enjoy satirizing or chiding herself for her own previous un-enlightened behaviour (i.e. for presuming that being single is a dire state when it clearly, as her book sets out to illustrate, has untold benefits for women). The narrative voice is often remarkably similar to the first-person narrator of much chick lit and is far less earnest than some of those considered in the previous section. Moreover, though these writers lack the 'psy' authority enjoyed by the earlier texts, the strategic use of the personal, as in much feminist writing, acts to authorize their accounts in specific ways (see Pearce, 2004).

The addressee of these texts may be in her mid-late 20s or 30s and, contra other examples of self-help literature aimed at women, does not appear beset by anxiety over her singleness. Overwhelmingly, their readers – like their authors – are seen as having moderate to high disposable incomes through which to 'pamper' themselves. That is, consumption is central and positioned as the provenance of single women; indeed, her ability to consume is seen as one of the core differences between her and her counterparts with children. This is one of the limitations of this style of text, and through which they can be seen to adhere to postfeminist logics, while concurrently their challenge to compulsory coupledom renders them outside its purview. Although perhaps suggestive of the infantilization of the single woman of which I have spoken previously, the fact that many in this style of book deploy the signifier 'girl' in their titles also locates them in relation to 'girl power' style discourses that have permeated popular culture since the mid-1990s. Moreover, in so 'girling' the single woman, they also reveal a debt to Brown's *Sex and the Single Girl* (see Chapter 2 here). In these books, like those considered in the previous section, being single is not conceptualized as a problem that needs to be solved; on the contrary, its desirability underpins all these narratives. Invocations of Bridget Jones and the foursome from *Sex and the City* are common, once again signalling some assumptions about readership and intertextual knowledge as well as generational location. Similarly, the importance of friendship (what in chick lit parlance is known as an 'urban family', the family one chooses), in terms of making single life more enjoyable, routinely features in these books.

Some of these texts focus on the prosaic elements of singleness, providing advice on the practicalities of living, travelling or socializing alone, from choosing an apartment to performing handiwork or DIY. They also address more nebulous aspects like strategies for coping with loneliness and the expectations of families, through which the 'Single Girl' continues to be infantilized: 'Until you get to grips with your relatives' concern about your SG status, it may mean you are still considered in childlike terms' (Lloyd Weber, 2007, pp. 106–7). Others focus on challenging dominant representations and hegemonic assumptions about the deficiency of the singular self. As Emily Dubberley argues in *I'd Rather be Single Than Settle: Satisfied Solitude and How to Achieve It*: 'As to the theory of your partner being your missing 'other half', this is all very romantic, but it has one massive flaw: it suggests that you're half a person until you have a partner. And that's just wrong. Who, after all, wants to be half a person?' (2007, p. 46). As she implies, this trope of an incomplete self has an enduring cultural currency, working to undermine the notion of a fully functioning autonomous self existing outside normative coupledom. To challenge this, such books foreground the often overlooked advantages of singleness for women.

The hidden benefits of singledom

Imogen Lloyd Webber's *The Single Girl's Guide* (2007), initially published in the UK, was also released in the US as *The Single Girl's Survival Guide*. Brandishing a hot pink back cover and a cartoon depiction of a stylish single Londoner, the blurb proclaims it 'a tongue-in-cheek but practical manual on life management for the fabulously free female'. It positions the book vis-à-vis popular culture's most well-known singletons: 'You've laughed and cried along with Bridget Jones and Carrie Bradshaw; now meet their real life counterpart Imogen.' Thus, Lloyd Webber's authority is predicated on her own experiences as a late 20s urban Singleton and her apparent proximity to these fictional icons of singleness. With the same type of intertextuality that marks chick lit's revisions of various Jane Austen plots, *The Single Girl's Guide* commences with the following epigraph: 'It is a truth which should be universally acknowledged that a single girl can be in possession of the most wonderful life' (17). The remainder of the text focuses on how to recognize, enjoy, and, most of all, 'manage' just such a life: 'A single girl is undoubtedly in possession of a good fortune, as she has the freedom to lead the life she wants – all it takes is a little management' (254). This idea of a self and a life to be managed borrows from traditional self-help rhetoric, but Lloyd Weber's text is of a less serious bent. Through its emphasis on social and personal freedom, the possibilities and myriad pleasures of singleness are glorified throughout. There is no rhetoric about 'the One' or the presumption that a single woman's life is a wasted life, and it is also free from panic about the female body's metaphorical timepiece. In fact, in Lloyd Weber's narrative, the SG is not suffering from the kinds of time-panic I have shown, following Negra, is usually thought to engulf the single woman: 'Today's world has bequeathed to the SG the gift of time – it is no longer the enemy of the SG it once was, but it is on your side, so panic not' (253–4). While she explicitly writes against this idea of a temporally challenged Single Girl, it is also apparent that her reader is presumed to be of an age yet capable of reproduction.

Of the book's focus, she warns readers early: 'This book is not about how to find a man' (20). In many ways, *The Single Girl's Guide* functions as an updated version of Brown's *Sex and the Single Girl*. Actually, many of these manuals reveal an intertextual debt to Brown's celebratory reassessment of the 'Single Girl' and her prototypical popular feminism. In this way, and despite the intervening years of profound social change in regards to gender, it seems that Brown's advice remains applicable, over 40 years after its initial appearance. *The Single Girl's Guide* deals with work, self (both interiority and exteriority), home, family, friendship, events, and 'distractions' (the book's code for men). Like Brown's Single Girl, Lloyd Weber foregrounds the importance of employment for the 'SG's' identity: 'The first crucial stepping stone to the SG's conquest of the world – whether debt-ridden graduate or lottery-winner – is employment of some description' (25). Belying the class specificity of the book's addressee, she presumes that the 'SG' has time and money to focus attention on herself, be it through various beauty regimes or redecorating one's own living space. The 'SG' is a racially and class specific subject; she is in receipt of a sizeable income which facilitates the at times hedonistic lifestyle endorsed throughout the text. For Lloyd Weber, the individual is prioritized and there is a pronounced emphasis on consumption and its transformative powers, making it consistent with the broader cultural logics of neoliberal postfeminism: 'When you're an SG [Single Girl], you can concentrate wholeheartedly on sorting YOU out from top to toe, both internally and externally' (57).

As is common in these Single Girl books, consumption is central and the idea that single women/readers desire – and have the means – to indulge is presumed. The 'single girl' is, Radner explains, 'a knowledgeable acolyte of feminine consumer culture' (2010, p. 11), a point such texts seem to substantiate. With money, it appears, singleness can be made to be enjoyable. That a pleasurable form of singleness is contingent upon excessive consumption means that such texts exclude a number of less privileged women, creating an implicit hierarchy of singles that is also staged in *Sex and the City*. Unlike judgemental popular narratives that condemn the single woman's supposed selfishness (see Chapter 2 here), Lloyd Weber is unapologetic in her celebration of this presumed ability to self-indulge. While the majority of the book does not position singleness as a transitory state nor is the idea that it is, or can be pleasantly, permanent advocated either. She situates singleness as a period in a woman life's where the focus on the self is possible in ways it will not be in other stages along the life course. With no partner or children, Lloyd Weber emphasizes, the 'SG' need not be guilt-ridden about spending more money or time on herself: 'Take pleasure from the knowledge that you are probably never going to feel less at fault, look more glamorous or have the possibility to play more than at this stage of your life' (28). Here, she positions singleness against (an inevitable) future wherein others will necessarily be foregrounded over the self: 'Being out is the oxygen, the very life blood, of the SG. We SGs are not tied to our abodes by any types of strings, apron or otherwise, and thus have the opportunity to get out there and enjoy ourselves more and better than any of our contemporaries obliged to consider their "better" half' (153–4). The 'SG', through her professional and social presence in the public sphere, is defined in opposition to these women limited by the domestic (women, it is implied, her readers will one day become).

In *The Single Girl's Guide*, the importance of an extensive, varied friendship network is recommended in the chapter on 'Friend Management'. Intersubjectivity is central and though a singular relationship may not be seen as desirable, other models of interaction and affective investment are promoted. She argues, in a tone reminiscent of a chick lit heroine, that friends 'are the family you get to pick; your playmates when you want to have fun, your support network when you are down, your DIY helpers who will also pick up their virtual tools when you are in need of fixing' (131). In terms of other core interpersonal relationships, she also includes a chapter on 'Family Management'. What are to be 'managed' are predominantly familial expectations about the need to be partnered and the assumption that, because the 'SG' is not, she is more available than other members of the family: 'Therefore, to become a happy SG, you may have to acknowledge that you will never wholly please your family, your parents in particular' (109).

While publications like Lloyd Weber's may challenge the centrality of a man in the Single Girl's life, most seem to emphasize the necessity of fulfilling one's sexual needs and desires (although this is not without its contradictions). Being a single woman, they argue, need not equate with celibacy. On the contrary, it leaves her open for varied sexual experiences. She presumes that the SG is not out to steer a man down the wedding aisle but, as she asserts, is seeking 'fun' and 'entertainment' from men (though she also questions women's ability to have sex without emotional investment, 230). In presumption of the postfeminist Single Girl's sexual appetite, Emily Dubberley (2007) also explicitly deals with this subject in her chapter 'In the mood for lust?' as does Sarah Ivens (author of the 2008 book, *A Modern Girl's Guide to the Perfect Single Life*), who invokes Brown in her chapter title: 'Sex and the Single Girl'. Moreover, in the attitude they articulate towards men as well as how they celebrate, and link a positive identity to, the Single Girl's ability to consume (Radner, 2010), these books can be seen to mirror Brown's.

'Stupendously Superior Singles'

As is common in this type of text, Jerusha Stewart's *The Single Girl's Manifesta: Living in a Stupendously Superior Single State of Mind* (2005) has a bright pink cover, myriad busy fonts and text boxes with mantras and platitudes, and a self-reflexive narrator who draws upon her experience of singleness as an authorizing gesture: Stewart is a 45-year-old African American woman for whom being single is definitely not a transitory state. This text, and others such as Nika C. Beamon's *I didn't work this hard just to get married* (2009), are important as they work to disrupt the normative whiteness of the broader cultural conversation over women's singleness. That said, Stewart's assumptions about class privilege and clear postfeminist emphasis on consumption means that it is not without its limitations, and – unlike Beamon – she does not foreground the way racial difference can delimit how women's singleness is lived and interpreted (either by oneself or by others). Nonetheless, her 'manifesta' represents a distinctly politically engaged form of the 'Single Girl' manual, and also deploys feminist rhetoric similar to DePaulo's (2006).

In terms of methodology, Stewart (2005) outlines that she interviewed over two hundred single people of various races, sexualities, and ages about how they perceive their own singleness. Her text consists of autobiography, biographies, quizzes, advice, 'quickie facts' about singles, resources, and media criticism. Her addressees are single women in their 30s, 40s, and 50s, and, in addition to recounting her own experiences, throughout she cites numerous women who have embraced the single life – a gesture she figures as courageous and liberating, especially in light of the increased circulation of mythologies around romantic love: 'With the epidemic of televised "love" connections and the proliferation of dating websites, the whole world seems to be in dating overdrive. Would the real, truly single people please stand up?' (6). In this way, she advocates a kind of identity politics for singles (as do the bloggers considered in my next chapter), with 'real' singles being those who have consciously chosen singleness.

In bold font a text box outlines the book's overall philosophy: 'Being single is a choice – a choice you are free to make along with millions of other women just like you.' Here, readers are reassured they are but one of many, a device used to normalize their singleness. At the end of every chapter she provides a section called 'The Last Word', which all commence with 'Being single is a choice'. At the first chapter's end, what follows is 'A Single's Declaration of Independence', with the five following key affirmations:

I am an unmarried revolutionary.
I promise to value my single-mindedness.
I will indulge in random acts of selfishness.
I claim my space as a single person.
I embrace the 'L' word. I love my life.

(7)

In advocating these 'acts of selfishness', she reappropriates the common refrain about single women and invests it with positive meaning, while her politicization of singleness is also evident in her invocation of 'revolution'. Each chapter contains 'notes to self' such as 'Live single life like you mean it' which readers are encouraged to post somewhere they can see them every day (244).

For Stewart and the women she interviews, as she notes, 'having it all' means attaining a 'perfectly realized self' (215), which contradicts the postfeminist assumption that 'having it all' signals the desire for both career and marriage and children. She encourages single women to mentor their younger counterparts, to act as the embodiment of this alternative way of living (i.e. contented, prolonged singleness):

You, too, are an independent single woman excelling at living life on your own terms. Don't shy away from opportunities to present another way of being to young people around you. They'll receive plenty of marriage messages, but some may be looking for validation that there is life outside those bonds. Take the time to discuss the freedom and fulfillment of solo living with those around you.

(44)

Nonetheless, the neoliberal postfeminist subject is also evident in Stewart's book. Like others in this subgenre, including Lloyd Weber's, Stewart's text presumes that her single readers enjoy a certain level of class privilege and foregrounds the ability to consume as an exercise of autonomous subjectivity. In particular, she makes recommendations that reveal the presumed class privilege of her readers, especially as she exhorts them to invest in large scale purchases such as real estate (235).

In the celebratory rhetoric that marks her entire text, Stewart argues: 'Let's face it: if you are single it's because you *choose* to be not because you are doomed to be' (2005, p. 9, original emphasis). While the rhetoric of choice and its politics, especially within postfeminism, have been unpacked by feminists (Probyn, 1993, 1997), its strategic deployment in these books is itself an important political gesture, particularly given that the idea is rarely deployed in relation to public understandings of women's singleness. As previous chapters have shown, while singleness is commonly seen as a transitory state and not routinely figured as something one would actively choose, Stewart's book is unique for its focus on singleness as a permanent, actively chosen way of being. In so doing, she attempts to reinstate agency to singles, something which – as I have argued – is rarely granted. Invoking the urban tribe idea that I have shown underpins series such as *Friends* and *Sex and the City*, Stewart chooses to underscore the alternative forms of sociality and connection that help reconstitute the idea of family: 'Just because we're unattached doesn't mean we're not connected. Our replacement sisterhoods, brotherhoods, tribes, and village people are all part of the modern expansive neighborhood' (2005, p. 60).

In terms of how she has been socially positioned, Stewart remarks on the very invisibility of the single woman: 'Once I reached adulthood, I realized that drive to be *seen and heard* is one of the most compelling aspects of being single. In a world where couples are the norm, sometimes so much of your energy is spent trying to get someone's attention' (14, original emphasis). She refigures singleness inter alia by highlighting its transgressive dimensions; being happily single means defying societal expectations and romance mythologies that seek to cultivate a sense of absence (of which I have previously spoken). Throughout her text, and like Karen Lewis and Judy Ford, Stewart characterizes singleness as a unique form of power, a power that comes from the recognition of complete self-sufficiency and autonomy: 'At forty-five, I am a truly *single* person ... *and I love it!* I'm spoiled rotten. I've come to realize that being single was a deliberate choice [...] I enjoy flaunting the power of being one. This single sense that one is enough. My single-mindedness tells me I have everything I need – in fact, I had it all the time' (29, original emphasis). She finds this realization that being single is not only acceptable but desirable entirely liberating. In terms of sexuality, Stewart presumes that the single woman is sexually agentic and (like the books in the previous section) includes a chapter that addresses how to meet one's sexual needs as a single. As part her effort to foster a community of singles and social support, the book concludes with a 'Solo Living Resources' section, providing the addresses of a number of websites that single women may find valuable.

These Single Girl conduct manuals differ markedly from those considered at the start of this chapter (those which attempt to bring about the 'salvation' of the manless woman). In these books, single women are not to be pitied, feared or cured. Instead, in many ways, they are positioned as leading a type of carefree life to be envied, invoking of course the class privilege (and especially the ability and desire to consume) of their presumed readership. Moreover, this last set of texts is contradictory; in some ways they reinscribe postfeminist logics – in terms of their celebratory rhetoric around consumption and an active feminine sexual subject, for example. In others – such as challenging the necessity of a man for a contented life – they effect its destabilization. Nonetheless, they legitimize singleness in ways that the authors of books such as *The Rules* simply find unimaginable, demonstrating – as I suggested in the introduction – that self-help advice for the single woman covers a broad spectrum from its repudiation to its celebration.

Conclusion

In many senses, the single woman subgenre of self-help exemplifies the way in which singleness is being figured more broadly; that is, in competing ways, ranging from those more familiar narratives of angst seeking its transcendence at all costs to those that attempt to recuperate singleness. That said, they do all purport to offer 'solutions' for their readers; their fundamental difference lies in what they perceive to be the remedy for women's singleness: Is it finding a man? Remaking the relationship with the self? Challenging how single women are viewed? Enjoying singleness (including through consumption)? The self-help book addressed to single women is by no means a homogenous phenomenon; and, of course, as no genre is ever fixed but is consistently evolving, so too with this particular type of writing. In this way, within the genre of self-help for single women I have identified a level of heterogeneity that makes it difficult to dismiss this genre outright. And it is clear that it is addressing a readership. The proliferation of books on this subject, from the 1990s but especially in the 2000s, reflects not only the increasing number of single women but also suggests a market for interpretive guides on how to make sense of singleness – either through its transcendence, acceptance or celebration. Nonetheless, it is important to acknowledge that the single woman self-help books with the highest readers – those featured on bestseller lists – include *The Rules* and *The Surrendered Single*. So while the writers considered later in this chapter intervene in the contested conversation over women's singleness in significant ways, their broader cultural impact does not appear to have rivalled their more ideologically problematic counterparts.

It has been argued that self-help books celebrating singleness merely function to secure the married/single binary, thereby undercutting their progressive potential (Reynolds, 2008). However, in her interviews with readers Simonds found that one of the most significant outcomes in the consumption of self-help texts was the sense that reading enabled them to 'tap into a community of sorts'; that is, 'they "feel less alone" when reading' (1992, p. 227). Therefore, single women readers of the books considered in the final two sections of this chapter in particular, who may feel marginalized and/or stigmatized, can find validation of their way of being as well as the sense that they are part of a broader community of likeminded women authors and readers. In this vein, an ethnographic consideration of how these texts work to mediate single women's conceptualization of their own singleness and how readers may bring themselves into being as single subjects, either in line with or against the grain of such publications, would be insightful. Finally, rather than seeing such texts in any isolationist fashion, the work to symbolically validate single women that is undertaken in some of these books is best seen as part of a wider intertextual conversation and revaluation also taking place in the blogosphere.

6
Blogging Solo: Women Refiguring Singleness

Introduction

In this final chapter I turn my attention to the blogosphere as a potentially oppositional field where the dominant meanings around singledom can be contested, negotiated, and rewritten. The single women blogosphere can be seen to challenge the texts and forms previously addressed in two key ways. Firstly, by providing counter-narratives to those that position singleness as a problem to be rectified; secondly, many of these blogs do not appear marred by the postfeminist (and indeed neoliberal) logics that characterize the media forms considered in previous chapters. That said, as in these earlier examples, there are actually a number of competing discourses about women's singleness in the blogosphere – including blogs that presume women's desperation (especially those in their 30s and 40s) to be otherwise – that must temper any simplistic celebration about how it is used. There is a clear distinction between what can be called dating singles' blogs, which centre on how to find (and secure) a mate, and those considered here. That is, the blogosphere is not *a priori* oppositional or progressive as far as single women are concerned. As Graeme Turner argues, 'there is nothing inherent in these technologies which privileges the liberal, the tolerant or the progressive in terms of the opinions they carry' (2010, p. 140). I do not attend to such dating-focused sites as they simply reinscribe the types of cultural scripts and heteronormative ideologies that I have critiqued throughout this book. As one of the bloggers analyzed here remarks, 'There is little community/support for single people that isn't about hooking up' (*Singlutionary*), and it is this supposedly universal truth that all women wish to be partnered along with the lack of support for those contesting this assumption, including within the blogosphere, that the bloggers examined here explicitly seek to contest. The blogs upon which I do focus – including *Singlutionary, Dazzingly Single, Onely, Singletude, First Person Singular, The Spinster Chronicles, Rachel's Musings, Single Women Rule, Living Single* – are significant not just in terms of what they might tell us about women, mediated citizenship, and participation in the blogosphere but also about what they literally say about being a single woman in the twenty-first century West. Important here are not only the actual blogs themselves, but the textual community created when readers respond to various posts (i.e. how they function as an interactive space).

As I have shown throughout, single women in contemporary media culture are often yet pathologized, thought to be lacking, and as having failed to enter proper adulthood (i.e. not seen as viable citizens). Within these blogs, however, writers aim to refigure women's singleness as well as providing resources, support, and a textual community where others can intervene in and contribute to the revaluation of single women. They act, therefore, as an important avenue in which single women can 'talk back' to mainstream media culture, challenging postfeminism especially. Rather than only considering the form in isolation from its content (as many commentators have done), this chapter analyzes the discourses deployed by bloggers and within blogs and how women bloggers publicly perform their very singleness as part of a personal and political strategy of resignification. It also places the discussion within the context of broader debates about the (often overestimated) democratic possibilities of this sphere, especially in terms of women and mediated citizenship and what Axel Bruns (2008) has called 'produsage'. Moreover, in a context where feminism is now largely constituted within mainstream media culture and its presence therein is diffuse, it will show how these blogs, by acting to disrupt dominant media narratives around the woman without a man, can – like some of the book's considered in the previous chapter – work as instances of popular feminism. While not all single women bloggers explicitly identify as feminist (though some do), it is clear that in attempting to revalue single life for women they are drawing on a series of assumptions, and often specialist discourses, consistent with feminism.

In terms of Angela McRobbie's (2009) theorization of postfeminism as involving popular culture's 'double entanglement' with feminism (relying upon while yet repudiating it) that has throughout framed my analysis, here I suggest that these blogs have a more complicated, and less pessimistic, relationship to feminism. That is, they do not seek to actively distance themselves from (second-wave) feminism in the way that postfeminist and even third-wave writers have been routinely shown to do, nor do they even necessarily identify as feminist.[1] Moreover, in politicizing singleness and challenging the celebration and embrace of heterosexual romance constitutive of postfeminism they also challenge the 'postfeminist mode of address' which is believed to be 'ubiquitous' (Whelehan, 2010, p. 158). Using strategies akin to consciousness-raising; identity politics; deploying and reiterating the famous feminist dictum, the personal is political; and empathy and community-building, these blogs can be seen to be using so-called 'new' media for a form of what is now believed to be 'old' politics. While I am certainly not nostalgically seeking to identify second-wave modes of discourse and/or action in these blogs as a way of deeming them 'authentically' feminist, there are obvious similarities between these blogs and a politics and practice commonly associated with the second-wave. They also show the ongoing distillation of feminist ideas in the public sphere; the impossibility of a singular, 'authentic' feminism; and how the blogosphere works as a site where postfeminism and neoliberalism can be discursively contested.

Circulating oppositional discourse publicly has always been important to feminism as to other social movements, and while an underground network of production and distribution may have characterized the early women's movement, the online environment provides the opportunity for (some) 'ordinary' women to intervene in how single women are being made-to-mean.[2] My emphasis here is not simply that channels of user generated content are available to and being taken up in politically important ways by women, but on what this form is permitting them to say that may not be *sayable* in other spaces (whether it is heard is a correlative point which I will later address). Although not all blogs around singleness are solely addressed to women (or indeed authored by women), the majority of what I call 'legitimizing' blogs appear to be written by, for, and about single women and it is this subgenre that concerns me throughout this chapter.

Both mainstream and academic attention to the blog has been geared towards the topical 'filter blog', seen as the 'prototypical blog' (Karlsson, 2007, p. 138) and against which the 'personal blog' has been unfavourably compared. Filter blogs are seen to be those explicitly political blogs that focus on news and current affairs and seek to intervene in broader political debate, and are generally seen to 'produce more political knowledge than do personal journals' (Wei, 2009, p. 537). Personal bloggers are often dismissed as narcissists, a dismissal predicated on certain gendered ideas about what is 'legitimately' public (Cohen, 2006).

However, as I will show, the legitimizing single women blogs upon which I focus here are at once 'filter' blogs *and* forms of online diaries, interweaving and redefining – as so much women's and feminist writing does – the personal and the political throughout. In this way, representing a hybrid form, they put under strain the dominant critical ways of categorizing blogs and trouble the gendered political/personal binary upon which such criticism relies (Herring et al, 2004).

To date, critically both the content and the form of women's blogs, and indeed how they function in a broadly political sense, have been relatively neglected. That is, the discourses deployed and the subject positions adopted and how they may work in a contestatory fashion are often subordinated in critical narratives that tend to speak in broad brushstrokes about the democratizing potential of this field. But as Lopez argues, 'If the internet provides both a forum for the broadcasting of women's voices and the community to support that voice, then we should be paying much more attention to the work that is happening on these websites' (2009, p. 736); this is a critical aim with which this chapter is consistent. Before turning to alternative narratives of singleness proffered by and constructed within these blogs it is necessary to engage with the broader question of the political implications of the blogosphere, including the dangers of overestimating its democratic potentialities.

The blogosphere, women, and 'democratization'

What has been called 'the blogging revolution' (Loewenstein, 2008) is commonly believed to have occurred over the past decade, with the form reaching widespread popularity in the mid-2000s. As a form of communication theoretically available to all, blogs have been lauded for their ability to give voice to the formerly voiceless. As Melissa Gregg argues: 'Within a wider discourse of cyber-utopianism, blogs have been celebrated for their capacity to reflect experiences that have been trivialized, denigrated or ignored in the past, particularly the views of women and younger members of society' (2006, p. 153).[3] Such critics view the blogosphere as fulfilling the democratic role that the mainstream media is believed to have abrogated. For Axel Bruns, blogs and other collaborative digital media such as Wikipedia trouble the producer/user relation, thereby creating a new hybrid category of 'produsers' (2008). However, it is important to be wary of this celebratory rhetoric that often surrounds new media technologies, especially claims about the inherently democratic nature of electronic forms such as blogs.

In his recent book, *Ordinary People in the Media: The Demotic Turn* (2010), Graeme Turner cogently outlines the problems with the seemingly uncritical celebration of the democratization said to be enacted by, and within, the so-called blogosphere. There is what he calls a 'strong current of digital optimism around which predicts a dramatic shift in all kinds of potentialities as a result of what is understood as the consumer securing increased control over production and distribution of media content' (Turner, 2010, p. 127). 'Digital optimists', he argues, have used the rise of the blogger especially to predict 'a grass roots takeover of media space' (Turner, 2010, p. 128). That there is, as he emphasizes, little evidence to date substantiating such overblown claims does not impact upon their frequency nor dampen their enthusiasm.

In particular, for some critics the blog enables consumers to become the subjects of discourse; that is, it is a field key to contemporary self-presentation. In 'Blogging and the Politics of Listening', Steve Coleman has argued that 'as vehicles for self-presentation, blogs diminish people's need to be spoken for by others' (2005, p. 276). Given that feminism is a social movement based around ensuring the audibility of women's voices as well as their self-determination, it would seem then that blogging's potential to 'diminish people's need to be spoken for by others' is entirely consistent with feminism. That said, for women and those publicly identifying as feminist, this domain of apparently limitless discursive freedom needs to be approached with a little more caution. Feminists have long been attuned to the limitations of celebrating the universality or accessibility of any form of communication. In particular, such totalizing assumptions about the democratic potentialities of this sphere necessarily entail the elision of many women, who for material, geopolitical, and cultural reasons do not or cannot access or utilize so-called new media technologies. As Anne Travers argues, claims about democratization are troubled by the question of women's access: 'both to the hardware and to the software required for participation, the education required to make use of it, the information required to get on board, and, importantly, the sense of entitlement required to produce public written statements and to take up social space' (2003, p. 224). Certain modalities of difference are elided within the blogosphere as they are in other forums. It is always important to remain conscious of such factors when making broader claims about how new technologies act to empower women, especially as it is only ever *some* women who are thus empowered.[4] In particular, it appears that these singles' advocacy blogs are predominantly written by heterosexual women, but again this is presumably because these are the singles constituted the most problematic, as well as the most visible, in public discourse (see Chapter 1 here).

Moreover, while not necessarily identifying their blogs as feminist, it is not unremarkable that a number of women bloggers (including those considered here) choose, like their nineteenth century literary women counterparts, to remain anonymous or adopt pseudonyms; one can presume that such a deliberate cloaking gesture is used in an attempt to minimize the type of 'hostilities' often experienced by women (and especially feminists) online (Caden, 2007), as well as to facilitate forms of self-disclosure in which writers might otherwise be reluctant to engage. These caveats aside, there does appear to be some important cultural work, especially in the form of resignification and revaluation, being undertaken by single women bloggers. Furthermore, in terms of women's engagement with cyberspace, in quite literally 'claiming the space' and using it *as if it were yours* subverts traditional and exclusive assumptions about public space' (Travers, 2003, p. 233, original emphasis).

The personal and the political: Diaries, blogs and/as popular feminism

The personal web log, or blog, is often seen as a modern form of diary. As Viviane Serfaty argues in *The Mirror and The Veil*, 'weblogs and online diaries are but the latest avatars in the long history of self-representational writing' (2004c, p. 1). That literary genres such as the diary have historically been gendered feminine, and taken up predominantly by women, is well-known (as is their devaluation on such grounds). Debate over whether online diaries should be conceptualized on a continuum with their print counterparts has been pronounced (McNeil, 2003; Sorapure, 2003; van Dijck, 2004), especially given there are significant divergences as well as continuities between the two forms. In terms of personal blogs, that such writing could be potentially consumed by tens of millions of globally dispersed readers, and instantaneously by some, not surprisingly alters the cultural function and nuances the tenor of what is now routinely called 'life writing'. As part of the 'remediation' of the diary form, 'bloggers are retooling the practice of diary writing, meanwhile creating a new type of cultural knowledge and social interaction via their tools' (van Dijck, 2004).[5] The personal blog is, then, at once a descendent of earlier textual diary forms and a radically altered hybrid form of autobiography and self-construction not to mention community-creation.

Given that the single life is said to be characterized by a capacity for 'deeper introspection', it is perhaps not surprising that single women use the diary form – including in its online varieties – to make sense of, and self-reflexively analyze, that singleness (Kaufmann, 2008, p. 77). However, there are a number of key distinctions between traditional diaries (that is, those produced offline) and blogs. In addition to being potentially subject to editing or amending 'without the telltale signs of a ripped page' (McNeil, 2003, p. 37), the open-endedness of blogs precludes any sense of narrative closure. But perhaps one of the most obvious differences between diaries and blogs is the latter's *immediate* publicness and thus their mode of address and capacity for direct readerly intervention.[6] That is, they are not written simply for the self but for the other, who in turn is granted the ability to respond (Gokulsing & Dissanayake, 2009, p. 209). As I show here, these blogs cannot simply be defined as 'personal' blogs, as they also bear (to varying degrees) the characteristics of so-called 'filter' blogs especially when they seek to intervene in political debates about discrimination against single women or when they critique their representation in news coverage, for example. Moreover, in doing so, the kind of criticism levelled at the self-help discourses interrogated in the previous chapter – that their focus on the individual comes at the cost of political critique, a charge that can also be levelled at postfeminism and neoliberalism – is not applicable to these blogs, as they can be seen to have this dual focus.

Blogs, as public performances of particular selves, can be important sites of identity formation, making them particularly useful for those adopting overtly political identities. Although many of the blogs and bloggers attended to here may not directly identify as feminist (though some do), that their critique of how single women are stigmatized, devalued, and positioned subordinately within dominant narratives is informed by feminism is unquestionable; in this way, then, at the very least they are all implicitly feminist. That is, these bloggers deploy what Linda Grant has called a 'feminist interpretive lens' (1993, pp. 124–5) through which to make sense of their singleness and to critique the way single women are positioned within language, politics, and culture. In this way, I would argue that the contestatory work that each of these bloggers performs is essentially a form of popular feminism that seeks to discursively intervene in a complex system of institutional, political, and cultural privilege afforded to those who adhere to (heterosexual) models of coupledom and life-long co-habitation. Furthermore, given that it is now commonly recognized that there are myriad ways of 'being feminist and doing feminism' (Heywood & Drake, 1997) and as the idea of a homogenous feminist identity appropriately fades, it is of less concern to me whether these bloggers explicitly identify as 'feminist' than how they work to destabilize dominant ways of conceptualizing women's singleness through their own interventions into a broader cultural conversation about their material and symbolic subordination. In this way, they are consonant with what is occurring elsewhere in the women's blogosphere (or at least parts of it) particularly in what has been dubbed the 'mommy blog'. As Lopez emphasizes, 'mommy blogging' has been called 'a radical act' (Bradley in Lopez, 2009, p. 732) and the same can certainly be argued of single women bloggers seeking to contest hegemonic understandings of women's singleness. As Lopez argues, 'Mommy bloggers are creating a different picture of motherhood to what we see in the mainstream media' (2009, p. 732); likewise with women's singlehood and the blogs analyzed here.

The pro-single woman blog genre

Like any form of cultural product, single woman blogs are by no means homogenous and there are various subgenres within this category. The relative privilege of these bloggers also varies; some are journalists (*First Person Singular*'s Wendy Braitman) or psychologists (*Living Single*'s Bella DePaulo), drawing upon the capital afforded by these professional identities, while the expertise of other bloggers, as we will see, is grounded solely in their personal experience. A number of these blogs are jointly-authored by two or more writers (*Onely*, *Single Women Rule*, *Quirkyalone*), thereby offering a broader range of (though yet pro-single woman) perspectives. Some blogs are age specific such as *Single and Thirty-something* or *Sixty and Single in Seattle*, which is also geographically specific while other subgenres include the single Christian woman blog (the misleadingly titled *Radical Woman*) and the single mother (*Ms Single Mama*, *Solo Mother*). While these subcategories suggest some form of diversity among single bloggers, especially in age and positioning on the life course, in most instances bloggers do not foreground their racial identity so arguably the normative whiteness of the mainstream representations considered in previous chapters is reinscribed in this forum. We must also be conscious of the 'digital divide' (see Cullen, 2001) and recognize that these bloggers, and those who participate in the forum they provide, clearly possess cultural capital, time, and resources that others may not.

In terms of where such blogs are produced, those upon which I focus here emanate predominantly from the United States (although reader comments suggest that their audiences are more geographically dispersed), and are presumably written from regions within the US with the ICT infrastructure to facilitate the maintenance of their blogs. Perhaps it is no surprise that many of these legitimizing blogs have emerged from this context, given that a nascent political movement mobilizing around State sanctioned discrimination against singles – 'singlism' (DePaulo, 2006) – appears to be gaining momentum there. Moreover, a number of these single women blogs seem to have started in 2008 or 2009, suggesting that this form is a relatively recent phenomenon. The implied addressee of most of these blogs is a woman who, like the blogger herself, is single and likewise grappling with giving positive meaning to life in a broader cultural context yet governed by 'matrimania' (DePaulo, 2006), a process they concede to be fraught. Not insignificantly, DePaulo's work, and the terminology she has developed, is routinely deployed by these bloggers. Indeed, the widespread circulation of DePaulo's ideas, articulated comprehensively not just in her own blog (*Living Single*) but in her book *Singled Out* (2006; see Chapter 1 here) and sporadic op-ed pieces in the *New York Times* and the *San Francisco Chronicle*, suggesting some broader cultural reverberations, arguably constitutes her the quintessential celebrity singles' activist.

Table 6.1 given next provides a snapshot and the key features of some of the blogs upon which I focus here[7]. As this table suggests, these preambles or 'About me' sections perform important work in situating these blogs within a broader process of revaluing single women's lives. Drawing upon the work of Phillipe Lejune (whose work on the 'autobiographical pact' is well-known in literary studies), Vivianne Serfaty discusses the 'preamble' or the 'incipit' of personal blogs as 'cautionary warnings to unwanted readers': 'These pre-texts can be seen as guidelines to the reader, as tools to pilot and sometimes control the addressee's interpretation of the diaristic narrative' (2004a, p. 4). She emphasizes too, following Gerard Genette, how titles can work in tandem with the preambles to form and delimit readerly expectations (2004a, p. 5).[8] The majority of the blogs analyzed here deploy a title which gestures towards their content: *Singletude, Singlutionary, Dazzlingly Single, First Person Singular*, and *The Contented Single* and the level of detail provided in their preambles varies. They commonly take the form of an 'About' section, where it is not uncommon to find explicit articulations of the author's sense of their blog's purpose, revealing political investments in certain ways of viewing the world (in this case, as overwhelmingly biased against single women). As Laurie McNeil argues, such 'About me' as well as the 'Frequently Asked Questions' sections act as prefatory

Table 6.1 Single Women in the Blogosphere

Title	Features	Preamble/About section
Onely: Single and Happy	Onely is clearly informed by feminist discourses and frames; it has two authors, Lisa and Christina, who use their experiences to challenge how single women are positioned in various contexts. It regularly critiques media representation of single women & forms of discrimination against single women.	'[W]e believe that being single can be a satisfying and rewarding way of life, and in this blog, we hope to affirm and promote the joys of this lifestyle while highlighting and consistently questioning the heteronormative bias underlying most media representations of single people.'
Singlutionary	The Singlutionary's blog interweaves personal narrative with broader political critique. The blog has a confessional tone and often provides intimate insights into and, detailed deconstructions of, the author's relationships.	'I've done all the wrong things a single person can do and I FINALLY figured out how I can live a happy satisfying search-free life just where I am. And I want to share that because the path to here was pretty lonely and very frustrating.'
Singletude	Singletude is a non-gender specific site that covers how singles are represented in the media; political issues like discrimination through the tax system; and how to manage the expectations of others vis-à-vis singlehood.	'Singletude is a positive, supportive singles blog about life choices for the new single majority. It's about dating and relationships, yes, but it's also about the other 90% of your life – family, friends, career, hobbies – and flying solo and sane in this crazy, coupled world.'
First Person Singular	First Person Singular is written by a journalist and covers topics such as food for one; sex and dating; fashion; a 'daily life' section for her personal reflections; exposing myths and stereotypes about single women; and in a number of sections she celebrates the accomplishments of remarkable single women.	'FIRST PERSON SINGULAR is an online gathering place, resource guide (and yes, venting booth) for single women … We've been envied, feared, vilified and pitied throughout history, and much of the time, misunderstood. Who are we, anyway? How did we get here? And what's the best strategy to be happy ever after?'
Living Single	Bella DePaulo's Living Single focuses less on recounting personal experience, which is perhaps not surprising given that her blog is 'housed' or hosted by Psychology Today and her authority therein is predicated upon her status as a psychologist and academic with a high public profile on discrimination against singles. That is not to say she does not speak about her own experiences as a contentedly single woman, but her posts read more like newspaper opinion pieces than personalized narratives.	'The truth about singles in our society.'

Single Women Rule	This blog has two key women authors, Terry McDonald and Keysha Whittaker, with regular guest bloggers and contributing writers; it has a type of self-help feel about it. As a membership organization, it seeks to connect and mobilize single women.	'SingleWomenRule.com is a blog and membership organization that encourages unmarried women to revel in life's magic and feel truly fulfilled, whether the knight in shining (or newly refurbished) armor ever arrives.'
The Spinster Chronicles	The Spinster Chronicles, whose author goes by the pseudonym, Spinster Leese, is also a diary-style blog that uses personal reflection as the basis for broader ruminations on how single women are made to feel aberrant.	'A line-by-line account of all the ways I'm defying our society's expectations, and loving every minute of it.'
Rachel's Musings	Rachel's Musings, originally entitled 'Singles by Choice', is a deeply politicized consciousness-raising-style blog that seeks to expose and challenge discrimination against single women. It is also grounded in narratives of the author's personal experience.	'This blog contains my musing on topics from singlism and feminism to atheism and religion. Themes that are of most interest to me revolve around meaning and the difficulty we have in finding it in today's world.'
Ms Single Mama	Ms Single Mama, unsurprisingly, is focused on the difficulties of being a single mother. That said, it too seeks to revalue single life for women.	'During my first year as a single mom, I was hunting – searching for someone to rescue me. Then something happened. I opened my eyes and realized that I didn't need a man at all' (original emphasis).
Solo Lady	Solo Lady is a website where readers are encouraged to write their own blogs. Often provides advice on topics like travelling on your own; financial issues for single women; politics; and health care.	'Welcome to your Solo Lady community, created for single women everywhere. We'll help you realize and enjoy the many options and opportunities of living solo. Solo Lady is now in its fourth year, and continues growing. So please enjoy, and please participate with us. We'll expand your horizons, enhance your world, and enrich your independent life!' (original emphasis).
Quirkyalone	A multi-authored blog, featuring inter alia a weekly post by the authors of Onely. It is non-gender specific and suggests the term is a 'tool for singledom and relationships in a new era where unmarried households are becoming a majority'. It routinely critiques the one-dimensional focus on coupledom, but does not exclude couples.	'Quirkyalones are people who enjoy being single (but are not opposed to being in a relationship) and prefer being single to dating for the sake of being in a relationship. It's a mindset … We prefer to be single rather than settle. In fact, the core of quirkyalone is the inability to settle. We spend a significant chunk of our lives single because we hold relationships to a high standard.'

pages that 'enable an audience to make quick decisions about whether to read this diary, or move on' (2003, p. 31). Such pages, she continues, also enable new readers to quickly acquire knowledge about a particular community, a move which facilitates their entry into that community (2003, p. 34).

The extent to which the blogs are explicitly political, as in offering a broader critique of how women are positioned within hetero-patriarchy, also varies, a distinction often evident in the preambles and what have been called 'capsule biographies' (McNeil, 2003, p. 31). For example, in their preamble, or what appears to be their mission statement, the authors of *Onely*, Christina and Lisa, somewhat polemically outline the aim of their blog:

> We chose the name *Onely* because the word helps reverse popular conceptions of what it means to be single. Here at *Onely*, we reject the negative connotations associated with being 'alone' promoted by contemporary American culture, connotations that suggest emptiness – such as 'lonely' or 'looking' – or that pathologize those who exist in the world outside of a coupled romantic relationship. Instead, we believe that being single can be a satisfying and rewarding way of life, and in this blog, we hope to affirm and promote the joys of this lifestyle while highlighting and consistently questioning the heteronormative bias underlying most media representations of single people–even and especially those that emerge within supposedly 'pro-single' rhetorics.

Onely in particular clearly mobilizes feminist discourses throughout, and purports to offer both a critique of hetero-patriarchal bias against single women and a celebration of the single lifestyle. These bloggers offer an explicitly feminist critique of how single women are positioned within dominant media narratives, and blog with the expressed goal of offering an alternative, not to mention a demystification of '"pro-single" rhetorics', to such limited representations. *Onely* exemplifies, perhaps better than any other, the counter-discursive potentialities of these legitimizing single women blogs as well as demonstrating how they disrupt the logics of postfeminism. That said, they all act politically given their attempts to contest the dominant meanings around women's singleness.

Some clearly appropriate the kinds of self-help discourses, and their accompanying revaluation of the single self, analyzed in the previous chapter. For example, *Dazzlingly Single.com* is introduced with: 'Never base your happiness on someone else. Fall in love with that wonderful person – you!!' Likewise, *Singultionary.Com* pronounces: 'No more desperate dating, pitiful pinning, and wahhhh wahhhh waiting!' *Singletude* (with the subtitle: 'A Positive Blog for Singles') in its preamble purports to decentralize the role of the significant other and re-prioritize other aspects of the quotidian:

> *Singletude* is a positive, supportive singles blog about life choices for the new single majority. It's about dating and relationships, yes, but it's also about the other 90% of your life – family, friends, career, hobbies – and flying solo and sane in this crazy, coupled world. *Singletude* isn't about denying loneliness. It's about realizing that whether you're single by choice or by circumstance, this single life is your life to live.

As this quotation makes evident, the rhetoric around singleness by these bloggers is largely celebratory. Although such a celebration may appear to merely invert the married/single binary, and thus fail to destabilize it, these discursive interventions are strategic and work to combat the pathologization of women's singleness occurring elsewhere in the public sphere. Clearly, these bloggers are attempting to recuperate women's singleness from the negative connotations it still evokes; they do this largely through telling their own single stories.

Telling single stories: The autobiographical 'I' of singles' blogs

Axel Bruns argues, 'By personalizing content, blogs go beyond a purely informative role and provide a platform for debate, deliberation, and the expression of a personal identity in relation to the rest of the (blogging) world' (2006, p. 5). But beyond this, they function not merely for the 'expression' of self to which Bruns alludes but to the constitution of particular selves in and through the narrative form of the blog. This constitution of the self in narrative as an iterative process is now widely critically accepted. As a number of theorists and Anthony Giddens in particular have argued, the self of late modernity is marked by perpetual invention and self-invention of a 'reflexive biography' (1991). Moreover, an increasing confessional culture (Plummer, 1995; Smith & Watson, 1996; Pearce, 2004) has seen the uses of the narrative 'I' extend into new forums and formats, like the blog. In this sense, blogs are fast becoming one of the most popular discursive sites for the public constitution of self; and, like the blog, the self is perpetually in process and subject to rewriting and refashioning. The location of the self in relation to material discussed (as well as the very constitution of that self) is central to the cultural work performed by single women blogs; these seemingly micro vignettes more often than not provide the basis for a broader critique of the operations of the macro. That is, the personal is indubitably political in these textual spaces as they work to challenge the neoliberal and postfeminist privatization of the field of intimate life. Further, online diary-style blogs can serve to disrupt our ideas about 'whose lives should be written' and indeed how (McNeil, 2003, p. 45).

The 'discursive repertoires' (Hermes, 1995) mobilized by these bloggers vary but generally personal experience is evoked as an authorizing gesture and bloggers regularly construct their own consciousness-raising narratives. For some, the blog's preamble appears central to a broader goal of contributing to social change through self-disclosure (Serfaty, 2004c, p. 9). In *The Spinster Chronicles*, the author professes to offer 'a line by line account of how I'm defying our society's expectations, and loving every minute of it'. Their so-called 'expertise', and consequently their authority to speak, is grounded in (narratives of) their own experience. Similarly, in her 'About Me' section, the author of *Singlutionary* tells readers:

> I am an expert at being single.
> Oh, I've been that single girl who did everything a desperate, horny, lovesick loser does. And I lived to tell about it.
> Now, I live a happy, healthy, pity-free life and I seek to share my love for single (and desperation free) living with the world.

Here, she constructs a past self against which her current pro-single blogging self is defined. Similarly, the author of *Ms Single Mama* explains:

> I started this blog one year later in the fall of 2007. During my first year as a single mom, I was hunting – *searching* for someone to rescue me. Then something happened.
> I opened my eyes and realized that I didn't *need* a man at all, I just wanted one. *There's a big difference.*
> We'll definitely hit a few bumps and maybe a pothole or two. Join my Single Moms Forum to vent or learn from each other, this way we can keep each other company along the way.
>
> (original emphasis; see also *Solomother*)

This comment is indicative of the self-reflexivity characterizing online diary-style blogs, especially as bloggers seek to unpack their own motivations and provide self-justifications for their use of this very public form of writing (Serfarty, 2004b).

All these bloggers imply that they have had some sort of epiphany or 'click moment' (as it was termed in the second-wave), forcing them to recognize that the single life need not be seen as pathetic, lonely, or the province of the hyper-selfish (as it is commonly seen in popular discourse). In this way, as Wood has argued of women's sex blogs, although not entailing the face-to-face element of the traditional feminist practice they act as a 'mediated consciousness-raising (c-r) space' (2008, p. 481). Within feminism, the concept of consciousness-raising was central during the second-wave in particular; in so-called CR groups women would interact and share personal stories of their subordinate positioning under patriarchy and come to view the world through new, highly politicized, eyes (see Hogeland, 1998). Similarly, the authors of these blogs speak to how single women have been marginalized and devalued, a stigmatization they explicitly seek to contest after themselves having experienced some kind of personal awakening. In this way, a re-politicization of the single woman and a validation of the single identity occurs in and through these blogs.

In terms of the importance of self-representation, Shelley Budgeon, drawing on Ken Plummer's work in *Telling Sexual Stories* (1995), argues that such narratives are not 'authority stories' but rather are the 'stories that can be told when people make a claim to the legitimacy of their own lives' (2008, p. 320). As I argue here, the blogosphere has become central for some single women (and indeed their participatory readers) in claiming such legitimacy in a way that rarely seems possible in mainstream postfeminist media culture. In this vein, the Singlutionary, in her 'Frequently Asked Questions' section, responds to a question about her personal motivation for creating this blog:

I have been single for almost ALL of my adult life (and before that also). Not just single-as-in-not-married but single-as-in-not-even-a-successful-relationship-in-sight. So why then, was I the recipient of everyone's midnight calls seeking advice about marriage or engagement or lack of engagement or potential date or lack thereof? I have no bloody clue. What I do know is that I've done all the wrong things a single person can do and I FINALLY figured out how I can live a happy satisfying search-free life just where I am. And I want to share that because the path to here was pretty lonely and very frustrating.

Here, she tracks a very personal journey which she shares with the aim of freeing others from the types of affective strain associated with the relentless search for a partner. The Singlutionary, then, wants to spare her single sisters the pain that she had to experience before conceding her own value as a single woman. Challenging the dominant ideology around coupledom and societal expectations, she now seeks, like other bloggers, to spread the single word regarding the possibility of a viable alternative for women. In this way, these bloggers seek to 'rewrite the meanings of singlehood', especially through refiguring it as a positive identity (Budgeon, 2008, p. 310). Unlike 'postfeminist Singletons', therefore, their energies are not devoted to 'defeating' their singleness but to making it a more inhabitable subject position. This trajectory – the process of conscious rejection of normative assumptions about women and the taking up not of the pen but of the keyboard – is mapped in most of these capsule biographies and again demonstrates the similarity between what is occurring in these blogs and earlier feminist processes of consciousness-raising (or indeed any resistance to interpellation). *Singletude*'s 'Clever Elsie' outlines the purpose of her blog:

> Clever Elsie is a 30-something unmarried female in New York, plowing upstream with just one paddle. She started this blog to combat the treatment of singles as second-class citizens. Single-headed homes now tip the scales at 50.8% of the population, so she thinks it's time we threw our weight around!) Singletude isn't about false positivity but about recognizing that a human life doesn't need to be paired to have value.

Like most others considered here, Elsie positions herself firmly within the realm of singles' advocacy.

These blogs function not just for the bloggers to construct their own single stories but provide a space for their readers to do so as well. As we will see, when bloggers 'reserve part of their site to [sic] others, they are taking steps ... towards the formation of a stable community' (Serfaty, 2004c, p. 60). For example, in the 'Single by Choice' section of *Rachel's Musings*, she encourages readers to share their experiences of singlehood as a way of providing vital social support:

> This part of the blog is designed to stimulate discussion about choosing being single as a lifestyle, whether temporary or permanent. It is also a place where we can share our stories of why we have chosen to be single, including our battle-scars and doubts. I hope that we can give each other encouragement and support in those times of doubt.

While the rhetoric of choice has been associated with – and indeed seen as a key marker of – postfeminism, its deployment in these blogs has a different inflection altogether, particularly as single life as a conscious choice, as opposed to unwanted happenstance, retains a radical dimension for women especially. That is, as I have shown in previous chapters, the idea that a woman would choose to remain without a male partner (for heteronormativity reigns) for any length of time has been largely unrepresentable. As Bella DePaulo remarked in an interview in the *Sydney Morning Herald*: 'It is not even a part of our cultural imagination that you could embrace being single and want to be single' (in Thomas, March 19, 2009). These blogs seek to make this a viable choice; that is, to make it 'part of our cultural imagination'.

Some of these single bloggers are at pains to emphasize that they are not anti relationship (or, more specifically, anti-men); that said, their personal narratives reaffirm that women do not need men to feel complete (see *Single and Thirty-something*). A number seek to debunk prince charming or man-as-saviour-style mythologies entirely (*Onely*, *Singlutionary*, *Rachel's Musings*). For example, on the satirically entitled *Bridget Jones Has Nothing On Me*, its author writes:

> As young girls, we're fed fairy tales of what life will be like when we grow up. We'll live in castles with Prince Charming, a slew of dwarfs, and fluffy Forrest creatures. We'll have closets full of designer hand bags and matching shoes. We'll either be high powered executives, successful entrepreneurs, or perfectly happy housewives/mothers. Those are dirty vicious lies.
>
> ('About Little Ole Me' section)

Also emphasizing that men are not integral to women's happiness, *The Contented Single*'s by-line reads: 'For the single that's happy to stay that way.' Similarly, on *Original Diva: Be the Amazing Woman You Are*, readers are encouraged to: 'Stop waiting for a man to make you happy! … If you are a single or divorced woman and you are looking to transcend the man obsession, then you are in the right place!' There are many ways such discursive transcendence is performed in these blogs, including through underscoring, and subsequently deconstructing, the naturalization of such an 'obsession' in various forms of postfeminist media culture.

Discursive activism: Bloggers contesting 'singlism'

Given that, according to postfeminist logics, activism (whether discursive or more traditional forms) is deemed redundant, these blogs challenge not just problematic narratives of singleness proffered in postfeminist media culture but postfeminist ways of figuring feminism and political practice. The nature and scope of specific posts not surprisingly varies widely: the representation of single women in popular culture; sex for the single; recipes when cooking for one; when and if to have children; book, music, television and film reviews; how to deal with nauseatingly coupled friends; travelling on your own; and political commentary are all staples within the single woman blogosphere. To varying degrees, these bloggers often post relevant clips from sites such as *YouTube* or advertisements; photographs; links to books they may be consuming as well other relevant websites; newspaper or magazine articles; and hyperlinks to other blogs. This introduction of different forms of media – images, video, or audio files – has the effect of preventing 'the construction of a unified, linear, ordered portrait of the self while simultaneously creating new meanings and opening up new spaces for interpretations defying the control of the diarists themselves' (Serfarty 2004c, pp. 28–9).

Perhaps not surprisingly, criticism on how single women are discursively constructed in mainstream media culture routinely features. Bloggers express their deep sense of frustration at the limited meanings granted to women's singleness in and through postfeminist discourse. For example, *Onely* also turns its attention to the self-help manuals considered in the previous chapter, arguing that those books focusing on working on the self to reach the other employ 'the classic "bait and switch" technique used by faux singles advocates: *Here's how to live a great single life, so that you can become unsingle!?'* (*Onely*, 8 December, 2009, original emphasis). In another post they critique reality television programmes like those considered here in Chapter 4. This excerpt also demonstrates the importance of humour and satire in these blogs[9]:

> we need a show that, instead of reversing the way married men and women are portrayed on TV, would subvert the way that singles are (most often) portrayed on TV — as desperate, lonely losers always struggling to find a mate. And where has television cornered the market on this portrayal of single people? That's right — Reality TV! Take your pick — from *The Bachelor* and *The Bachelorette* (those old standards), to *Rock of Love*, *More to Love*, or a *Shot at Love*, to *Blind Date* (which, I'll admit, is a personal fave), to *Joe Millionaire*, to *Who Wants to Marry My Dad*, and even *Married by America* — the basic premise of all these shows is that if you're single, it's time for an intervention!
>
> (*Onely*, 30 July, 2009)

In response, they outline their plans, with tongues firmly in cheeks, for a new reality programme called 'I complete me'. This represents an obvious rewriting of the well-known line uttered by Tom Cruise's character in the film *Jerry Maguire* where he confesses to his love interest: 'You complete me.' Similarly, on the DVD release of *He's Just Not That Into You*, *Onely* suggests: 'HJNTIY takes every stereotype about single people (especially single women) and conflates each one like a big ball of cotton-candy fluff, producing a lame series of (poorly connected) stories that ultimately repeat the same old (heteronormative) messages that we single people are so used to (not to mention tired of!) hearing' (10 June, 2009). The community of *Onely* readers not surprisingly agreed, posting a number of similar comments as well as links to their own blog reviews. For example, *Singletude*'s author uploaded a hyperlink to her own review of February 2009. In a similar manner, Bella DePaulo offers regular critiques on the portrayal of single women on television and in advertising. In addition to representations in popular culture, she regularly uses press coverage as the basis for her blog, citing specific articles as further evidence of singlism and matrimania in the public sphere. Likewise, *Singletude* offers a weekly wrap up entitled 'Singles in the News'.

In addition to challenging how single women are represented in popular culture, *Onely*'s 'Singled Out' section explicitly addresses political issues relevant to single women, especially around the time of the 2008 US Presidential election. These bloggers refuse to allow singleness to be privatized, thereby contesting the idea that the individual must simply act as the 'entrepreneurial actor' promoted in neoliberal political culture to personally manage the difficulties of singleness (Brown, 2003). Instead, they highlight the links between state-sanctioned forms of discrimination and living as a single woman on a daily basis, emphasizing how single women must attempt to intervene to effect political change – even if only through exercising their democratic right to vote. One of the two *Onely* bloggers, Christina, draws attention to the importance of the single woman's vote (29 September, 2009): 'Single women only earn 56 cents to every dollar a married man makes! *Newsweek*'s and *Time*'s coverage of the Sarah Palin VP campaign contains singlist rhetoric disparaging both childfree single women and single moms! (Even though single women form a key voting demographic that could sway the election).' Here, *Onely* critiques discrimination against single women through citing the pay gap between them and married men and underscoring how 'singlist rhetoric' is being deployed during the campaign as well as viewing single women as a key political constituency.

Likewise, on 'Super Tuesday' (where 24 US states hold their prima-
ries), Clever Elsie of *Singletude* urged singles to vote for a candidate that
would respond to the distinctive needs of singles: 'Singles, we are a
large demographic (up to 50% of the US population by some estimates),
and we have the power to tip this vote in the direction of a nominee
who will work to implement policies that will be singles-friendly'
(5 February, 2008; see also *Solo Lady*'s 'Single Women Must Vote!!' post,
1 April, 2008). The highly politicized discourse employed here, and on
Onely, further indicates how these blogs function as important forms of
political commentary and critique.

Onely also draws attention to cultural specificity and how different
forms of 'matrimania' are evident elsewhere in the world. After a post
regarding a report about Malaysia giving away free honeymoons in an
effort to increase the marriage rate, they seek out other similar stories
from readers:

> Does anyone have other examples of matrimania in different coun-
> tries? Does the matrimania of countries other than the U.S. make
> the U.S. matrimania look less bad, or does it make the U.S. look
> even worse? Regarding the latter, I think that for the U.S. to offer
> over 1,000 legal rights to married people at the expense of singles
> is almost *more* insidiously matrimaniacal than the Saudi govern-
> ment's wife-selling ideas, because at least the Saudis don't pretend to
> have a culture of sexual equality and freedom for all.
>
> (*Onely*, 19 October, 2009)

This emphasis on how 'matrimania' is institutionally supported, or
rather enacted, through benefits granted to couples unavailable to singles is a common thread throughout these legitimizing single women
blogs. In this way, as *Quirkyalone* notes of *Onely*, these blogs are effectively forms of 'singles' advocacy'.

Some writers provide practical information on how to negotiate, and
mitigate, the impact of policy or legislatively based discrimination.
Although its focus is not gender-specific, in *Singletude* readers are given
practical financial tips in a two part series 'Tax Tips for Single Filers' (19
& 28 March, 2008): 'As a single, you are a one-income family. Unless
you marry, you won't be able to rely on someone else's pension or Social
Security. So it's imperative that *you* prepare yourself for retirement now.
That means investing wisely, part of which is keeping as much of your
investment as possible in *your* pocket and out of the government's'
(original emphasis). The series follows a post entitled 'The Singles'

Penalty: Tax Code Discrimination' (18 March, 2008) which shows how singles pay more tax than married people in the same tax bracket. Such issues are also regularly canvassed in Bella DePaulo's *Living Single* blog on *Psychology Today*. For example, 'The High Price of Being Single' (5 October, 2009) also takes up the issue of financial disadvantage for singles. DePaulo, as mentioned, is a key figure in rendering visible the politics of singlehood, commonly drawing attention to how bias against single people and women in particular manifests such as through workplace discrimination. In this way, the difficulties experienced by singles are not attributed to the individual but seen as a part of a broader socio-political context that devalues them. In suggesting that structural remedies are necessary, these bloggers work to challenge the individualization and depoliticization characteristic of neoliberalism and indeed postfeminism (see Vavrus, 2007).

In *Rachel's Musings*, the author overtly seeks to make readers aware of how they are being discriminated against in her piece prior to the 2008 National Single's Week: 'Overcoming Singlism'. The three elements in how this can be achieved, she argues, are that 'We need to *recognize* singlism both in society and in ourselves'; 'We need to *raise awareness* by pointing out singlism wherever and whenever we see it and to counter the marriage myths'; and finally, 'We need to *counteract* singlism by embracing being single as a completely valid choice and by valuing all our relationships' (original emphasis, 21 September, 2008). Clearly, here, this blogger engages directly with the politics of being single and provides strategies on how singlism can be combated, both at the level of the self and of society. Rachel's comments here are reminiscent of feminist critiques of sexism and patriarchy; especially in her emphasis on singlism (like sexism) as an invisible, insidious form of inequity that requires two interrelated discursive tactics: firstly, it must be rendered visible, and secondly, it must be contested; this blog (like others) regularly performs this dual political manoeuvre. In this way, she advocates a form of activism predicated on the embrace of singleness as a distinct identity (i.e. an identity politics). In particular, she emphasizes what appears to be a form of discursive activism or what Stacey Young has called 'discursive politics' (1997), with bloggers like Rachel working to intervene and actively change the complex, intertextual network of meanings in which the single woman is implicated but also in laying bare the various forms of discrimination against her. In the same way that feminist publishing has been seen as integral to such 'discursive politics', and thus the performance of contemporary feminist activism (Young, 1997), so too with these blogs.

Continuing the trend of underscoring how single women are being pathologized in mainstream culture, *First Person Singular* features a section on 'Myths and Stereotypes'. Therein, Braitman engages with the hefty cultural baggage associated with the signifier 'spinster' (the politics of which I have discussed in previous chapters). She writes about her strategic deployment of the term, which she relates directly to other marginalized groups' subversive appropriation of derogatory signifiers: 'I liked watching people flinch when I described myself that way. I wanted to upend the stereotype, and reclaim the word, help make it hip, as gays and lesbians did with the word "queer."' However, she also notes that while she had originally intended to call her blog, *The Unexpected Spinster*, a literary agent suggested that her usage of the term would be sure to 'spell doom for any publishing prospects'. So recognizing, as the agent had implied, that the 'word has had a bad rap for hundreds of years', she relented and renamed the blog. The negative connotations of 'spinster', then, continue to be evoked – even in the blogosphere. Nonetheless, Braitman's emphasis on the politics of naming also sees her writing positioned broadly within a feminist discursive realm. In contrast, the author of *The Spinster Chronicles* has adopted the pseudonym 'Spinster Leese' and calls her links section 'Sites for Spinsters'.

Likewise, in a March 2009 post unambiguously entitled, 'I'm a Spinster', the author of *Singlutionary* (she offers no other nomenclature) defiantly proclaims: 'Apparently the word "Spinster" used to mean a financially independent woman who made her own living spinning! Well. That is me! I'm a Spinsty for reals now!' Here The Singlutionary even affectionately shortens the term, dubbing herself a 'Spinsty'. Another blog seeks to reclaim 'spinster' too. The preamble of *The Spinsterlicious Life* suggests it is a place 'where delightful single women, who know how to live and love life, and the people who love them (...or wonder about them) engage with each other. We're putting a spin on Spinster!' Unlike the anxious singles of postfeminist media culture, these women revel in their singleness. This point leads into the question of how these women are using their singleness as the basis for a distinct, textually performed identity.

One of the significant aspects of the self-making that occurs in these blogs is the way being single comes to function as a form of identity politics. While the limitations of a politics based on identity claims have been emphasized by many critics, including feminists, the authors of these legitimizing singles' blogs come to define themselves as single women in ways that are clearly political and as the basis for the mobilization of women.[10] For example, in the 'My story as a single' section of

Rachel's Musings, she links being single to other forms of subordinated and socially marginalized identities, even (not unproblematically) appropriating the politicized trope of 'coming out':

> It is slowly but surely dawning on me that maybe it's time to come out as single. Yes, just like gays and lesbians had to consciously proclaim their otherness, their homosexuality, it's time for me to embrace being single, to consciously proclaim that I am single and that I want to build my life as a single woman. I am not waiting for a guy to carry me off. I am not waiting for a soulmate anymore. It's scary, yes, but it's also liberating.

By invoking the Otherness of the single woman, especially she who chooses to remain so, she highlights how taking up the subject position of 'single woman' can function as a potentially empowering gesture. These bloggers write themselves into being as an oppositional gesture. That is, these public identifications as unashamedly single can be transgressive in that the blogger refuses to recognize the aberrance of being single and instead works to normalize it as an identity. In so doing, they also provide a forum for others to become part of a public forged from this shared recognition of singleness as more than a default way of being in the world.

Interactivity or 'mini public spheres'

As these blogs suggest, networks of women then are constituted, and communicate with each other, in this virtual arena. Blogs, as David Perlmutter argues, are 'porous portals not meant to be one-stop journeys. Even the most solipsistic blogs tend to link to friends or buddies or fellow conspirators' (2008, p. 17). Much has been written on the ways in which the internet can function as a public, or counter public, sphere, work that is often predicated upon the types of democratizing assumptions problematized earlier in this chapter. To signal the heterogeneity of online communities and contest the idea of a singular, uniform public sphere (as per Jurgen Habermas' original ideal), Gillian Youngs uses the term 'mini public spheres' in a way that aptly describes the kinds of cultural work being undertaken in and through these single woman blogs: 'Self-selecting interactive engagement is a characteristic of the new web world, which may be considered to be generating perhaps large numbers of mini-public spheres through specific blogs or groupings of blogs focused on similar issues or concerns' (2009, p. 132).

Moreover, the fact that the blogger both joins and creates communities necessarily informs both the type of text and the type of self that she produces (McNeil, 2003, p. 32).

In terms of online community, Paul Hodkinson has shown that there has been a migration of those formerly involved in online discussion groups to personalized online interactive journals where networked communities are maintained in much the same way (2007, p. 627). Some of these bloggers explicitly outline how they, and the textual space they have created, attempt to foster a sense of community and a movement of similarly disposed singles. For example, The Singlutionary purports to be involved in – or rather precipitating – a singles' revolution: 'The singlution is a fledgling movement, started right here, which supports single people in living full and satisfying lives just the way they are. It celebrates single living and offers hope and community to people who struggle with single life.' Here, she conceives of her blog as a valuable form of social support and she refers to this as the 'happily single online community' (11 November, 2010).[11] In using this idea of a movement and supportive network of single women she clearly invokes second-wave feminism as well as *Bridget Jones's* celebration of the 'Singleton' lifestyle. Likewise, *Quirkyalone* purports to be the 'online home of the quirkyalone movement!' Being 'quirkyalone' is 'about resisting the tyranny of coupledom, the prevailing notion that you must be in a relationship at all times in order to be happy'.[12]

Journalist Wendy Braitman, author of *First Person Singular*, tells readers that she started her blog after she 'unwittingly became an expert' (a claim made by many other single bloggers) on the single woman's life and felt the need to offer a textual site for women to gather to discuss their singleness:

> FIRST PERSON SINGULAR is an online gathering place, resource guide (and yes, venting booth) for single women. In January, 2007 we officially tipped the scales, when our ranks swelled to more than half of all American women. Magazines are devoted to us, politicians court our votes, and realtors have made it easier for us to get home loans. That doesn't mean a single life is always easy. It's not. We've been envied, feared, vilified and pitied throughout history, and much of the time, misunderstood. Who are we, anyway? How did we get here? And what's the best strategy to be happy ever after?

In Braitman's 'About' section, cited above, the centrality of the 'I' is missing. Instead, she invokes a community of like-minded single women as well as emphasizing their value as a political constituency with their own concerns and agendas. Like other bloggers, she also alludes to how single women have been historically denigrated. In her concluding series of questions she deploys the pronoun 'we', again fostering the sense of a supportive online community for a group of women that, by conscious choice or circumstance, challenge societal expectations by not being partnered. In fostering, and hosting, such a community, these blogs mirror the kinds of coalition and community-building activities that characterized feminism's second-wave. Thereby, they challenge the rhetoric of individualism dominant in mainstream media culture and which is a constitutive part of both neoliberal and postfeminist discourses. There is also a sense of sisterhood, especially in the way bloggers support each other through cross-posting and guest appearances.

In attempting to form such publics, as well as in drawing attention to the way singles are treated by the State, such bloggers work to disrupt the governing neoliberal rhetorics critiqued here in previous chapters. As Wendy Brown argues, 'The model neo-liberal citizen is one who strategizes for her/himself among various social, political and economic options, not one who strives with others to alter or organize these options. A fully realized neo-liberal citizenry would be the opposite of public-minded, indeed it would barely exist as a public' (2003, p. 3). In such a context, she argues, there is no 'body politic' but just a 'group of individual entrepreneurs and consumers' (2003, p. 3). These bloggers, however, clearly attempt to bring into being a pro-single (if not feminist) virtual public that challenges limited ways of figuring singleness in both politics and various sites of mainstream media.

On *Solo Lady.com*, consisting of a web page, links to resources, a message board, and a blog page where readers can post their own entries, creator Lea Lane (aka The Solo Lady) introduces the site:

> Welcome to *your Solo Lady community, created for single women everywhere*. We'll help you realize and enjoy the many options and opportunities of living solo.
> Solo Lady is now in its fourth year, and continues growing. So please enjoy, *and please participate with us*. We'll expand your horizons, enhance your world, and enrich your independent life!
>
> (original emphasis)

As on *First Person Singular*, Lane highlights how the site functions as a community and also invokes the 'we' of this discursive support network, creating the sense that there are many others who also recognize the 'enriching' potentialities of women's singlehood (i.e. that the reader is not aberrant). Moreover, the ability of readers to post their own entries (as opposed to simply responding to those of others) further augments this idea of a textual space created for its readers.

The so-called blog roll, or links to other blogs, also works to help establish this community, as readers are encouraged to consider and participate in other 'sanctioned' blogs. As one post on *singlewomenrule. com* emphasizes, 'So there's definitely strength in numbers. As we journey through internet land we've found a few more blogs by us for us. We'll be featuring content from these gals so check 'em out!' (31 March, 2009). For National Singles Week 2009 in the US, a number of these bloggers took part in a 'blog crawl' from September 20 to 27, further cementing this sense of a discursive community engaged in politicizing singleness. As *Onely* explains to readers: 'In the virtual world, a blog crawl works like a pub crawl, or museum crawl in the real world; each day, you'll visit a designated blog to read featured blog posts from our favorite voices in the singles community.' The blog crawl, featuring other though likeminded voices, appears to function as a concentrated exemplification of the processes of feedback, interactivity, and cross-referencing that routinely occur in these blogs. It is also worth noting, however, that those voices authorized to speak during the blog crawl become the designated celebrities of the pro-single women blogosphere, ensuring that some women are read over others. In this way, certain women, through their celebritization, become what P. David Marshall calls 'privileged epistemological players' (1997) in this realm. That said, such voices also have more chance of being taken up firstly in internet news sites (as they sometimes are) and subsequently through mainstream media outlets, thereby extending their critique of singlism to a wider audience.

These bloggers are often reflexive about the processes of community-building and the establishment of support networks; importantly, that single women *need* this online form of public validation and support because it is not elsewhere available is an assumption underpinning each of these blogs. For example, in a recent post on *The Spinster Chronicles*, Spinster Leese expresses a debt to other bloggers similarly working to validate single life:

> *The Spinster Chronicles* is coming up on its first year anniversary and its popularity has grown thanks in part to others who explore the topic of 'singles in society' in the blogging community. In particular

I want to thank the writers from *The Singlutionary, Singletude,* and *Onely* for helping to promote my blog and generate awareness about 'the spinster lifestyle' to the rest of the world.

(7 October, 2009)

Here, she positions her blog (and its apparent success) within a broader – indeed, overstatedly, global – conversation around women's singleness that is being staged in and through the blogosphere. Likewise, the unambiguously titled *Single Women Rule.com* defines itself as: 'A global network of single women reveling in life's magic and feeling truly fulfilled – whether the knight in shining (or newly refurbished) armor ever arrives!' Moreover, that they share an important, activist goal is evident in hortatory posts like this one from the aforementioned *singlewomenrule.com*: 'Sisters in the struggle: single women blog up!' (31 March, 2009). In exhorting their 'sisters' to take action, the resonances between the discourses used in many of these blogs and second wave feminist writing are clear; though in this case the action refers to blogging. The collective, collaborative elements of this form constitute an important site for single women to mobilize and critique how they are being positioned in public discourse. One of the most important ways in which this collaboration manifests is through reader posts.

The direct participation of readers in the form of responses to previous posts, links, and/or questions also creates the sense of a dialogic public, and readers can help shape the blog through their own interventions (although, like newspaper editors, of course, the host of the blog has a degree of editorial control). In this way, the blog differs significantly from other forms of life writing. The principle difference between the blog as an online form of diary and the 'regular' diary form is 'the online diarist is always irreducibly dialogic, expecting an audience and a response. It accounts for the other, and writes in response to the response of the Other' (Gokulsing & Dissanayake, 2009, p. 209). As Serfaty also emphasizes, one of the most innovative features of blogs is their authors' active attempts to seek collaboration, through the comments system in particular, with an actual audience (2004a, pp. 3–4). So, then, what does the Other say in the comments sections of these blogs?

As is the case with other participatory forums, such as the letters to the editor section of newspapers, the level of response differs depending on the specific post and readers' own affective investments. And it is also important to 'remember that the additions provided by others are subordinated to and incorporated into the [blogger's] text ... whose voice remains the main center of the self-representational text'. Nonetheless, the provision of this space also reveals their desire for reciprocity (Serfaty, 2004c, p. 62). Indicative of the blog as a conversational site, *Onely*'s two authors regularly pose questions at the end of their posts, encouraging reader response. After a post providing links to a fellow blogger's recently published article on Salon.com, *Onely* asks: 'I know we're constantly celebrating the perks of being alone here at *Onely*, but it never hurts to add a few more — what do you appreciate most TODAY about being alone?' (13 August, 2009). Most responses relate to the pleasures of living alone and being able to make one's own decisions. This question, however, is indicative of the collaborative style of blogs like *Onely* and shores up the sense of a vibrant discursive community: 'What interesting and thought-provoking responses you've posted here! I'm so happy to be reminded of the diversity and intelligence of our audience – I (we) feel really lucky to be (virtually) surrounded by such a supportive and interesting community' (*Onely*, 30 July, 2009). As Fitzpatrick argues, because of their ongoing conversation with other bloggers, and into which readers themselves can intervene, blogs can be seen as having a 'collective and intersubjective authorship' (2007, p. 177). This is especially the case with blogs like *Quirkyalone* which, although initially written by the author of the book of the same name, Sasha Cagen, in April 2009 became a group-authored blog (including a weekly advice column by the authors of *Onely*).

In addition to posting their own personal narratives, common especially are expressions of gratitude for the type of revaluing work being undertaken by these bloggers. For example, one reader-writer responding to *Rachel's Musings* remarks:

> I want to thank you for creating this website. I can relate to so much of what you have written – especially your struggles with what you call 'internalized matrimania.' I too am a 40 year old single woman – never been married with no children. And while I love being single and have absolutely no interest in ever marrying, it can feel frightening going it alone – particularly when everyone else is safely coupled-up.

Likewise, another respondent notes: 'Thank you for your clear view of relationships, including the relationship we have with our selves!' Readers of *Onely* often express similar sentiments: 'I just found this site & I love it … Thank you for a refreshingly honest portrayal of LIFE as a single person (yes, we do have very active, fulfilling lives!!).' (*Onely*, 1 October, 2009). Invoking the solidarity of sisterhood, another writes: 'Hiiii I'm so glad I've found you lovely sisters! It's so nice to know that there are women like me out there. I just love your blog' (*Onely*, 11 October, 2009). For such reader-writers, these blogs function as unique cultural spaces of support and validation. Moreover, even though the vast majority of readers will not post their opinions, they are still granted the sense that they are part of a broader network (Tremayne, 2007, p. xiii). These blogs also suggest, as Karlsson's research on blog readers has shown, that readerly investment in blogs is linked to their 'sameness' to the author (2006, p. 29). As readers rarely provide detail of their geographical location or include markers of class or race, it is impossible here to extend this point in demographic terms. Nonetheless these readers' comments suggest that their appreciation of the blog derives primarily from its personal resonances and its (re)affirmation of single women. Such audience collaboration also has important effects on the self-construction of the blogger. In this way, 'blogging is the event of "rewriting oneself" through interaction with the audience' (Gurak & Antonijevic, 2008, p. 65). These single women identities, then, like the blogs themselves, are developing out of this communal process.

Conclusion

Although these legitimizing blogs by single women seek, as we have seen, to legitimize and tell a story about single women that runs counter to those proffered in mainstream genres examined in earlier chapters, it is vital to conclude with a few remarks about their reach. While theoretically accessible to anyone with a computer, it is obvious that the cultural reach (and thus impact) of the alternative narratives about single women circulating in and through the blogosphere nowhere near rivals that of those texts by multinational production companies, with global distribution channels and marketing machines (not to mention the celebrities that are key in this commercial process). In such texts, as earlier chapters have shown, pervasive heteronormative ideologies work to ensure the continued aberrance of the 'man-less' woman. However, these blogs do not operate like the other forms of mass media interrogated here; arguably their audience is comparatively small and targeted. The sheer quantity of consumers of, say, the film *Bridget Jones's Diary* compared to what we can presume would be the audience of the *Singlutionary* blog, offers a salutary reminder that their cultural impact cannot be commensurate.

Nonetheless, these blogs are gaining visibility through more mainstream news sites; one example of the flow between these blogs and the journalistic field occurred recently in Australia. In 2009, the *Sydney Morning Herald* published a story entitled 'Single and Loving It' (Thomas, 19 March), in which the author draws attention to the singles' advocacy groups gaining momentum on-line: 'The movement has spawned the obligatory outpouring of blogs and websites with titles like Onely, Singletude, Sexless in the City and Singlutionary.' In addition to reporting on these sites, the article cites Bella DePaulo and concludes with a number of quotations from the *Onely* blog on 'what if married people were treated like singles?' This journalistic engagement with the singles' blogosphere represents an instance of how it comes to permeate the mainstream and perhaps help change the stories privileged therein. Moreover, suggesting how the singles advocacy blogosphere has an 'offline' function, blogs like *Quirkyalone* are part of 'an organized grass-roots movement constituted in large part by online communities but it also operates as a means of facilitating face-to-face meetings and events' (Budgeon, 2008, p. 301).

As Graeme Turner has argued, drawing on the work of Mathew Hindman (2009), it is crucial that we emphasize 'the importance of recognizing the difference between who gets to speak on the internet, and who gets to be heard' (2010, pp. 128–9). However, in the case of these blogs, if readerly interaction is anything to go by, it does appear that they are being heard by other single women whose way of being then receives a form of validation that they may not find elsewhere. Moreover, they underscore the necessity of a critique of how singleness is gendered; the lived realities of single women, they argue, are delimited by both the kinds of dominant narratives circulating about them, be it in government policy documents or a television program like *The Bachelor*. In offering an alternative, they are fulfilling an important personal, cultural, and political function.

A number of critics have argued that many forms of political practice have been displaced to media culture, a claim certainly substantiated by these blogs; they are, Perlmutter argues, 'the new political battleground' (2008), making them an important site for the construction and circulation of various forms of feminist discourse. Like second-wave feminist activists, although shifting the focus from sexism against all women to 'singlism' against those not in heterosexual partnerships, these bloggers use this communicative form for clearly political purposes. In so doing, they crucially disrupt postfeminist and neoliberal frames. These bloggers adopt distinct identities as the basis for a mobilization of women, and they also track their own experience of consciousness-raising as a way of imploring their audience to do the same. Here, second-wave feminism does not so much appear to have been disavowed (as in postfeminism) but thoroughly incorporated, part of the vocabulary, politics, and rhetorical strategies of these bloggers. The way these blogs operate as a form of popular feminism, even if not explicitly self-defined as such, suggests that feminist frames continue to be productively deployed to interpret the personal, including being contentedly single. The stories of women's singleness they proffer clearly work to destabilize the centrality, and celebration, of heterosexual coupledom that I have shown to be evident elsewhere in postfeminist media culture. As these blogs and some of the books considered in the previous chapter suggest, there are some textual sites in which an often liberatory story is being told about women's singleness. As well as putting under strain the hegemony of postfeminist discourse, such texts demonstrate how the scripts limiting the way women experience and make sense of their singleness are able to be rewritten.

Notes

Introduction

1. See Ringrose and Walkerdine's work on how the boundaries of femininity are policed, constituting some subject positions – those against which normative femininity comes to be defined – 'uninhabitable' (2008, p. 234).

1 Theorizing Women's Singleness: Postfeminism, Neoliberalism, and the Politics of Popular Culture

1. Lewis and Moon (1997) have observed that women's singleness is at once glamorized and stigmatized, however I suggest, and explore how, this is a particular feature of postfeminist media culture.
2. As Jill Reynolds argues, 'the cultural context today incorporates new representations of singleness while continuing to draw on older, more devalued notions that being single is a problem for women: generally to be resolved through commitment to a heterosexual relationship' (2008, p. 2).
3. In early feminist studies of how women were represented in the media, the 'images of women' style criticism dominated, arguing that women were misrepresented in and through the mainstream media and that such 'negative' representations had deleterious effects on the women who consumed them. This is a position that has been thoroughly critiqued and replaced by more nuanced approaches to both signification and consumption. See Walters' chapter 'From Images of Women to Woman as Image' for a rehearsal of these debates (1995).
4. For example, in her critical text *Postfeminisms*, Ann Brooks (1997) conceptualizes it in terms of the intersections of feminism, poststructuralism, postmodernism, and postcolonialism. Others have theorized it primarily as a popular manifestation which effectively represents an updated form of antifeminism (Faludi, 1991; Walters, 1995; Kim, 2001).
5. The idea that postfeminism is itself constituted by contradiction, 'the product of competing discourses and interests' (Genz & Brabon, 2009, p. 6), has been explored by a number of critics (see Genz, 2009; Genz & Brabon, 2009).
6. The persistence of these ideas can also be understood in psychoanalytic terms, as Joanne Brown argues in *A Psychosocial Exploration of Love and Intimacy* (2006): '[T]he organisation of life around an axis of exclusive coupledom will focus on our entry into life as one half of a mother/father infant dyad and suggest that it is this union (and primary attachment figure and relationship) that we need to restore, in order to live an ontologically secure life' (203).
7. Catherine Belsey emphasizes how the romance narrative is involved in the work of establishing, and purporting to fill, this lack (1994).
8. In the United States, a political movement mobilizing around singleness appears to be gaining momentum. In this regard, each year in the third week of September, 'Unmarried and Single Americans Week' is celebrated.

9. As Michelle Hammers argues, both postfeminism and third-wave discourses seek to disavow second-wave feminism around issues of individualism and sexuality especially: 'Although these discourses hold different positions on the continued relevance of feminism per se, they share a shift in emphasis from collective action directed toward systemic change toward individual action, along with the fact that both these discourses embraced a celebratory attitude toward increased female sexuality and individual expression of that sexuality, provides a fulcrum upon which these discourses can be leveraged to undermine women' (2005, p. 170).

10. As Leonard similarly posits, 'Postfeminist culture both assumes and creates a female subject who desires marriage' (2006, p. 55).

11. As Ahmed argues, 'Feminists do kill joy in a certain sense: they disturb the very fantasy that happiness can be found in certain places. [...] It is not just that feminists might not be happily affected by the objects that are supposed to cause happiness but that their failure to be happy is read as sabotaging the happiness of others' (2010, p. 66).

12. Although beyond the scope of this study, a number of critics have shown that the 'single mother' as a discursive category is also viewed to be especially troublesome.

13. For an analysis of the discursive limits of the married/single binary, see Geller, 2001.

14. Moreover, others have attended to celluloid divorcees in films such as *It's Complicated* and *Something's Gotta Give* (see Negra, 2009); these portrayals are telling in terms of how mature women come to be visible in mainstream texts. See also Sadie Wearing (2007) on the ageing female body in *Something's Gotta Give* and the makeover reality programme, *What Not to Wear*.

15. The differences between how men's and women's singleness has been historically figured is well documented. As Budgeon observes, 'For men, however, bachelorhood, unlike the term 'old maid', carries the connotations of choice and hence these men are granted agency. There is no direct male counterpart to the old maid stereotype and arguably the status of 'bachelor' following the logic of the sexual double standard has enjoyed a favourable position in the cultural imaginary' (2008, p. 308).

2   From the Second-wave to Postfeminism: Single Women in the Mediasphere

1. For other historical overviews of the single woman in modern popular culture, see Genz, 2009; Kingston, 2004.

2. Siegel (2002) also argues that these claims regarding the 'triumph of the Single Girl' have been overblown.

3. The use of the term 'new femininities' is not without significant limitations; see my critique, 2003.

4. In drawing upon these articles, I concur with Negra's comments that 'While individual popular press articles are imperfect indices of the complexities and contradictions of a broad and diverse culture, they can be important and resonant snapshots of the state of play on key issues such as gender and class' (2009, p. 1).

5. Citing interviews with Cynthia Nixon (Miranda), Kim Cattrall (Samantha), and Sarah Jessica Parker (Carrie), Deborah Siegel notes that this gesture of the *SATC* actors disassociating themselves from their characters in the popular press is common (2002, p. 8).

6. The question of how single women are constructed as consumers through various advertising campaigns is beyond the scope of this study but is worthy of further critical attention. Perhaps the most prominent campaign has been the marketing of the DeBeers right-hand ring for single women (see Henderson, 2009). See also Gennaro for an analysis of consumption and 'perpetual adolescence' (2007).

7. This term comes from Masahiro Yamada's book, *The Age of the Parasite Single* (1999).

8. As Angela McRobbie notes, among all newspapers, the *Daily Mail* has the highest number of women readers in the UK, despite the fact that it commonly displays a hostile stance in relation to feminist issues (2009, p. 23).

9. Though this article foregrounds Diaz and Minogue, Jennifer Aniston in particular would offer an important case study into the figure of the (pitiable) celebrity single (see Hills, 2010).

10. The so-called 'enfreakment' of the single woman has been explored by DiCicco (2010).

11. Gillard's decision not to mother became the subject of heated media debate in 2006 when she – then the deputy opposition leader – was negatively described by a political opponent as 'deliberately barren'. One article rather unsubtlely featured an empty fruitbowl in her kitchen as a metaphor for 'barren' womb.

12. The choice not to reproduce remains coded as an aberrant one for women, by and large discursively constructed as a failure. A woman who actively chooses not to have children is routinely described pejoratively as selfish and self-absorbed, her choice devalued and her agency disavowed. The single woman without children, then, is seen as especially problematic in the mainstream cultural imaginary.

13. A revisioning of that film, *Down with Love*, representing a further fictionalization of Brown, was released in 2004. The film was replete with multiple intertextual allusions, including through the casting of Renee Zellweger, who had played the quintessential single girl in the form of Bridget Jones, in the lead role (see Taylor, 2010).

14. The role of *Cosmopolitan* in constructing the independent single woman as its addressee should not be underestimated. As Imelda Whelehan argues, 'even though the relationship of *Cosmo* to feminism has been ambivalent, it has for decades headed the field of women's magazines in championing the image of the independent and successful career woman' (2002, p. 29).

15. See Siegel (2002) for a comparative analysis of *Sex and the Single Girl* and *Sex and the City* and their ambivalence around women's singleness. As she makes clear, these perpetual anxieties make it difficult to celebrate these ostensibly 'new' representations of single women.

16. Feminist response to the sexual revolution was, unsurprisingly, ambivalent (see Jeffreys, 1997).

17. Hilary Radner has recently reconceptualized Brown's impact on modern popular culture, through she calls neo-feminism, see 'Chapter 1: Neo-Feminism and The Rise of the Single Girl' (2010).

18. While its politics are laudable, Faludi's 'backlash' relies upon the idea that the media operates as an amorphous patriarchal machine, with little possibility for feminist intervention let alone pleasures for women as audience members.

19. Significantly, in 2006 (5 June) – 20 years following its initial publication – *Newsweek* published what was in effect a retraction, stating its grim predictions that an educated, white, 40-year-old single woman was more likely to be 'killed by a terrorist' than marry had failed to play out (McGinn, 2006). However, in the *New York Times* Jessica Yellin argued that the damage had already been done (4 June, 2006): 'For a lot of women, the retraction doesn't matter. The article seems to have lodged itself permanently in the national psyche ... A number of experts and publications eventually challenged the magazine's conclusions, but the message was out. It wasn't just *Newsweek*. The so-called marriage crunch study on which the article was based was widely reported across the country, and the terminally single woman – another magazine's term – became a popular trope.'

20. As *Murphy Brown* attests, television from this era conversely approached this figure with more sophistication and less overtly reactionary politics (Dow, 1996).

21. The intertextual significance of Michael Douglas being the male lead, or rather the male 'victim' of an excessively powerful woman, in these films cannot be ignored (see Leonard, 2009, p. 79–80).

22. Faludi notes that originally the character of Alex was set to commit suicide, but test audiences apparently viewed this ending as 'insufficient punishment' for her disruption to the patriarchal nuclear family, so the film's producers opted to reshoot the ending at a cost of $1.3 million (1991, p. 151).

23. Like Bridget after discovering what a cad Daniel Cleaver is, Ally McBeal in one episode is shown to watch *Fatal Attraction* (in 4.10) while *SATC*'s Samantha Jones moves into New York's meat packing district, where Alex Forrester had also lived.

24. For a more detailed reading of this film, see Hollinger, 1998.

25. That said, for Garrett, in modern films like *Fatal Attraction*, 'the *femme fatale*'s reincarnation as professional woman rather than desperate, frustrated wife is, in itself, a kind of progress' (2007, p. 164).

26. For a different reading of such 'girly' films, see Radner's (2010) analysis of films such as *Legally Blonde* (2001) and *The Devil Wears Prada* (2006), she argues have focused largely on women's fulfilment through the world of work and thereby downplayed romantic relationships.

27. This is a quote from Kingston, 2004, p. 218.

28. This refers to the series and the episode number being discussed.

29. Whelehan remarks upon the cross-cultural flow of these characters: 'UK viewers saw Ally McBeal through the lens of Bridget Jones and American viewers saw in Bridget the legacy of both Ally McBeal and Candace Bushnell's newspaper column and later novel, *Sex and the City*' (2005, p. 175).

30. Once again speaking back to public criticism, in one episode Ally is charged with contempt of court after a Judge requires her to wear longer skirts and she refuses to capitulate (2.4).

31. That is not to say that more nuanced approaches, which emphasize the potential complexity of audience engagement with the text and indeed the

very contradictory discourses at operation within the text itself, have not been produced (see Nurka, 2002; Lotz, 2006).

32. Moreover, the show's normative whiteness and limitations in terms of racial stereotypes, around Renee Raddick and Ling Woo especially, has also been the subject of criticism (Patton, 2001; see also Kim, 2001).
33. The broader discursive reverberations of *Sex and the City*, as well as shifting demographics, are evidenced by the way a certain type of single woman voter came to be identified as a key political constituency in the 2004 US election – the 'Sex and the City voter' was a 'construct that invoked a homogenized view of women as young, white consumers who are sexually available' (Anderson & Stewart, 2005, p. 603).
34. While *SATC* predates its popular usage, in the past few years a new discursive category of single woman has emerged: the cougar. In popular parlance, the cougar is a woman over 40, often presumed divorced, who dates much younger men. In 2009 an American television sitcom was developed centring on this figure. Starring *Friends'* Courtney Cox, as an exemplification of the denigration of (newly) single women in mainstream popular culture, *Cougartown* is striking.
35. See Negra's reading of this episode, 2009, pp. 10–12.
36. In its filmic incarnations the transgressive possibilities of the series are totally disavowed, especially in the most recent film. In *Sex and the City 2*, released in June 2010, three of the characters were married, with only Samantha being without a partner at the film's end. However, the film generates comics moments through her extreme efforts to defy ageing through a regime of prescription drugs, reducing a formerly strong, autonomous woman to a caricature, and therefore her abjection relates to both to her singleness and her ageing body.

3   Spinsters and Singletons: *Bridget Jones's Diary* and its Cultural Reverberations

1. It is not necessary here to restage well-known feminist debates about romance fiction, how it – as a form of mass culture – has been gendered feminine and thus devalued, or how its predominantly female audience have been seen as 'cultural dupes'. See Tania Modleski's *Loving With A Vengeance* (1986) and Janice Radway's *Reading the Romance* (1984).
2. It is worth noting that although a racially-specific subgenre, 'Sistalit', has been produced, generally the genre is marked by its (invisible) whiteness.
3. In addition to Fielding's texts, Jane Green's *Jemima J* (1998) and *Perfect Ten* for weight loss chick lit narratives.
4. Chick lit's core characters are almost always in fulltime employment; glamorous, hyper-public careers that tend to resurface are publishing, advertising (*Love is Four Letter Word*), marketing, public relations (*Getting Personal* (2002), *Mr Maybe* (1999)), journalism – women's magazines in particular – *Flipside* (1999), *The Girl Most Likely* (2003), *Pants on Fire* (2000), *Pride, Prejudice and Jasmin Field* (2000), *Jemima J* (1998)), art galleries (*Just Friends*) (2002), fashion *The Devil Wears Prada* (2003)), and television (*Bridget Jones* and *Straight Talking* (2003)).

5. The most well-known example of this emphasis on conspicuous consumption, in addition to Candace Bushnell's *Sex and the City* (1997) is Lauren Weisberger's *The Devil Wears Prada* (2003). See also Sophie Kinsela's *Shopaholic* series, including *Confessions of a Shopaholic* (2001) and Jane Green's *Mr Maybe* (2002). For a reading of consumerism in chick lit, see Philips, 2000 and Smith, 2008.

6. Jane Green's novels in particular underscore the emptiness of sexual liaisons outside monogamous partnerships. See *Jemima J* (1998) and *Mr Maybe* (2002).

7. See pages 7–8 in Chris Manby's *Getting Personal* (1999).

8. See, for example, the endings of *Having it and Eating It* (Durrant, 2003) and *The Devil Wears Prada* (2003).

9. For developments in the genre, see Chapter 9 of Whelehan, 2005.

10. It was published in the US in 1998, and has reportedly been translated into 33 languages (Whelehan, 2002, p. 14).

11. For a comparative analysis of *Bridget Jones's Diary* and *Pride and Prejudice*, see Ferris, 2006.

12. Imelda Whelehan has explored the connections between earlier forms of feminist writing and chick lit in *The Feminist Bestseller* (2005)

13. As Whelehan notes, the film adaptation 'broke all records in the UK for a domestic film in its opening weekend by making nearly £7 million' (2002, p. 73).

14. Though as Gamble makes clear, Shazzer's feminism is clearly tied to her explication of a theory about men's 'emotional fuckwittage', which she sees as entirely consistent with the 'book's central preoccupation with getting a man' (2006, p. 64).

15. For analysis of the film and questions of adaptation, especially around postfeminism, see Cobb, 2008. In particular, she shows how the novel's transgressive dimensions are undercut by the postfeminist tropes dominating the film (294).

16. Dorney (2004) uses Zizek in her reading of chick lit novels and consumption.

17. Her one professional triumph appears to be her interview with a woman accused of murder, Elena Rossini, which is due solely to the intervention of Mark Darcy, who was her barrister (240–2).

18. As Vavrus argues (2007, p. 50), news stories on what has been called the 'Opt Out Revolution' exemplify the 'fusion of postfeminism and neoliberalism', discussed here in Chapter 1, and show how rather than advocating structural remedies to address the difficulties yet faced by 'working mothers' the onus is placed on the individual to resolve them. Discourses of 'opting out' and 'retreatism' (see Negra, 2009) suggest how the apparent obstacles to the postfeminist narrative of 'having it all' become highly individualized and privatized.

19. Gorton conversely argues that such 'failures' are actually successes, suggesting Bridget's refusal to conform (2008).

20. Feminist literary critic, Elaine Showalter, also argues that Fielding's character is altered by her move to the big screen. The film, she notes, 'is a charming and frothy fairy tale with no feminist consciousness whatsoever. The bright, ambitious, neurotic Bridget of Helen Fielding's novel has been turned into an adorable airhead, a pratfalling idiot, "Bridget Jones, wanton sex goddess"' (2001).

21. Both books were re-released following the film adaptations, in 2001 and 2003 respectively, with a photograph of Zellweger as Bridget on their covers.
22. For example, the women interviewed for Macvarish's (2006) study invoked Bridget – recounting especially her fear of dying alone – as someone they wished to avoid becoming.

4   Desperate and Dateless TV: Making Over the Single Woman

1. *Tough Love* has received hardly any critical attention, while cultural critics have extensively covered *The Bachelor*.
2. Other dating reality TV shows to have been critically analyzed in terms of their limitations for women include Fox's *Paradise Hotel*. For example, Marla Harris observes that 'not only does the show assume that men and women are heterosexual, but also that women can be happy only when they are part of a heterosexual couple. Here, where each newly arrived woman must endure a week without a male roommate, the notion of "a room of one's own" is redefined as punishment' (2004, p. 357).
3. In this area, as per their 2010 conference paper, Storey & Xiaohu are currently working on a project about how love is mediated through the texts of popular culture.
4. In Little's study of British farmers who participated in a magazine of *The Farmer Wants a Wife* scheme, interviews with farmers revealed that 'fashionable and hyperfeminine appearances were seen as "unsuitable"' to rural living (2007, p. 858).
5. See, for example, Gray, 2004 and Frank, 2007 for a more celebratory approach to such narratives.
6. This is a well-known quote from John Berger's *Ways of Seeing* (1972). See also Foucault, 1977.
7. That said, at times women do refuse to accept the Bachelor's rose but this is a rarity. As Dubrofsky shows, in the second season two Asian American women chose to depart (see Dubrofsky, 2006 for her analysis of the racial dynamics of this episode).
8. See Cloud, 2010 for an analysis of audience reaction to this narrative twist.
9. 'Enlightened sexism', as Douglas clarifies in her book of the same name, 'is a response, deliberate or not, to the perceived threat of a new gender regime. It insists that women have made plenty of progress because of feminism – indeed, full equality has allegedly now been achieved – so it's now okay, even amusing, to resurrect sexist stereotypes of girls and women' (2010, p. 9).
10. The operation of race within season 12 is worthy of further analysis. The only African American contestant, Marshana, is repeatedly referred to as a 'drama queen' and the major confrontations in the series involve her.
11. See Dubrofsky's (2005) chapter on how, in her opinion, the series works to complicate critical accounts of postfeminism.
12. On viewer discussion boards, most participants viewed the move as a cynical ploy to garner ratings. Moreover, viewers repeatedly call her 'fake', 'manipulative', and 'immature' (http://realitytv.about.com/b/2010/02/08/ali-leaves-the-bachelor-did-ali-do-the-right-thing.htm).

13. It is worth noting, however, that she did go on to feature on *The Bachelorette* and thus continued to invest in this televised process to become unsingle.
14. Indeed, viewers on forums hosted by 'Television Without Pity' certainly demonstrate the degree to which viewers critically engage with the programme but they also reveal a degree of contempt towards certain competitors, troubling claims that such sites are necessarily progressive and/or counterhegemonic (see http://www.televisionwithoutpity.com/show/the-bachelor).

5 Self-Help and the Single Girl: From Salvation to Validation

1. Self-help books for so-called 'bachelor girls' are said to have flourished in the 1920s and 30s, the period following the First World War when there was quite literally a surplus of women (Nicholson, 2007, pp. 89–90). While 'husband-catching manuals' were common, books like Marjorie Hillis' 'adopted a bracing, no-nonsense tone aimed at rallying the spinsters out of their gloom and passivity' (Nicholson, 2007, p. 90). For Hillis, singleness was a state that women should 'make the best of' (2005, p. 12). Nonetheless, she does identify a number of benefits: 'Living alone, you can – within your own walls – do as you like. The trick is to arrange your life so you really do like it' (2005, p. 14).
2. In this emphasis on the biologically based incommensurability of the sexes, Gray's books – including *Men Are From Mars, Women Are From Venus* (1990) – became an important part in the 'reassertion of sexual difference' that Gill views as an integral part of postfeminist media culture. Of how his ideas came to circulate, she notes 'Gray's work has become an important part of postfeminist media culture in its own right, as well as in its citations in other popular cultural texts from magazines to 'chick lit', and its inauguration of the notion of (interplanetary) translation' (2007, pp. 158–9).
3. Lest it seem that the Rules philosophy is now outdated, in 2007 British author, Kate Taylor, reinscribed Fein and Schneider's suggestion that women should disavow their sexual agency. In *Not Tonight, Mr Right: The Best (Don't Get) Laid Plans for Finding and Marrying the Man of Your Dreams*, as the title implies, readers are advised that their success with men will be guaranteed by simply withholding sex.
4. As Peta Boyton emphasizes, the authors of *The Rules* paradoxically claim that their approach is feminist. As she argues, however, they presume that women can be feminists but not in the realm of romantic relationships (Boynton, 2003, p. 239).
5. Indeed, Hazleden suggests that relationships manuals ostensibly about how to find and maintain a romantic relationship are predominantly concerned with 'the care for, and nurturance of, self' (2003, p. 415).
6. Nonetheless, like Ford's, the book directly contradicts this maxim as it presumes that all women do want to be partnered. By the book's conclusion her pro-single rhetoric appears under strain, and she confesses, 'As great as it is to be single, for most of us the ultimate goal is to meet the right guy, get married and start a family' (Scheftt, 2007, pp. 246–7).
7. As Riley makes clear, there is a danger in attempting to valorize singleness as a way of countering its current abjection. Instead, she suggests: 'The question "how single is single" could ask: how might such singleness neither be

considered pathological nor be swept up, in an ostentatious depathologizing, into a compulsive sociability?' (2006, p. 9).

8. This is a phrase used by Gloria Steinem and which has been criticized for its emphasis on personal change at the attitudinal level (Dubrofsky, 2009, p. 266).

6   Blogging Solo: Women Refiguring Singleness

1. While engagement with new media technologies is often viewed to mark 'third-wave' feminism, as I have argued elsewhere (Taylor, 2008), I find the use of term of the term third-wave and attendant familial metaphors and generational tropes of limited use at the best of times but especially in relation to these blogs. These women do not self-identify along a generational axis, and often not even as feminist, and they position themselves, not against a certain form of feminism (as third-wavers often do), but against a hetero-patriarchal cultural imaginary that fails to validate their way of being in the world.

2. However, this use of the term 'ordinary' is not entirely unproblematic. Such celebrations of the 'ordinary' person's ability to make media, or to become its object as a celebrity, have been critiqued by Graeme Turner in his work on the so-called 'demotic turn' (2010).

3. While it is common to anecdotally claim that the blogosphere is populated by at least 50 per cent women, studies such as Mathew Hindman's have shown that the political blogs most read, and those thus having the most public impact, are 'well-educated white male professionals', leading him to suggest that, despite celebrations of the field's democratizing capacity, 'many voices are still left out' (2009, p. 128). See also Herring et al., 2004.

4. See, for example, Oreoluwa Somolu's article on how African women are using, or prohibited from using, blogs (2007, pp. 485–6).

5. It is important to recognize that blogs pose significant critical challenges, especially given that they are 'inherently unstable objects-constantly changing, sometimes disappearing altogether' (Sorapure, 2003, p. 19). As Sorapure emphasizes, then, the object of analysis is constantly shifting and also varies 'depending on the path the reader has taken through it' (2003, p. 19).

6. This is not to suggest that other forms of diary are not written with an addressee in mind. As Van Dijck emphasizes, the idea that the diary is a 'private genre, strictly written for oneself, is as misleading as it is persistent' (2004). That said, there is a difference between the immediate accessibility of the online diary and the idea that all diaries are theoretically written for consumption by an Other at some point in time. As McNeil emphasizes, blogs allow writers to 'carry on daily conversations that will no longer be monologic, where the response will not just be imagined but actual' (2003, p. 29).

7. These blogs were all accessed throughout January 2010.

8. Also drawing on Genette, Lena Karlsson compares the 'About Me' section of blogs to a book jacket, in terms of how it can work to delimit readerly expectations (2006, p. 25).

9. Signalling its prevalence, Serfaty (2004c) devotes an entire chapter to the operation of humour in blogs; see 'Chapter 3: Humor in Cyberspace', pp. 71–82.

10. See Reynolds (2008, p. 153) for a consideration of women's singleness and identity politics.
11. Not insignificantly, these bloggers often refer to, and indeed themselves organize, off line events for single women for face-to-face support, extending the network of supportive single women.
12. That said, *Quirkyalone* emphasizes that its followers enjoy being single but are not 'opposed to being in a relationship': '*Quirkyalone* is not anti-love. It is pro-love. It is not anti-dating. It is anti-compulsory dating. We tend to be romantics. We prefer to be single rather than settle. In fact, the core of *Quirkyalone* is the inability to settle. We spend a significant chunk of our lives single because we hold relationships to a high standard' (Quirkyalone.net).

References

Ahmed, S. (2007) 'The Happiness Turn', *New Formations*, 63 (Winter 2007/2008): 7–14.

―――― (2010) *The Promise of Happiness*, Durham: Duke University Press.

Akass, K. & McCabe, J. eds. (2004) *Reading Sex and the City*, London: I. B. Tauris.

Alderson, M. (2000) *Pants on Fire*, Melbourne: Penguin.

Anderson, K. V. & Stewart, J. (2005) 'Politics and the Single Woman: The "Sex and the City" Campaign', *Rhetoric and Public Affairs*, 5.4: 595–616.

Andrejevic, M. (2004) *Reality TV: The Work of being Watched*, Maryland: Rowman & Littlefield Publishers.

Arnst, C. (1998) 'Single Women in a Hostile World', 13 July, *BusinessWeek*, accessed via http://www.businessweek.com/1998/28/b3586044.htm (retrieved on 20 April 2010).

Arthurs, J. (2003) '*Sex and the City* and Consumer Culture: Remediating Postfeminist Drama', *Feminist Media Studies*, 3.1: 83–98.

Aslama, M. & Pantti, M. (2006) 'Talking Alone: Reality TV, Emotions and Authenticity', *European Journal of Cultural Studies*, 9.2: 167–84.

Attwood, F. (2005) 'Fashion and Passion: Marketing Sex to Women', *Sexualities*, 8.4: 392–406.

―――― (2006) 'Sexed Up: Theorizing the Sexualization of Culture', *Sexualities*, 9.1: 77–94.

Auerbach, N. (1991) 'Foreword', pp. ix–xv in L. L. Doan ed. *Old Maids to Radical Spinsters: Women in the Twentieth-Century Novel*, Chicago: University of Illinois Press.

Babener, L. (1992) 'Patriarchal Politics in *Fatal Attraction*', *Journal of Popular Culture*, 26.3: 25–34.

Bartky, S. L. (1990) *Femininity and Domination: Studies in the Phenomenology of Oppression*, New York: Routledge.

Bauman, Z. (2003) *Liquid Love: On the Frailty of Human Bonds*, Cambridge: Polity.

Bawden, J. (2002) *Get A Life, Then Get A Man*, New York: Plume.

Beamon, N. C. (2009) *I Didn't Work This Hard Just To Get Married: Successful Single Black Women Speak Out*, Chicago: Lawrence Hill.

Beck, U. & Beck-Gernsheim, E. (1995) *The Normal Chaos of Love*, Cambridge: Polity.

Bellafante, G. (1998) 'Feminism: It's All About Me!', *Time Magazine*, 29 June, accessed via http://www.time.com/time/magazine/article/0,9171,988616,00.html (retrieved on 15 January 2010).

Belsey, C. (1994) *Desire: Love Stories in Western Culture*, Oxford: Blackwell.

Benjamin, J. (1990) *The Bonds of Love: Psychoanalysis, Feminism and the Problem of Domination*, London: Pantheon.

Bennett, T. & Woollacott, J. (1987) *Bond and Beyond: The Political Career of a Popular Hero*, Basingstoke: Palgrave Macmillan.

Benstock, S. (2006) 'Afterword: The New Woman's Fiction', pp. 253–6 in S. Ferris & M. Young eds. *Chick Lit: The New Woman's Fiction*, New York: Routledge.

Berger, J. (1972) *Ways of Seeing*, London: Viking.

Berlant, L. (2008) *The Female Complaint: The Unfinished Business of Sentimentality in American Culture*, Durham: Duke University Press.

Bernherdt, G. & Cuccillo, L. (2004) *He's Just Not That Into You: The No Excuses Truth to Understanding Guys*, New York: Simon Spotlight Entertainment.

Biressi, A. & Nunn, H. (2005) *Reality TV: Realism and Revelation*, London: Wallflower.

Blackman, L. (2004) 'Self-Help, Media Cultures and the Production of Female Psychopathology', *European Journal of Cultural Studies*, 7: 219–36.

—— (2010) '"It's Down To You": Psychology, Magazine Culture, and the Governing of Female Bodies', pp. 19–39 in L. Reed & P. Saukko eds. *Governing the Female Body: Gender, Health, and Networks of Power*, Albany: State University of New York.

Boynton, P. (2003) 'Abiding by *The Rules*: Advising Women in Relationships', *Feminism & Psychology*, 13.2: 237–45.

Brett, S. (2008) 'Strictly a Solo Act', 7 April, *Sydney Morning Herald*, accessed via http://www.smh.com.au/news/people/strictly-a-solo act/2008/04/06/1207420189506.html (retrieved on 9 February 2010).

'Bridget Jones Fear is Making Women Want to Wed Earlier' (2010), 13 April, *Daily Mail*, accessed via http://www.dailymail.co.uk/news/article-1265520/Bridget-Jones-fear-making-women-want-wed-earlier.html (retrieved on 15 September 2010).

'"Bridget Jones Syndrome" Makes Kids Want to Marry Early' (2010), 13 April, accessed via http://timesofindia.indiatimes.com/life/relationships/parenting/Bridget-Jones-syndrome-makes-kids-want-to-marry-early/articleshow/5794563.cms (retrieved on 10 December 2010).

Brooks, A. (1997) *Postfeminisms: Feminism, Cultural Theory, and Cultural Forms*, London: Routledge.

Brown, H. G. (1962, 2003 edn) *Sex and the Single Girl*, New York: Barnes and Noble.

—— (1964, 2004 edn) *Sex and the Office*, New York: Barnes and Noble.

Brown, J. (2006) *A Psychosocial Exploration of Life and Intimacy*, Basingstoke: Palgrave Macmillan.

Brown, M. (2010) 'Bridget Jones: The TV Show?' 26 February, *The Guardian*, accessed via http://www.guardian.co.uk/media/2010/feb/26/nbc-universal-working-title (retrieved on 25 January 2011).

Brown, W. (2003) 'Neoliberalism and the End of Liberal Democracy', *Theory & Event*, 7.1, accessed via http://muse.jhu.edu/journals/theory_and_event/v007/7.1brown.html (retrieved on 2 August 2010).

Bruns, A. (2008) *Blogs, Wikipedia, Second Life, and Beyond: From Production to Produsage*, New York: Peter Lang.

—— (2006) 'Introduction', pp.1–8 in A. Bruns & J. Jacobs eds. *The Uses of Blogs*, New York: Peter Lang.

Brunsdon, C. (1997) *Screen Tastes*, London: Routledge.

Budgeon, S. (2006) 'Friendship and Formations of Sociality in Late Modernity: The Challenge of "Post Traditional Intimacy"', *Sociological Research Online*, 11.3, accessed via http://www.socresonline.org.uk/11/3/budgeon.html (retrieved on 29 January 2010).

—— (2008) 'Couple Culture and the Production of Singleness', *Sexualities*, 11.3: 301–25.

Bushnell, C. (1997) *Sex and the City*, New York: Grand Central Publishing.

Butler, J. (1990) *Gender Trouble: Feminism and the Subversion of Identity*, New York: Routledge.

Byrne, A. & Carr, D. (2005) 'Caught in the Cultural Lag: The Stigma of Singlehood', *Psychological Enquiry*, 16.2/3: 84–91.

Caden, G. (2007) 'The Carnival of Feminists', *thirdspace*, 7.1 (Summer), accessed via http://www.thirdspace.ca/journal/article/view/resources_carnivals/46 (retrieved on 7 January 2010).

Calman, C. (2000) *Love is a Four Word*, London: Transworld.

Cannold, L. (2005) *What, No Baby? Why Women Are Losing Their Freedom to Mother, and How They Can Get It Back*, Fremantle: Fremantle Arts Press.

Carpenter, L. (2007) 'We Never Had It So Good', 11 March, *The Observer*, accessed via http://www.guardian.co.uk/lifeandstyle/2007/mar/11/familyandrelation-ships.features1 (retrieved on 6 December 2010).

Carter, D. & Ferres, K. (2001) 'The Public Life of Literature', pp. 140–60 in T. Bennett & D. Carter eds. *Culture in Australia*, Melbourne: Cambridge University Press.

Case, A. (2001) 'Authenticity, Convention, and *Bridget Jones's Diary*', *Narrative* 9.2: 176–81.

Chapman, J. (2008) 'Bridget Jones generation "to blame for breakdown of family"', 29 September, *Daily Mail*, accessed via http://www.dailymail.co.uk/femail/article-1063792/Bridget-Jones-generation-blame-breakdown-family.html (retrieved on 27 January 2011).

Clements, M. (1998) *The Improvised Woman: Single Women Redefining Single Life*, New York: W. W. Norton & Co.

Cloud, D. (2010) 'The Irony Bribe and Reality Television: Investment and Detachment in *The Bachelor*', *Critical Studies in Media Communication*, 27.5: 413–37.

Cobb, S. (2008) 'Adaptable Bridget: Generic Intertextuality and Postfeminism in *Bridget Jones' Diary*', pp. 281–304 in J. Boozer ed. *Authorship in Film Adaptation*, Austin: University of Texas Press.

Cochrane, K. (2008) 'Did Bridget Destroy Family Life?', 30 September, *The Guardian*, accessed via http://www.guardian.co.uk/lifeandstyle/2008/sep/30/women.family (retrieved on 27 January 2011).

Cohen, K. (2006) 'A Welcome for Blogs', *Continuum*, 20.2: 161–73.

Coleman, S. (2005) 'Blogs and the Politics of Listening', *Political Quarterly*, 76.2: 273–80.

Corral, J. & Miya-Jervis, L. eds. (2001) *Young Wives' Tales: New Adventures in Love and Parternship*, Berkeley: Seal Press.

Coupland, D. (1991) *Generation X: Tales For An Accelerated Culture*, New York: St Martin's Press.

Cowlishaw, B. R. (2001) 'Subjects are From Mars, Objects are From Venus: Construction of the Self in Self-Help', *Journal of Popular Culture*, 35.1: 169–84.

Cranny-Francis, A. (1990) *Popular Feminist Fiction*, Kensington: UNSW Press.

Crawford, M. (2004) 'Mars and Venus Collide: A Discursive Analysis of Marital Self-Help Psychology', *Feminism and Psychology*, 14.1: 63–79.

Creed, B. (1993) *The Monstrous Feminine: Film, Feminism, Psychoanalysis*, London: Routledge.

Crittenden, D. (2000) *What Our Mothers Didn't Tell Us: Why Happiness Eludes the Modern Woman*, London: Simon & Schuster.

Crown, S. (2007) '"1984" is definitive book of the 20th century', 2 June, *The Guardian*, accessed via http://www.guardian.co.uk/books/2007/jun/02/uk.hay2007authors (retrieved on 14 September 2010).

Crozier, S. (2008) 'Making It After All: A Reparative Reading of *The Mary Tyler Show*', *International Journal of Cultural Studies*, 11.1: 51–67.

Cullen, R. (2001) 'Addressing the Digital Divide', *Online Information Review*, 25.5: 311–20.

Davies, C. (2008) 'Single and Happy: It's the Freemales', 13 April, *The Observer*, accessed via http://www.guardian.co.uk/lifeandstyle/2008/apr/13/women.familyandrelationships3 (retrieved on 20 March 2010).

Denholm, D. (2011) 'Leftist Lara Giddings still looking for Mr Right', 25 January, *The Australian*, accessed via http://www.theaustralian.com.au/national-affairs/leftist-lara-giddings-still-looking-for-mr-right/story-fn59niix-1225993919278 (retrieved on 25 January 2011).

DePaulo, B. (2006) *Singled Out: How Singles are Stereotyped, Stigmatised, and Ignored, and Still Live Happily Ever After*, New York: St Martin's Griffin.

DePaulo, B. & Morris, W. (2006) 'The Unrecognized Stereotyping and Discrimination Against Singles', *Current Directions in Psychological Science*, 15.5: 251–4.

DiCicco, L. (2010) 'The Enfreakment of America's *Jeune Fille a Marier*: Lily Bart to Carrie Bradshaw', *Journal of Modern Literature*, 33.3: 78–98.

Di Massa, C. M. (1998) 'Up and Down', 27 September, *Los Angeles Book Review*, accessed via http://bridgetarchive.altervista.org/bjd_up_down.htm (retrieved on 17 December 2010).

Doan, L. L. (1991) 'Introduction', pp. 1–16 in L. L. Doan ed. *Old Maids to Radical Spinsters: Unmarried Women in the Twentieth-Century Novel*, Chicago: University of Illinois Press.

Dobson, R. & Johnson, A. (2004) 'V Bad News for the Bridget Jones Generation: Staying Single is Worse for You than Smoking', 29 August, *The Independent*, accessed via http://www.independent.co.uk/news/uk/this-britain/v-bad-news-for-the-bridget-jones-generation-staying-single-is-worse-for-you-than-smoking-558181.html (retrieved on 27 January 2011).

Dolby, S. K. (2005) *Self Help Books: Why Americans Keep Reading Them*, Champaign: University of Illinois Press.

Dorney, K. (2004) 'Shop Boys and Girls! Interpellating Readers as Consumers in Chicklit and Ladlit', *Diegesis: Journal of the Association for Research in Popular Fictions*, 8 (Winter): 11–21.

Douglas, S. (1994) *Where the girls are: Growing up female with the mass media*, New York: Times Books.

—— (2010) *Enlightened Sexism: The Seductive Message that Feminism's Work is Done*, New York: Times Books.

Dow, B. (1996) *Prime Time Feminism: Television, Media Culture, and The Women's Movement from 1970*, Philadelphia: University of Pennsylvania Press.

—— (2002) '*Ally McBeal*, Lifestyle Feminism and the Politics of Personal Happiness', *The Communication Review*, 5: 259–64.

—— (2006) 'The Traffic Men and the *Fatal Attraction* of Postfeminist Masculinity', *Women's Studies in Communication*, 29.1 (Spring): 113–31.

Doyle, L. (2002) *The Surrendered Single: A Practical Guide to Marrying the Man Who's Right for You*, New York: Fireside.

Dubberley, E. (2007) *I'd Rather Be Single Than Settle: Satisfied Solitude and How to Achieve It*, London: Fusion Press.

Dubrofsky, R. E. (2002) 'Ally McBeal as Postfeminist Icon: The Aestheticizing and Fetishizing of the Independent Working Woman', *The Communication Review*, 5.4: 264–84.

—— (2005) *The Bachelor Industry: The Surveillance and Governing Women*, unpublished doctoral thesis, University of Illinois.

—— (2006) 'The Bachelor: Whiteness in the Harem', *Critical Studies in Media Communication*, 23.1: 39–56.

—— (2007) 'Therapeutics of the Self: Surveillance in the Service of the Therapeutic', *Television and New Media*, 8.4: 263–84.

—— (2009) 'Fallen Women in Reality TV: A Pornography of Emotion', *Feminist Media Studies*, 9.3 (September): 353–68.

Durrant, S. (2003) *Having it and Eating It*, New York: Riverhead Books.

Dux, M. & Simic, Z. (2008) *The Great Feminist Denial*, Melbourne: Melbourne University Press.

Ebert, T. (2009) *The Task of Cultural Critique*, Chicago: University of Illinois Press.

Edwards, T. M. (2000) 'Who Needs A Husband?' *Time Magazine*, 15.9, 28 August, accessed via http://www.time.com/time/magazine/article/0,9171,997804,00.html (retrieved on 9 February 2010).

Falk, F. (2008) *On my Own: The Art of Being a Woman Alone*, London: Rider.

Faludi, S. (1991) *Backlash: The Undeclared War Against Women,* New York: Vintage.

Fein, E. & Schneider, C. (1995) *The Rules*, New York: Warner Books.

—— (1998) *The Rules II: More Rules to Live and Love By*, New York: Grand Central Publishing.

—— (2002) *The Rules for Marriage: Time-Tested Secrets for Making Your Marriage Work*, New York: Grand Central Publishing.

—— (2002) *The Rules for Online Dating: Capturing the Heart of Mr. Right in Cyberspace*, New York: Simon and Schuster.

Felski, R. (2000) *Doing Time: Feminist Theory and Postmodern Culture*, New York: New York University Press.

Ferris, S. (2006) 'Narrative and Cinematic Doubleness: *Pride and Prejudice* and *Bridget Jones's Diary*, pp. 71–84 in S. Ferris, & M. Young eds. *Chick Lit: The New Woman's Fiction*, New York: Routledge.

Ferris, S. & Young, M. (2006), 'Introduction', pp. 1–16 in S. Ferris & M. Young eds. *Chick Lit: The New Woman's Fiction*, New York: Routledge.

—— (2008) 'Introduction: Chick Flicks and Chick Culture', pp. 1–25 in S. Ferris & M. Young *Chick Flicks: Contemporary Women at the Movies*, New York: Routledge.

Fielding, H. (1996, 2001 edn) *Bridget Jones's Diary*, London: Picador.

—— (1999, 2003 edn) *Bridget Jones: The Edge of Reason*, London: Picador.

—— (2001) *Bridget Jones's Guide to Life*, London: Penguin Books.

Fitzpatrick, K. (2007) 'The Pleasure of the Blog: The Early Novel, The Serial and The Narrative Archive', in T. Burg & J. Schmidt eds. *BlogTalks Reloaded*, Norderstedt: Books on Demand.

Ford, A. (2007) *Kiss Me, I'm Single: An Ode to the Single Life*, San Francisco: Red Wheel.

Ford, J. (2004) *Single: The Art of Being Satisfied, Fulfilled and Independent*, Massachusetts: Adams Media.

Forleo, M. (2008) *Make Every Man Want You*, New York: McGraw-Hill.

Foucault, M. (1977) *Discipline and Punish: The Birth of the Prison*, New York: Pantheon.

Frank, K. (2007) 'Primetime Harem Fantasies: Marriage, Monogamy, and a Bit of Feminist Fanfiction on ABC's *The Bachelor*', pp. 91–118 in M. Johnson ed. *Third Wave Feminism and Television: Jane Puts It In A Box*, London: I. B. Tauris.

Freeman, J. (1999) *Flipside*, Sydney: Bantam Books.

Friedan, B. (1963) *The Feminine Mystique*, New York: Penguin.

Furedi, F. (2004) *Therapy Culture: Cultivating Vulnerability in an Uncertain Age*, London: Routledge.

Gabriel, J. (1998) *Whitewash: Racialized Politics and the Media*, London: Routledge.

Gamble, S. (2006) 'Growing Up Single: The Postfeminist Novel', *Studies in the Literary Imagination*, 39.2 (Fall): 61–78.

Gardiner, J. (2000) '"What is an Author?" Contemporary Publishing Discourse and the Author Figure', *Publishing Research Quarterly*, Spring: 63–76.

Garrett, R. (2007) *Postmodern Chick Flicks: The Return of Woman's Film*, Basingstoke: Palgrave Macmillan.

Geller, J. (2001) *Here Comes The Bride: Women, Weddings and the Marriage Mystique*, New York. Four Walls, Eight Windows.

Genette, G. (1997) *Paratextuality: Thresholds of Interpretation*, Cambridge: Cambridge University Press.

Gennaro, S. (2007) 'Sex and the City: Perpetual Adolescence Gendered Feminine', *Nebula*, 4.1: 246–74.

Genz, S. (2009) *Postfemininities in Popular Culture*, Basingstoke: Palgrave Macmillan.

—— (2010) 'Singled Out: Postfeminism's "New Woman" and the Dilemma of Having It All', *The Journal of Popular Culture*, 43.1: 97–119.

Genz, S. & Brabon, B. (2009) *Postfeminism: Cultural Texts and Theories*, Edinburgh: Edinburgh University Press.

Gerhard, J. (2005) 'Sex and the City: Carrie Bradshaw's Queer Postfeminism', *Feminist Media Studies*, 5.1: 37–49.

Giddens, A. (1991) *Modernity and Self Identity: Self and Society in the Late Modern Age*, Cambridge: Polity.

—— (1992) *The Transformation of Intimacy*, Cambridge: Polity.

Gill, R. (2007) 'Postfeminist Media Culture: Elements of a Sensibility', *European Journal of Cultural Studies*, 10.2: 147–66.

—— (2008) 'Culture and Subjectivity in Neoliberal and Postfeminist Times', *Subjectivity*, 25: 432–45.

—— (2009) 'Mediated Intimacy and Postfeminism: A Discourse Analytic Examination of Sex and Relationships Advice in a Women's Magazine, *Discourse and Communication*: 3.4: 345–69.

Gill, R. & Herdieckerdoff, E. (2006) 'Rewriting the Romance: New Femininities in Chick Lit?' *Feminist Media Studies*, 6.4: 487–504.

Gleick, E. (1998) 'A V Fine Mess', 31 May, *New York Times*, accessed via http://www.nytimes.com/books/98/05/31/reviews/980531.31gleickt.html (retrieved on 27 January 2011).

Gokulsing, K. M. & Dissanayake, W. (2009) *Popular Culture in a Globalised India*, London: Routledge.

Gorton, K. (2008) *Theorising Desire: From Freud to Feminism to Film*, Basingstoke: Palgrave Macmillan.

Gottlieb, L. (2010) *Marry Him: The Case for Settling for Mr Good Enough*, New York: Dutton.

–––– (2008) 'Marry Him! The Case for Settling for Mr Good Enough', *The Atlantic Magazine*, March, accessed via http://www.theatlantic.com/magazine/archive/2008/03/marry-him/6651/# (retrieved on 10 March 2010).

Grant, B. K. (1996) 'Rich and Strange: The Yuppy Horror Film', *Journal of Video and Film*, 48.1/2: 4–16.

Grant, L. (1993) *Fundamental Feminism*, London: Routledge.

Gray, J. (1990) *Men are From Mars, Women are From Venus*, New York: Harper Collins.

Gray, J. (2004) 'Cinderella Burps: Gender, Performativity, and the Dating Show', pp. 260–77 in S. Murray & L. Ouellette eds. *Reality TV: Remaking Television Culture*, New York: New York University Press.

Green, A. (2009) *Sexy and Confident: How to Be the Dreamgirl Men Want, Have a Better Life and Improve Your Self-esteem*, New York: Artrum Media.

Green, J. (1998) *Jemima J*, London: Penguin.

–––– (1999) *Mr Maybe*, London: Penguin.

–––– (2003) *Straight Talking*, London: Penguin.

Greer, G. (1999) *The Whole Woman*, London: Double Day.

Gregg, M. (2006) 'Posting with Passion: Blogs and the Politics of Gender', pp. 151–60 in A. Bruns & J. Jacobs eds. *Uses of Blogs*, New York: Peter Lang.

Guenther, L. (2006) 'Bridget Jones's Diary: Confessing Post-feminism', pp. 84–99 in J. Gill ed. *Modern Confessional Writing*, New York: Routledge.

Gurak, L. J. & Antonijevic, S. (2008) 'The Psychology of Blogging: You, Me, and Everyone in Between', *American Behavioral Scientist*, 52.1: 60–8.

Hale, E. (2009) 'Meet the TWITs–Teenage Women In Their Thirties', 2 August, *Herald Sun*.

Hamer, M. (2010) 'Aussie Girls Prefer Single Life', 14 February, *Herald Sun*, accessed via http://www.heraldsun.com.au/news/national/aussie-girls-prefer-single-life/story-e6frf7l6-1225830050103 (retrieved on 14 February 2010).

Hamilton, C. (1909) *Marriage as a Trade*, New York: Moffat, Yard and Company.

Hamilton, J. (2008) 'Girls Fear Bridget's Single Life', 13 April, *The Sun*, accessed via http://www.thesun.co.uk/sol/homepage/woman/2929643/Girls-fear-Bridgets-single-life.html (retrieved on 20 August 2010).

Hammers, M. L. (2005) 'Cautionary Tales of Liberation and Female Professionalism: The Case Against *Ally McBeal*', *Western Journal of Communication*, 69.2: 167–82.

Hanson, C. (2004) 'Fiction, Feminism and Femininity from the Eighties to the Noughties', pp. 16–27 in E. Parker ed. *Contemporary British Women Writers*, Wiltshire: The Cromwell Press.

Harris, M. (2004) 'Gender Trouble in *Paradise (Hotel)*, or a Good Woman is Hard to Find', *Feminist Media Studies*, 4.3: 356–58.

Hausseger, V. (2005) *Wonder Woman: The Myth of Having it All*, Crows Nest: Allen & Unwin.

Hawkins, G. (2001) 'The Ethics of Television', *International Journal of Cultural Studies*, 4.4: 412–26.

Hazleden, R. (2003) 'Love Yourself: The Relationship of the Self with Itself in Popular Self Help Texts', *Journal of Sociology*, 39.4: 413–28.

–––– (2004) 'The Pathology of Love in Contemporary Relationship Manuals', *The Sociological Review*: 201–17.

Heath S. & Clever, E. (2003) *Young, Free and Single?: Twenty-somethings and Household Change*, Basingstoke: Palgrave Macmillan.

Henderson, F. D. (2009) 'Successful, Single, and "Othered": The Media and the "Plight" of Single Black Women', pp. 374–91 in D. Kellner & R. Hammer eds. *Media/Cultural Studies: Critical Approaches*, New York: Peter Lang.

Hennessy, R. (1993) *Feminism and the Materialist Politics of Discourse*, London: Routledge.

Henry, A. (2004a) *Not My Mother's Sister: Generational Conflict and Third Wave Feminism*, Boston: University of Indiana Press.

————— (2004b) 'Orgasms and Empowerment: *Sex and the City* and the Third Wave Feminism', pp. 65–82 in K. Akass & J. McCabe eds. *Reading Sex and the City*, New York: I. B. Taurus.

Hermes, J. (2006) '"Ally McBeal", "Sex and the City" and the Tragic Success of Feminism', pp. 79–96 in R. Moseley & J. Read eds. *Feminism in Popular Culture*, Oxford: Berg.

————— (1995) *Reading Women's Magazines*, Cambridge: Polity.

Herring, S. C., Kouper, I., Scheidt, L. A., & Wright, E. I. (2004) 'Women and Children Last: The Discursive Construction of Weblogs', in L. J. Gurak, S. Antonijevic, L. Johnson , C. Ratliff, & J. Reyman eds. *Into the blogosphere: Rhetoric, community, and culture of weblogs*, accessed via http://blog.lib. umn.edu/blogosphere/women_and_children.html (retrieved on 15 October 2010).

Hewlett, S. A. (2002) *Baby Hunger: The New Battle for Motherhood*, London: Atlantic.

Heywood, L. & Drake, J. eds. (1997) *Third Wave Agenda: Being Feminist, Doing Feminism*, Minneapolis: University of Minnesota Press.

Hill, A. (2005) *Reality TV: Audiences and Popular Factual Television*, London: Routledge.

Hillis, M. (1936, 2005 edn) *Live Alone and Like It: The Classic Guide For The Single Woman*, London: Virago.

Hills, R. (2010) 'Why is Jennifer Aniston the Poster Girl for Single Angst?', 11 October, *Sunday Life Magazine*, accessed via http://www.theage.com. au/lifestyle/lifematters/why-is-jennifer-aniston-the-poster-girl-for-single-angst-20101011-16ey4.html?comments=53 (retrieved on 11 October 2010).

Hindman, M. (2009) *The Myth of Digital Democracy*, Princeton: Princeton University Press.

Hochschild, A. R. (1983) *The Managed Heart: The Commercialisation of Human Feeling*, Berkeley: University of California Press.

————— (1994) 'The Commercial Spirit of Intimate Life and the Abduction of Feminism: Signs from Women's Advice Books', *Theory, Culture and Society*, 11.2: 1–24.

Hodge, W. (1998) 'Bridget Jones? She's Any (Single) Woman, Anywhere', 17 February, *New York Times*, accessed via http://www.nytimes.com/library/books/021798britain-bridget.html (retrieved on 27 January 2011).

Hodkinson, P. (2007) 'Interactive Online Journals and Individualization', *New Media and Society*, 9.4: 625–50.

Hogeland, L. (1998) *Feminism and its Fiction: The Consciousness Raising Novel and the Women's Liberation Movement*, Philadelphia: University of Pennsylvania Press.

Holden, K. (2007) *The Shadow of Marriage: Singleness in England, 1914–1960,* Manchester: Manchester University Press.

Hollinger, K. (1998) *In the Company of Women: Contemporary Female Friendship Films,* Minneapolis: University of Minnesota Press.

Holmes, K. (1998) 'Spinsters Indispensable: Feminists, Single Women and the Critique of Marriage, 1890–1920', *Australian Historical Studies,* 29.110: 68–90.

Holmes, S. (2010) 'Dreaming a Dream: Susan Boyle and Celebrity Culture', *The Velvet Light Trap,* 65 (Spring): 74–6.

Hornby, G. (2008) 'David Willetts Misses the Angst of Bridget Jones', 20 September, *The Telegraph,* accessed via http://www.telegraph.co.uk/comment/personal-view/3562487/David-Willetts-misses-the-angst-of-Bridget-Jones.html.

Hymowitz, K. S. (2007) 'The New Girl Order', *City Journal,* 17.4 (Autumn), accessed via http://www.city-journal.org/html/17_4_new_girl_order.html (retrieved on 12 April 2010).

Illouz, E. (2008) *Saving The Modern Soul: Therapy, Emotions and the Culture of Self-Help,* Berkeley: University of California Press.

Ingraham, C. (1999) *White Weddings: Romancing Heterosexuality in Popular Culture,* New York: Routledge.

——— (2005) 'Introduction: Thinking Straight', pp. 1–14 in C. Ingraham ed. *Straight: The Power, The Promise, and The Paradox of Heterosexuality,* London: Routledge.

Irigaray, L. (1985) *This Sex Which Is Not One,* Ithaca: Cornell University Press.

'Is Feminism Dead?' (1998), *Time Magazine,* 29 June, 151.29, accessed via http://www.time.com/time/magazine/0,9263,7601980629,00.html (retrieved on 15 January 2010).

Israel, B. (2002) *Bachelor Girl: The Secret History of Single Women in the Twentieth Century,* New York: William Morrow.

Ivens, S. (2008) *A Modern Girl's Guide to the Perfect Single Life: How to be single and love it!,* London: Piatkus.

Jeffreys, S. (1997) *The Spinster and Her Enemies,* Melbourne: Spinifex.

Johnston, E. (2006) 'How Women Really Are: Disturbing Parallels Between Reality Television and 18th Century Fiction', pp. 115–32 in D. S. Escoffery ed. *How Real is Reality TV?: Essays on Truth and Representation,* Jefferson: McFarland & Company.

Johnston, L. (2006) 'Bridget Jones Generation Being Urged to Freeze Eggs', 7 September, *The Independent,* accessed via http://www.independent.co.uk/life-style/health-and-families/health-news/bridget-jones-generation-urged-to-freeze-eggs-414979.html (retrieved on 27 January 2011).

Jong, E. (1973) *Fear of Flying,* Austin: Holt, Rinehart, & Winston.

Joshel, S. R. (1992) 'Fatal Liaisons and Dangerous Attraction: The Destruction of Feminist Voices', *Journal of Popular Culture,* 26.3 (Winter): 59–70.

Kaminer, W. (1992) *I'm Dysfunctional, You're Dysfunctional: The Recovery Movement and Other Self Help Fashions,* Reading: Addison-Wesley.

Karlsson, L. (2006) 'Acts of Reading Diary Weblogs', *HUMAN IT,* 8.2: 1–59.

——— (2007) 'Desperately Seeking Sameness', *Feminist Media Studies,* 7.2: 137–53.

Kaufmann, J. (1999, 2008 edn) *The Single Woman and the Fairytale Prince,* London: Polity.

Kavka, M. (2008) *Reality Television, Intimacy and Affect: Reality Matters*, Basingstoke: Palgrave Macmillan.

Kean, L. (2005) *Perfect Ten*, London: Harper Collins.

Kellner, D. (1995) *Media Culture: Cultural Studies, Identity and Politics Between the Modern and Postmodern*, New York: Routledge.

Kim, L. (2001) '"Sex and the Single Girl" in Postfeminism: The F Word on Television', *Television and Media*, 2.4 (November): 319–34.

Kingston, A. (2004) *The Meaning of Wife*, New York: Farrar, Strauss and Giroux.

Kinsela, S. (2001) *Confessions of a Shopaholic*, 2001, New York: Dial Press.

Kipnis, L. (2003) *Against Love: A Polemic*, New York: Pantheon Books.

Kitzinger, C. & Wilkinson, S. (1994) 'Dire Straights: Contemporary Rehabilitations of Heterosexuality', pp. 75–91 in G. Griffin, M. Hester, S. Rai and S. Roseneil eds. *Stirring It: Challenges for Feminism*, London: Taylor & Francis.

Koropeckyj-Cox, T. (2005) 'Singles, Society, and Science: Sociological Perspectives', *Psychological Inquiry*, 16.2/3: 91–6.

Lehman, K. J. (2007) *Whose Girl?: Representations of Single Women, Sexual Politics and the Workplace in 1960s and 1970s Film and Television*, unpublished doctoral thesis, The University of New Mexico.

Leonard, S. (2006) 'Marriage Envy', *Women's Studies Quarterly*, 3/4 (Fall-Winter): 43–64.

—— (2009) *Fatal Attraction*, London: Blackwell.

Lewis, K. & Moon, S. (1997) 'Always Single and Single Again Women: A Qualitative Study', *Journal of Marital Therapy*, 23.2: 115–34.

Lewis, K. (2004) *With or Without A Man: Single Women Taking Control of Their Lives*, Maryland: Bull Publishing.

Lewis, T. (2008) *Smart Living: Lifestyle Media and Popular Expertise*, New York: Peter Lang.

Little, J. (2007) 'Constructing Nature in the Performance of Rural Heterosexualities', *Environment and Planning D: Society and Space*, 25.5: 851–66.

Little, J. & Panelli, R. (2007) '"Outback" Romance? A Reading of Nature and Heterosexuality in Rural Australia', *Sociologia Ruralis*, 47.3 (July): 173–88.

Lloyd Webber, I. (2007) *The Single Girl's Guide*, Kent Town: Wakefield Press.

Loewenstein, A. (2008) *The Blogging Revolution*, Carlton: Melbourne University Press.

Lopez, L. K. (2009) 'The Radical Act of "Mommy Blogging": Redefining Motherhood Through the Blogosphere', *New Media and Society*, 11: 729–47.

Lotz, A. (2006) *Redesigning Women: Television After the Network Era*, Illinois: University of Illinois Press.

Mabry, A. R. (2006) 'About a Girl: Female Subjectivity and Sexuality in Contemporary "Chick" Culture', pp. 191–206 in S. Ferris & M. Young eds. *Chick Lit: The New Woman's Fiction*, New York: Routledge.

Macvarish, J. (2006) 'What is "the Problem" of Singleness?', *Sociological Research Online*, 11.3, accessed via http://www.socresonline.org.uk/11/3/macvarish. html (retrieved on 5 February 2010).

—— (2008) 'Intimacy in the 21st Century: The Negotiation of Divergent Rationalities', ISA Conference September, accessed via http://www.riskandun-certainty.net/TG04/Macvarishpaper.pdf (retrieved on 5 December 2010).

Maddison, S. & Storr, M. (2004) 'The Edge of Reason: The Myth of Bridget Jones', pp. 3–16 in J. Hands & E. Siapera ed. *At the Interface: Continuity and Transformation in Culture and Politics*, Amsterdam: Rodopi.

Maher, J. (2004) 'What Do Women Watch?: Tuning in to the Compulsory Heterosexual Channel', pp. 197–213 in S. Murray & L. Ouelette eds. *Reality TV: Remaking Television Culture*, New York: New York University Press.

Manby, C. (2002) *Getting Personal*, London: Coronet Books.

Marsh, K. A. (2004) 'Contextualizing Bridget Jones', *College Literature*, 31.1 (Winter): 52–72.

Marshall, P. D. (1997) *Celebrity and Power*, Minneapolis: University of Minnesota Press.

Matthews, D. M. (2008) *Every Man Sees You Naked: An Insider's Guide to How Men Think*, Tucson: Wheatmark Inc.

McClanahan, A. M. (2003) *Completely Single? Representations of Single Women through Multiple Media Narratives*, unpublished doctoral thesis, Ohio University.

―――― (2007) '"Must Marry TV": The Role of the Heterosexual Imaginary in *The Bachelor*', pp. 303–19 in M. Galician & D. Merskin eds. *Critical Thinking About Sex, Love, and Romance in the Mass Media: Media Literacy Applications*, New Jersey: Lawrence Erlbaum.

McGee, M. (2005) *Self Help, Inc: Makeover Culture in America*, Oxford: Oxford University Press.

McGinn, D. (2006) 'Marriage by the Numbers; Twenty Years Since the Infamous "Terrorist" Line, States of Unions Aren't What We Predicted They'd Be', 5 June, *Newsweek*.

McMahon, A. (1999) *Taking Care of Men: Sexual Politics in the Public Mind*, Melbourne: Cambridge University Press.

McNair, B. (2002) *Striptease Culture: Sex, Media and the Democratization of Desire*, London: Routledge.

McNeil, L. (2003) 'Teaching an Old Genre New Tricks: The Diary on the Internet', *Biography*, 26.1: 24–47.

McRobbie, A. (1994) *Postmodernism and Popular Culture*, London: Routledge.

―――― (2007) 'Postfeminism and Popular Culture: Bridget Jones and the New Gender Regime', pp. 27–39 in Y. Tasker & D. Negra eds. *Interrogating Postfeminism: Gender and the Politics of Popular Culture*, Durham: Duke University Press.

―――― (2009) *The Aftermath of Feminism: Gender, Culture and Social Change*, London: Sage.

Merkin, D. (1998) 'The Marriage Mystique', *The New Yorker*, 3 August, 74.22: 70–6.

Michaels, S. (2010) 'Lily Allen to Score Bridget Musical?' 2 June, *The Guardian*, accessed via http://www.guardian.co.uk/music/2010/jun/02/lily-allen-bridget-jones-musical (retrieved on 1 December 2010).

Miller, R. (2009) *Man Magnet: How to be the best woman you can be in order to get the best man*, New York: Artrum Media.

Modleski, T. (1986, 2008 edn) 'Introduction to the Second Edition', pp. xi–xxvii, *Loving With A Vengeance: Mass Produced Fantasies for Women*, New York: Routledge.

Moran, J. (2000) *Star Authors: Literary Celebrity in America*, London: Pluto.

Moran, R. (2004) 'How Feminism Forgot the Single Woman', *Hofstra Law Review*, Fall: 1–78.

Morreale, J. (2007) 'Faking It and the Transformation of Personal Identity', pp. 95–106 in D. Heller ed. *Makeover Television: Realities Remodelled*, New York: I. B. Tauris.

Moseley, R. & Read, J. (2002) 'Having It Ally: Popular Television (Post-)Feminism', *Feminist Media Studies*, 2.2: 231–49.

Mulvey, K. (1999) 'Eat Your Heart Out Bridget; Parties Galore, a Dinner Date Every Night and Weekend Adventures. One Woman Shows that the Bridget Jones Generation are not all Desperate to meet Mr Right', 3 June, *Daily Mail*.

——— (2003) 'From Sexy Single to Bridget Moans; or How Being Alone is Only Fun When You're Young...', 16 January, *Daily Mail*.

——— (2006) 'Duped Out of Motherhood', 24 February, *Daily Mail*.

Nakomoto, S. (2002) *Men Are Like Fish: What Every Woman Needs to Know about Catching a Man*, New York: Java Books.

Nathan, M. (2000) *Pride, Prejudice and Jasmin Field*, London: Judy Piatkus Publishers.

Negra, D. (2004) '"Quality Postfeminism": Sex and the Single Girl on HBO', *Genders*, 39, accessed via http://www.genders.org/g39/g39_negra.html (retrieved on 17 January 2010).

——— (2006) 'Where the Boys are: Postfeminism and the New Single Man', *Flow: A Critical Forum on Television and Media*, 4.3 (April), accessed via http://flowtv.org/?p–223 (retrieved on 17 January 2010).

——— (2009) *What a girl wants: Fantasizing the reclamation of self in postfeminism*, London: Routledge.

——— (2010) 'Picturing Family Values', *The Velvet Light Trap*, 65 (Spring): 60–1.

Nehring, C. (2002) 'Mr Goodbar Redux', *The Atlantic*, January, accessed via http://www.theatlantic.com/past/docs/issues/2002/01/nehring.htm (retrieved on 5 June 2010).

Nelson, A. (2004) 'Sister Carrie Meets Carrie Bradshaw: Exploring Progress, Politics and the Single Woman in *Sex in the City* and Beyond', pp. 83–95 in K. Akass & J. McCabe eds. *Reading Sex and the City*, New York: I. B. Tauris.

Nicholson, V. (2007) *Singled Out: How Two Million Women Survived Without Men after the First World War*, London: Viking.

Nochimson, M. P. (2000) 'Brightness Falls from the Air', *Film Quarterly*, 53.3: 25–32.

Nurka, C. (2002) *Postfeminist Autopsies*, unpublished doctoral thesis, University of Sydney.

Oram, A. (1992) 'Repressed and Thwarted, or Bearer of the New World? The Spinster in Inter-war Feminist Discourses', *Women's History Review*, 1.3: 413–33.

Ouelette, L. (2002) 'Victims No More: Postfeminism, Television, and *Ally McBeal*', *The Communication Review*, 5.4: 315–35.

Ouellette, L. & Hay, J. (2008a) *Better Living Through Reality TV*, Oxford: Blackwell.

——— (2008b) 'Makeover Television, Governmentality and the Good Citizen', *Continuum*, 22.4: 471–84.

Ouellette, L. & Murray, S. (2004) 'Introduction', pp. 1–28 in L. Ouellette & S. Murray eds. *Reality TV: Remaking Television Culture*, New York: New York University Press.

Page, S. (1988, 2003 edn) *If I'm So Wonderful, Why am I Still Single: Ten Strategies That Will Change Your Love Life Forever*, New York: Three Rivers Press.

Patton, T. O. (2001) 'Ally McBeal and her Homies: The Reification of White Stereotypes of the Other', *Journal of Black Studies*, 32.2: 229–60.

Payette, P. (2002) 'The Feminist Wife? Notes From A "Political Engagement"', pp. 139–70 in M. Johnson ed. *Jane Sexes It Up: True Confessions of Feminist Desire*, New York: Nation Books.

Pearce, L. (2004) *The Rhetorics of Feminism*, London: Routledge.

Perlmutter, D. (2008) *Blogwars: The New Political Battleground*, New York: Oxford University Press.

Philips, D. (2000) 'Shopping for Men: The Single Woman Narrative', *Women: A Cultural Review*, 11.3: 238–51.

Plummer, K. (1995) *Telling Sexual Stories*, London: Routledge.

Potts, A. (2002) *The Science/Fiction of Sex: Feminist Deconstruction and the Vocabularies of Heterosex*, London: Routledge.

Pozner. J. (2010) *Reality Bites Back: The Troubling Truth About Guilty Pleasure TV*, Berkeley: Seal Press.

Prince, R. (2008) 'Tory Party Conference: Bridget Jones Generation Blamed', 28 September, *The Telegraph*, accessed via http://www.telegraph.co.uk/news/newstopics/politics/conservative/3097489/Tory-party-conference-Bridget-Jones-generation-blamed.html (retrieved on 17 January 2011).

Probyn, E. (1993) 'Choosing Choice: Images of Sexuality and "Choiceoisie" in Popular Culture', pp. 278–93 in S. Fisher & K. Davis eds. *Negotiating at the Margins: The Gendered Discourses of Power and Resistance*, New Jersey: Rutgers University Press.

—— (1997) 'New Traditionalism and Post-Feminism: TV Does the Home', pp. 126–39 in C. Brunsdon, J. D'Acci, L. Spigel eds. *Feminist Television Criticism: A Reader*, Oxford: Clarendon Press.

Projansky, S. (2001) *Watching Rape: Film and Television in Postfeminist Culture*, New York: New York University Press.

Radner, H. (1999) 'Introduction: Queering the Girl', pp. 1–35 in H. Radner & M. Luckett eds. *Swinging Single: Representing Sexuality in the 1960s*, Minneapolis: University of Minnesota Press.

—— (2010) *Neo-Feminist Cinema: Girly Films, Chick Flicks and Consumer Culture*, New York: Routledge.

Radway, J. (1984) *Reading the Romance: Women, Patriarchy, and Popular Literature*, Chapel Hill: University of North Carolina Press.

Rapping, E. (1996) *The Culture of Recovery: Making Sense of the Self Help Movement in Women's Lives*, Boston: Beacon Press.

Razer, H. (2004) 'Bridget Jones as Everygirl', 11 November, *The Age*, accessed via http://www.theage.com.au/articles/2004/11/10/1100021859539.html?from=storyrhs (retrieved on 27 January 2011).

Rees, G. & Ballinger, L. (2008) 'Rise of the Freemale: The Women Who'd Rather be Single than Share their Time and Money', 2 June, *Daily Mail*, accessed via http://www.dailymail.co.uk/femail/article-1023532/Rise-freemale-The-women-whod-single-share-time-money.html (retrieved on 25 February 2010).

Reynolds, J. (2008) *The Single Woman: A Discursive Analysis*, London: Routledge.

Reynolds, J. & Wetherell, M. (2003) 'The Discursive Climate of Singleness: The Consequences for Women's Negotiation of a Single Identity', *Feminism and Psychology*, 13.4: 498–510.

Reynolds, J., Wetherell, M., & Taylor, S. (2007) 'Choice and Chance: Negotiating Agency in Narratives of Singleness', *The Sociological Review*, 55.2: 331–51.

Rich. A. (1980) 'Compulsory Heterosexuality and Lesbian Existence', *Signs*, 5.4: 631–60.

Riley, D. (2002) 'The Right to Be Lonely', *Differences*, 13.1: 1–13.

Rimke, H. M. (2000) 'Governing Citizens Through Self Help Literature', *Cultural Studies*, 14.1: 61–78.

Ringrose, J. & Walkerdine, V. (2008) 'Regulating the Abject: The TV Make-Over as Site of Neoliberal Reinvention Towards Bourgeois Femininity', *Feminist Media Studies* 8.3: 227–46.

Riviere, J. (1929) 'Womanliness as Masquerade', *International Journal of Psychoanalysis*, 10: 303–13.

Rojek, C. (2000) *Celebrity*, New York: Reaktion Books.

Rosa, B. (1994) 'Anti-monogamy: A Radical Challenge to Compulsory Heterosexuality?' pp. 107–20 in G. Griffin, M. Hester , S. Rai, & S. Roseneil eds. *Stirring It: Challenges for Feminism*, London: Taylor and Francis.

Rose, N. (1989, 1999 edn) *Governing the Soul*, London: Free Association Books.

——— (1996) *Inventing Ourselves: Psychology, Power and Personhood*, Cambridge: Cambridge University Press.

Salerno, S. (2005) *Sham: How the Self-Help Movement Made America Helpless*, New York: Random House.

Salt, B. (2008) *Man Drought and Other Social Issues of the New Century*, Prahan: Hardie Grant Books.

Sandfield, A. (2006) 'Talking Divorce: The Role of Divorce in Women's Constructions of Relationship Status', *Feminism & Psychology*, 16.2: 155–73.

Sandfield, A. & Percy, C. (2003) 'Accounting for Single Status: Heterosexism and Ageism in Heterosexual Women's Talk about Marriage', *Feminism and Psychology*, 13.4: 475–88.

Scanlon, J. (2009) 'Sensationalist Literature or Expert Advice? Helen Gurley Brown's *Sex and the Single Girl* in its Publishing Context', *Feminist Media Studies*, 9.1 (Spring): 1–15.

——— (2010) *Bad Girls Go Everywhere: The Life of Helen Gurley Brown*, Oxford: Oxford University Press.

Schilling, K. M. & Fuehrer, A. (1993) 'The Politics of Women's Self Help Books', *Feminism and Psychology*, 3.3: 418–22.

Schrager, C. D. (1993) 'Questioning the Promise of Self-Help: A Reading of *Women Who Love Too Much*', *Feminist Studies*, 19.1 (Spring): 177–92.

Scheftt, J. (2007) *Better Single Than Sorry: A No-Regrets Guide to Loving Yourself and Never Settling*, New York: Harper Collins.

Serfaty, V. (2004a) 'From Self-explanation to Self-justification: Online Diaries and Blogs in America', *Recherches Anglaises et Nord-Américaines (RANAM)*, Université Marc Bloch, 37 (October): 247–56.

——— (2004b) 'Online Diaries: Towards a Structural Approach', *Journal of American Studies*, 38: 457–71.

——— (2004c) *The Mirror and the Veil: An Overview of Online Diaries and Blogs*, Amsterdam: Rodopi.

Shalit, W. (1999) 'Sex, Sadness and the City', pp. 1–7, Autumn, *City Journal*, accessed via http://www.city-journal.org/html/9_4_a4.html (retrieved on 12 June 2010).

Showalter, E. (2001) 'Sex Goddess', *The American Prospect*, 21 May, 12.9: 38–40.

Shulman, N. (1996) 'Some Consolations of the Single State', *Times Literary Supplement*, 1 November, p. 26.

Siegel, D. (2002) 'Sexing the Single Girl', Centre for the Education of Women, University of Michigan: 1–14, accessed via http://www.umich.edu/~cew/PDFs/pubs/siegel.pdf (retrieved on 3 March 2010).

Simonds, W. (1992) *Women and Self-Help Culture: Reading Between the Lines*, New York: Rutgers University Press.

——— (1996) 'All Consuming Selves: Self-Help Literature and Women's Identities', pp. 15–29 in D. Grodin & T. R. Lindlof eds. *Constructing the Self in a Mediated World*, London: Sage.

Simpson, R. (2006) 'The Intimate Relationships of Contemporary Spinsters', *Sociological Research Online*, 11.3, accessed via http://www.socresonline.org.uk/11/3/simpson.html (retrieved on 20 February 2010).

'Singing Scottish Spinster a Global Sensation' (2009), 17 April, *Sydney Morning Herald*, accessed via http://www.smh.com.au/news/technology/web/2009/04/17/1239475033673.html (retrieved on 21 January 2010).

'Singles and the City: The Bridget Jones Economy' (2001), *The Economist*, 22 December, 361.8253: 68–70, accessed via http://www.economist.com/node/883664?Story_ID=883664 (retrieved on 3 May 2010).

Sisman, R. (2002) *Just Friends*, London: Ballantine Books.

Smith, C. J. (2008) *Cosmopolitan Culture and Consumerism in Chick Lit*, London: Routledge.

Smith, J. (2009) 'The Susan Boyle Freakshow', *The Guardian*, 1 June, accessed via http://www.guardian.co.uk/commentisfree/2009/jun/01/susan-boyle-britains-got-talent (retrieved on 7 April 2010).

Smith, S. & Watson, J. (1996) *Getting a Life: Everyday Uses of Autobiography*, Minneapolis: University of Minnesota Press.

Smyczynska, K. (2007) *The World According to Bridget Jones*, Frankfurt: Peter Lang.

Somolu, O. (2007) 'Telling Our Own Stories: African Women Blogging for Social Change', *Gender and Development*, 15.3: 477–89.

Sorapure, M. (2003) 'Screening Moments, Scrolling Lives: Diary Writing on the Web', *Biography*, 26.1: 1–23.

Sparrow, R. (2003) *The Girl Most Likely*, St Lucia: University of Queensland.

'SPUDs, Single Women Taking Over Australia' (2008), 12 March, accessed via http://www.news.com.au/single-women-now-have-the-upper-hand/story-e6frfkp9-1111115778111 (retrieved on 24 July 2010).

Spurr, P. (2008) 'Forget This Tosh About "Freemales" – Single Women Who Say They Are Happy Are Lying', 5 June, *Daily Mail*, accessed via http://www.dailymail.co.uk/femail/article-1024317/Forget-tosh-freemales–single-women-say-happy-lying.html (retrieved on 7 March 2010).

Squires, C. (2007) *Marketing Literature: The Making of Contemporary Writing in Britain*, Basingstoke: Palgrave Macmillan.

Starker, S. (1989) *Oracle at the Supermarket: The Americ an Preoccupation With Self-Help Books*, New Brunswick: Transaction Publications.

Stephens, R. L. (2004) 'Socially Soothing Stories? Gender, Race and Class in TLC's *A Wedding Story* and *A Baby Story*', pp. 191–210 in S. Holmes & D. Jermyn *Understanding Reality Television*, London: Routledge.

Stewart, J. (2005) *The Single Girl's Manifesta*, Illinois: Sourcebooks.

Storey, J. & Xiaohu, Z. (2010) 'Media Love', Unpublished paper presented at the 'Crossroads' Cultural Studies Conference, Linghan University Hong Kong.

Storr, A. (1988) *Solitude: A Return to the Self*, New York: Free Press.

Straus, J. (2006) *Unhooked Generation: The Truth About Why We're Still Single*, New York: Hyperion.

Summers, A. (1994) *Damned Whores and God's Police*, Ringwood: Penguin.

Tasker, Y. & Negra, D. (2007) 'Introduction', pp. 1–25 in Y. Tasker & D. Negra eds. *Interrogating Postfeminism: Gender and the Politics of Popular Culture*, Durham: Duke University Press.

Taylor, A. (2003) 'What's so new about "The New Femininity?": Feminism, Femininity and the Discourse of the New', *Hecate: An Interdisciplinary Journal of Women's Liberation*, 29.2: 182–98.

—— (2008) *Mediating Australian Feminism: Re-reading the First Stone Media Event*, Oxford: Peter Lang.

—— (2010) 'Celebrity (Post)feminism, the Sixties Feminist Blockbuster and *Down with Love*', *The Sixties: A Journal of Politics, History and Culture*: 3.1: 79–96.

Taylor, K. (2007) *Not Tonight, Mr Right: The Best (Don't Get) Laid Plans for Finding and Marrying the Man of Your Dreams*, Cambridge, MA: Da Capo Books.

'The Singles Issue' (2000), 5 November, *The Observer*, accessed via http://www guardian.co.uk/theobserver/2000/nov/05/life1.lifemagazine (retrieved on 10 January 2010).

Thomas, S. (2009) 'Single and Loving It', 19 March, *Sydney Morning Herald*, accessed via http://www.smh.com.au/news/lifeandstyle/lifematters/single-and-loving-it/2009/03/18/1237054864876.html (retrieved on 2 February 2010).

Thornham, S. (2007) *Women, Feminism and Media*, Edinburgh: Edinburgh University Press.

Thorton, S. (2010) 'The Burning of Miss Havisham: Dickens, Fire and the "Fire-Baptism"', pp. 79–98 in H. Bloom ed. *Charles Dickens's Great Expectations*, New York: Infobase Publishing.

Travers, A. (2003) 'Parallel Subaltern Feminist Counterpublics in Cyberspace', *Sociological Perspectives*, 46.2: 223–37.

Tremayne, M. ed. (2007) *Blogging, Citizenship, and the Future of Media*, New York: Routledge.

Trimberger, E. K. (2005) *The New Single Woman*, Boston: Beacon.

Tseelon, E. (1999) *The Masque of Femininity*, London: Sage.

Turner, G. (2004) *Understanding Celebrity*, London: Sage.

—— (2010) *Ordinary People and the Media: The Demotic Turn*, London: Sage.

Umminger, A. (2006) 'Supersizing Bridge Jones: What's Really Eating the Women in Chicklit', pp. 239–52 in S. Ferris & M. Young eds. *Chick Lit: The New Woman's Fiction*, New York: Routledge.

US Census Bureau News (2010), 19 July, accessed via http://www.census.gov/newsroom/releases/pdf/cb10ff-18_single.pdf (retrieved on 8 January 2011).

Ussher, J. (1997) *Fantasies of Femininity: Reframing the Boundaries of Sex*, London: Penguin.

Van Dijck, J. (2004) 'Composing the Self: Of Diaries and Lifeblogs', accessed via http://www.journal.fibreculture.org/issue3/issue3_vandijck.html. (retrieved on 10 January, 2010).

Van Slooten, J. L. (2006) 'A Truth Universally (Un)Acknowledged: *Ally McBeal*, *Bridget Jones' Diary* and the Conflict Between Romantic Love and Feminism', pp. 36–54 in E. Watson ed. *Searching the Soul of Ally McBeal: Critical Essays*, Jefferson: Macfarland & Co.

Van Zoonen, L. (1994) *Feminist Media Studies*, London: Sage.

Vavrus, M. D. (2007) '*Opting out* Moms in the News: Selling New Traditionalism in the New Millennium', *Feminist Media Studies*, 7.1: 47–63.

Vernon, P. (2005) 'Does Bridget Still Speak for Single Women?' 7 August, *The Guardian*, accessed via http://www.guardian.co.uk/books/2005/aug/07/fiction. features1 (retrieved on 15 September 2010).

Vint, S. (2007) 'The New Backlash: Popular Culture's Marriage with Feminism, or Love is All You Need', *Journal of Popular Film and Television*: 161–68.

Walters, S. D. (1995) *Materials Girls: Making Sense of Cultural Theory*, Los Angeles: University of California Press.

Wardop, M. (2010) 'Four in 10 Women Confess to "Bridget Jones" Love Life', 13 April, *The Telegraph*, accessed via http://www.telegraph.co.uk/news/ uknews/7581505/Four-in-10-women-confess-to-Bridget-Jones-love-life.html (retrieved on 17 January 2011).

Watters, E. (2003) *Urban Tribes: Are Friends the New Family?* London: Bloomsbury.

Wearing, S. (2007) 'Subjects of Rejuvenation: Aging in Postfeminist Culture', pp. 277–310 in Tasker, Y. & Negra, D. eds. *Interrogating Postfeminism: Gender and the Politics of Popular Culture*, Durham: Duke University Press.

Weber, B. R. (2007) 'Makeover as Takeover: Scenes of Affective Domination on Makeover TV', *Configurations*, 15.1 (Winter): 77–99.

——— (2009) *Makeover TV: Selfhood, Citizenship, and Celebrity*, Durham: Duke University Press.

Whelehan, I. (2000) *Overloaded: Popular Culture and the Future of Feminism*, London: The Women's Press.

——— (2002) *Helen Fielding's Bridget Jones*, London: Continuum.

——— (2005) *The Feminist Bestseller: From Sex and the City to Sex and the Single Girl*, Basingstoke: Palgrave Macmillan.

——— (2010) 'Remaking Feminism: Or Why Is Postfeminism So Boring?' *Nordic Journal of English Studies*, 9.3: 155–72.

Whitehead, Dafoe B. (2002) *Why There Are No Good Men Left: The Romantic Plight of the New Single Woman*, New York: Broadway Books.

Wei, L. (2009) 'Filter Blogs vs. Personal Journals: Understanding the Knowledge Production Gap on the Internet', *Journal of Computer-Mediated Communication*, 14: 532–58.

Weisberger, L. (2003) *The Devil Wears Prada*, London: Harper Collins.

Williams, K. (2006) 'Singled Out: In Seeking a Mate, Men and Women Find Delicate Balance', 8 October, *The Washington Post*, accessed via http://www. washingtonpost.com/wpdyn/content/article/2006/10/07/AR2006100701070. html (retrieved on 19 September 2010).

Winship, J. (1987) *Inside Women's Magazines*, London: Pandora.

Wood, E. A. (2008) 'Consciousness-raising 2.0: Sex Blogging and the Creation of a Feminist Sex Commons', *Feminism and Psychology*, 18.4: 480–87.

Wood, H. & Skeggs, B. (2004) 'Notes on Ethical Scenarios of Self on British Reality TV', *Feminist Media Studies*, 4.1: 205–08.

——— (2008) 'The Labour of Transformation and Circuits of Value around Reality TV', *Continuum*, 22.4: 559–72.

Yamada, M. (1999) *Parasaito shinguru no jidai [The Age of the Parasite Single]*, Tokyo: Chikuma Shobo.

Yellin, J. (2006) 'Single, Female and Desperate No More', *New York Times*, June 4, accessed via http://www.nytimes.com/2006/06/04/weekinreview/04yellin.html (retrieved on 10 March 2010).

York, P. (1997) 'The Things that Shaped our Year: Bridget Jones Goes Global', 28 December, *The Independent*, accessed via http://www.independent.co.uk/arts-entertainment/the-things-that-shaped-our-year-bridget-jones-goes-global-1290871.html (retrieved on 12 September 2010).

Young, S. (1997) *Changing the Wor(l)d: Discourse, Politics and the Feminist Movement*, London: Routledge.

Youngs, G. (2009) 'Blogging and Globalization: The Blurring of the Public/Private Spheres', *Aslib Proceedings: New Information Perspectives*, 61.2: 127–38.

Zizek, S. (1989) *The Sublime Object of Ideology*, London: Verso.

Film and television

27 Dresses, 2008, Dir. Anne Fletcher.

The Age of Love, NBC, 2007, Creator: J.D. Roth.

Ally McBeal, Twentieth Century Fox, 1997–2002, Creator: David E. Kelley.

The Bachelor, ABC, 2002–present, Creator: Mike Fleiss.

The Bachelorette, ABC, 2003–present, Creator: Mike Fleiss.

Basic Instinct, 1992, Dir. Paul Verhoeven.

Bridget's Jones Diary, 2001, Dir. Sharon Maguire.

Bridget Jones: The Edge of Reason, 2004, Dir. Beeban Kidron.

The Cougar, MTV Land, 2009, Creator: Michael Fleiss.

Brothers and Sisters, ABC, 2006–11, Creator: Jon Robin Baitz.

Cougartown, ABC, 2009–Present, Creators: Kevin Biegel, Bill Lawrence.

Desperately Seeking Susan, 1985, Dir. Susan Seidelman.

Disclosure, 1994, Dir. Barry Levinson.

Down with Love, 2004, Dir. Peyton Reed.

Fatal Attraction, 1987, Dir. Adrian Lyne.

Friends, Warner Bros., 1994–2004, Creators: David Crane, Marta Kauffman.

The Farmer Wants a Wife, (Australia), 2007–present, Fremantle Media Enterprises.

Flavor of Love, VH1, 2006–2008, Creators: Cris Abrego, Mark Cronin.

He's Just Not That Into You, 2009, Dir. Ken Kwapis.

Joe Millionaire, Fox, 2003, Creator: Chris Cowen.

Keeping Up with the Kardashians, Bunim/Murray Productions, 2007–present, Creators: Eliot Goldberg, Ryan Seacrest.

The Mary Tyler Moore Show, CBS, 1970–77, Creators: James L. Brooks, Allen Burns.

Murphy Brown, CBS, 1988–1998, Creator: Diane English.

Offspring, Southern Star Entertainment, 2010–present, Creator: Debra Oswald.

Poison Ivy, 1992, Dir. Katt Shea.

Rock of Love, VH1, 2007–2009, Creators: Cris Abrego, Mark Cronin.

Sex and the City, HBO, 1998–2004, Creator: Darren Starr.

Sex and the City, 2008, Dir. Michael Patrick King.

Sex and the City 2, 2010, Dir. Michael Patrick King.

Single White Female, 1992, Dir. Barbet Schroeder.

Single White Female 2: The Psycho, 2005, Dir. Keith Samples.

Sleepless in Seattle, 1993, Dir. Nora Ephron.

Tough Love, VH1, (2009–2010), Creator: Steve Ward.
The Wedding Date, 2005, Dir. Clare Kilner.
When Harry Met Sally, 1989, Dir. Rob Reiner.
You've Got Mail, 1998, Dir. Nora Ephron.

Blog addresses

Bridget Jones Has Nothing On Me: http://catherinette.wordpress.com/about/.
Dazzlingly Single: http://www.blogcatalog.com/blogs/dazzlingly-single.
First Person Singular: http://www.firstpersonsingular.org.
Living Single: http://www.psychologytoday.com/blog/living-single.
Ms Single Mama: http://www.mssinglemama.com/.
Onely: Single and Happy: http://onely.org/.
Original Diva: http://www.originaldiva.com/.
Quirkyalone: http://www.quirkyalone.net/.
Rachel's Musings: http://www.rabe.org/about/.
Radical Woman: http://solofemininity.blogs.com/
Single and Thirty-something: http://singlethirtysomethingwordpress.com/.
Single Women Rule: http://singlewomenrule.com/.
Singlutionary: http://singlutionary.blogspot.com/.
Singletude: http://singletude.blogspot.com/.
Sixty and Single in Seattle: http://marysreallife.blogspot.com/.
Solo Lady: http://www.sololady.com/.
Solo Mother: http://www.solomother.com/.
The Contented Single: http://thecontentedsingle.blogspot.com/.
The Spinster Chronicles: http://spinningleese.blogspot.com/.
The Spinsterlicious Life: http://www.thespinsterliciouslife.com/.

Index

CPSIA information can be obtained at www.ICGtesting.com
Printed in the USA
LVOW010606111212

311042LV00023B/479/P

DATE